THE
HAUNTING
OF AMERICA

THE
HAUNTING
OF AMERICA

TROY TAYLOR

Ghosts and Legends *of*
America's Haunted Past

BARNES
& NOBLE
NEW YORK

Text design by Maureen Slattery

2006 Barnes & Noble Publishing

ISBN-13: 978-0-7607-8252-1
ISBN-10: 0-7607-8252-0

Printed and bound in the United States of America

3 5 7 9 10 8 6 4 2

TABLE OF CONTENTS

THE HAUNTED HOUSE

Unhinged, the iron gates half-open hung,
Jarred by the gusty gales of many winters,
That from its crumbled pedestal had flung
One marble globe in splinters.

The wood-louse dropped, and rolled into a ball,
Touched by some impulse, occult or mechanic;
And nameless beetles ran along the wall
In universal panic.

The subtle spider, that from overhead
Hung like a spy on human guilt and error
Suddenly turn'd, and up its slender thread
Ran with a nimble terror.

O'er all there hung the shadow of a fear;
A sense of mystery the spirit daunted;
And said, as plain as whisper in the ear,
The place is haunted!

—Tom Hood

Introduction

THE AMERICAN GHOST STORY

Along the banks of a small river in North Carolina, the light of a ghostly lantern still glows. The legends say that it is carried in the hands of a grim old man who once prowled the land along the darkened river each night, watching for thieves and trespassers. The light moves down along the bushes and between the trunks of curving trees, wandering slowly and gently swaying back and forth as though its bearer limps and hobbles with age.

But the eerie light is not the only phantom artifact of the past to be reported here. This land has a strange and mysterious history.

The property once belonged to a man named Adam Springs and a house that he built still stands on the edge of McAdenville, North Carolina. Few people have ever heard of this place but those who have cannot deny its strange links to not only the annals of ghostlore, but to American history as well.

There are a number of legends that surround this old, antebellum home, which was built by Adam Springs and is located above the South Fork River in McAdenville. He called the house Long Shoals but it came to be known simply as the Springs House. One of the most prominent legends of the place concerns a young woman who was once in the employ of Springs whose name was Nancy Hanks.

Springs was a gruff, middle-aged man who always dressed in conservative clothing and who even occasionally toted a Bible under one arm. Regardless, young Nancy caught his eye on the first day that she arrived for work at the mansion. It was only a matter of time before Springs pressured the girl into an affair.

However, when Nancy discovered that she had become pregnant, Springs wanted no part of it. Knowing that he would be unable to explain the situation to his wife, the townsfolk and the local church members, he decided that Nancy needed to be sent away someplace where no one knew him.

He spent a number of sleepless nights over this problem and then one afternoon, he met a young man named Thomas Lincoln, who was passing through McAdenville for points further west. He was a stranger in town and having little money, he was unable to find a place to stay. Hearing of his plight, Springs befriended him and allowed him to stay at Long Shoals as a houseguest. Springs had more than hospitality on his mind though and around the time that Lincoln was planning to depart for Kentucky, he took the young man aside and offered him a large sum of money to take Nancy with him.

Lincoln agreed and the couple soon departed for Kentucky, where they fell in love. When the child conceived with Adam Springs was born, he was named Abraham. He would leave an indelible mark on the historic landscape of America.

While few scholars or books on the life of Abraham Lincoln have acknowledged what may be simply a legend, people who knew Grat Springs, Adam's legitimate son, often commented on his striking resemblance to President Lincoln.

While it is well known that Lincoln's ghost is said to still walk the earth, few realize that Adam Spring's ghost is still said to be roaming around as well. According to other legends of the house, Springs was often harassed by thieves who would sneak down to the river near his house and steal from his fish traps. On occasion, with lantern in hand, Springs would go down to the river, where he would put out the light and wait. When the thieves arrived, he would relight the lantern and hold it next to his face, pretending to be some vengeful river specter, and would frighten the robbers away.

Springs was so obsessed with protecting his traps that he wrote a provision into his will that stated he should be buried in an upright position in the grave. His body was supposed to face the river so that he could watch over the traps. There has been some dispute as to whether or not he was actually buried this way. No one has ever exhumed him to see, which may be the reason his ghost still haunts the place!

Perhaps because he was not buried in the manner that he requested, his lantern is said to appear on certain dark nights. It will blink on and float down along the river as if searching for the thieves who are stealing from the fish traps.

The river has changed much since the days when Springs lived nearby. A textile mill was later built along the banks below the house, along with a row of small company houses for the workers. From here comes another of the local legends. . .

According to the story, there was a man who worked for the mill and lived in one of these houses with his daughter. It was said that her father arranged a marriage for her to a man that she didn't want to marry. She argued bitterly with her father, but he refused to call off the wedding. So, on the night before the ceremony, she put on her wedding dress and walked down the river's edge. Slowly, she waded out into the muddy water and drowned herself. The legends now say that if a bride, on the night before her wedding, puts on her gown and walks to the same spot on the riverbank, the ghost of the dead girl will appear to her.

Along with the ghost stories, the Springs mansion still stands. Some years ago, a family was serving as the caretakers of the place. They were sitting out on the front porch one evening, enjoying the night air, and one of the daughters got chilled and went inside for a sweater. When she didn't return after a little while, her sister went into the house to look for her. Moments later, their parents heard a blood-chilling scream! Inside, they found the two girls standing at the bottom of the staircase, looking up the steps in terror. At the top of the stairs was a man, dressed in old-fashioned clothing and carrying what appeared to be a Bible in one hand. When the girl's father started to call out to the intruder, the apparition simply vanished!

There have been other reported sightings of Adam Springs at the old house. Tenants have also told of slamming doors and completely dry floors that inexplicably become so slippery that no one can walk on them. One woman, who lived in the mansion as a child, claimed that when she and other family members would walk through the house at night, they would feel a soft object strike them in the face, "something that felt like a horse's tail." When the lights were switched on, they would find nothing there.

In recent years, the Springs house has been restored and has been used as the administrative offices for a local textile company. While the place certainly does not look haunted, staff members can tell you otherwise. Some of the folks who work here refuse to go up to the third floor of the house by themselves, and they tell of doors slamming shut behind them, even though there is no breeze, whispering sounds when no one else is present, and a strange feeling of never being alone.

"Do you ever look behind you to see if someone is there?", one of the employees was asked.

"No," the woman replied, shaking her head. "I've always been afraid of what might be standing behind me!"

It has already been stated in this book that the deeds of yesterday create the hauntings of today. Strange tales like the one that you have just read are what are considered classic American ghost stories—tales of not only ghostly happenings, but historical deeds and legends as well. I have always been of the belief that a tale is not worth telling unless it has a basis in truth and perhaps this explains my love of both history and hauntings.

Such a shared interest is what created the idea for this book and the series of volumes to follow. My purpose was to collect stories that contain not only historical background but ghosts and hauntings too. And while my books have always encompassed the haunted past and present, I wanted to take special note in this series of our haunted American history. Here, I hope to present both sides of each story. While I did not attempt to put together dry textbooks of facts and dates, I also tried to stay away from breathless accounts of waking up in the middle of the night to see Aunt Tilly standing at the foot of the bed. First-hand accounts of random encounters have never interested me much, but give me a story with a basis in the past and you have my attention!

I have always felt that the best way to find out why a location might be haunted is to look back and see what happened there in the past. This is true about individual houses, buildings and even graveyards and it's also true about America itself. I have a hard time thinking of any event in American history, from the founding of the colonies to the taming of the west, that does not have at least one ghost story connected to it. Some of them, like the Civil War, literally have dozens!

Of course, I can't hope to collect all of the hauntings of America in a single volume of the series for there are many tales to be told. Instead, I plan to present a number of books, each containing ghostly stories and haunted spots, that will have one very important thing in common—each of the stories will be grounded in the past. The stories will be both unusual and strange and while some may be old favorites, many of them you will have never heard before. I also hope that even the stories that are familiar will have a side to them that you have never encountered in your earlier reading.

13

And some may ask if each of the stories in this book is true? To that I can only tell you that each of them was documented as the truth. There are all real stories that have been told by real people. The truth of each story is up to the reader to decide.

But what do you think? Do you believe in ghosts? There are many readers who do believe that ghosts are real, who have had their own strange experiences over the years. Like many of us, they have tried to explain them away, but cannot. Many readers are not so open-minded though. Those who do not believe in ghosts say that spirits are merely the figments of our imagination. Such stories, these readers insist, are the creations of fools, drunkards and folklorists. Such a reader will most likely finish this book and still be unable to consider the idea that ghosts might exist. In that case, I can only hope to entertain this person with the history and horrific tales of America's eerie past.

However, I hope this person will not be too quick in assuming that he has all of the answers. There are stranger things, to paraphrase the poet, than are dreamt of in our philosophies.

Happy Hauntings!
Troy Taylor

THE HAUNTING OF AMERICA

Chapter One

NEW ENGLAND HAUNTS

America's First Ghost Story

The first recorded ghost in New England was reported in Machiasport, Maine in 1799. While the Native Americans undoubtedly had their own hauntings and spirits for centuries before the early settlers, the first writings of an encounter with a ghost came in that year.

A man named Abner Blaisdel and his family began to hear "knocking noises" in their home on August 9. The sounds continued on for some time and then escalated the following January 2 into a mournful voice from the cellar. The ghost, according to their account, claimed to be that of Captain George Butler's dead wife. Her name was Nelly Hooper, the spirit announced.

Abner Blaisdel was quite startled by this. David Hooper, the ghost's apparent father, lived but a few miles away. With that in mind, he summoned Hooper and, although skeptical about his daughter's ghost, he trekked through a snowstorm to the Blaisdel house. When he arrived, Blaisdel explained about the ghost and took Hooper down into the cellar. The doubtful old man soon became a believer when he heard his daughter's sweet voice in the gloomy basement. He asked questions and she replied with answers only she would have known. After awhile though, the voice faded away.

A few days later, Paul Blaisdel, Abner's son, became the first to actually see the ghost. He claimed to see her apparition floating in a field near the house, from which he ran in terror. The following night, Nelly's voice echoed in the cellar and gave Paul a tongue-lashing for not speaking to her when he saw her in the field.

By February 1800, Nelly had become famous in Machiasport and in the surrounding area. Crowds flocked to the Blaisdel house to hear her voice and to perhaps catch a glimpse of her. The constant stream of people sent Nelly into hiding for a time but by May 1800, she returned in grand form, appearing before 20 startled witnesses in the Blaisdel cellar. Some of them described her as a "bright light" and others as a shimmering female form in white clothing.

She remained a fixture in the small community and by the close of the year 1800, more than 100 people stated that they had seen Nelly's ghost. Such admissions came to the attention of a local minister named Cummings. He did not believe in ghosts and was quickly becoming upset with his parishioners for their foolishness. He decided to go and confront Abner Blaisdel, the man he believed was responsible for the hoax. He started down the road in a foul temper and but stumbled onto an experience that would forever change his life.

He saw a woman in the roadway, surrounded by a bright light. She came closer to him. "I was filled with genuine fear," Cummings said later, "but my fear was connected with ineffable pleasure." Nelly never spoke to the preacher, but she didn't have to either. Cummings had suddenly become a believer in ghosts. He later wrote a book about his experience and for the rest of his career, he preached widely about his belief in a life after death.

After confronting Reverend Cummings, Nelly only made one final appearance before departing from this world forever. Captain George Butler, Nelly's widowed husband, became the subject of her wrath. She appeared to him one night and berated him for daring to remarry after her death. You see, he had promised her as she lay dying that he would never take another wife!

DUDLEYTOWN

The Enigma of the Connecticut Mountains

In the far reaches of northwestern Connecticut, in the shadows of the mountains and lost in the pages of time, rests the remains of a small village called Dudleytown. The homes of this once thriving community are long gone, but the land where the town once stood is far from empty. Amidst the forest and rocks are tales of ghosts, demons, unexplained mysteries, curses and a rich history that dates back to the very beginnings of America.

Today, only the cellar holes and a few stone foundations remain. The roads that once traversed to this place are now little more than narrow trails where only a few adventurous hikers, and the occasional ghost hunter, dare to wander. Although it is forbidden, the most hardened curiosity-seekers still dare to venture down Dark Entry Road and into these shadowy woods at night.

Dudleytown, or at least the area where it was located, was first owned by a man named Thomas Griffis, one of the first to settle in this region, in the early 1740s. There are no records to say that he ever lived where Dudleytown later stood but he did own half of the land in 1741. A few years later, with the arrival of Gideon Dudley in 1747, the village would be named. Gideon was followed to the region by two brothers, and Dudleys have become known over the years as the men who brought a curse to this small town—a curse that has allegedly plagued the region ever since.

According to what have turned out to be both recent and fanciful accounts, the "curse" had its beginnings in England in 1510. At that time, Edmund Dudley was beheaded for being involved in a plot to overthrow King Henry VIII. Supposedly, a curse was placed on the family at this time, which stated that all of the Dudley descendants would be surrounded by horror and death. Proponents of the curse claim that the Dudleys then began to experience a rather disquieting run of bad luck.

Edmund's son, John Dudley, also attempted to control the British throne by arranging for his son, Guilford, to marry Lady Jane Grey, next in line for the crown. After Edward VI died, Lady Jane became the queen for a short time before the plan failed, ending with the execution of Lady Jane and the two Dudleys. To make matters worse, Guilford's brother returned from France, and being a military officer, brought home a plague that he spread to his officers and troops. The sickness wiped out massive numbers of British soldiers and eventually spread throughout the country, killing thousands.

John Dudley's third son, Robert, Earl of Leicester, a favorite of Elizabeth I, wisely decided to leave England and travel to the New World. It would be his somewhat luckier descendant, William, who would settle in Guilford, Connecticut. Three of William's descendants, Abiel, Barzallai and Gideon, would later buy a plot of land in Cornwall township.

While there are undoubtedly some grim events that surrounded the Dudley family in England and France, questions have been raised as whether or not any curse really followed them to America. The question has been raised because in order for the curse to have been passed along to account for the haunting of Dudleytown, then William Dudley would have had to have been the son of Robert, Earl of Leicester—but he wasn't. Robert Dudley had only two sons and one of them died while still a child. The other went to Italy and while he had children, all of them remained in that country. This means that there was no link between William, his sons who founded Dudleytown, and any so-called curse.

But while we may have established the fact that Dudleytown was never cursed, this does not mean that it was not tainted in some other way. There are many places across the country where odd things happen and where the land does not seem quite right. Records indicate that the land around Dudleytown was once Mohawk Indian tribal grounds but tell us little else before the coming of the first settlers. This region has gained a chilling reputation over the years. Could the weird stories and strange disappearances here be connected to the past in some way—or are they nothing more than just coincidence and imagination?

In the early 1740s, the mentioned Thomas Griffis bought a parcel of land that would later be considered the first lot in Dudleytown. The land today looks much as it did when Griffis first came here. It is covered in thick forest and the ground is strewn with rocks. The nearby mountains also heavily shadow the area, so it receives little sunlight. The woods were later dubbed with the rather ominous name of Dark Entry Forest.

In 1747, Gideon Dudley bought some land from Griffis to start a small farm. By 1753, Gideon's two brothers, Barzallai and Abiel Dudley, from Guilford, Connecticut, also purchased land nearby. A few years later, a Martin Dudley from Massachusetts also moved to the area but was from a different line of the family. He later married Gideon's daughter.

One thing that should be mentioned was that Dudleytown was never an actual town. It was a more isolated part of Cornwall. The village rested in the middle of three large hills, which accounts for the recollections of it being nearly dark at noon time. The Cornwall township was never a good area for farming, as is apparent by the rocks that were used to build the foundations and stone walls that still stand today. In spite of this though, settlers began to trickle into the area. The Tanner family, the Joneses, the Pattersons, the Dibbles and the Porters all took up residence here. The community grew even larger after iron ore was discovered nearby and farming became a secondary concern. However, there were never any stores, shops, schools or churches in Dudleytown. Provisions had to be purchased in nearby towns and when one died, a trip to Cornwall was necessary because, in addition to there being no church in town, there was no cemetery either. The population of Dudleytown was never large and according to an 1854 map, the peak number of families who lived here only reached 26.

In spite of all of these things, the town did thrive for a time. Dudleytown was noted for its timber, which was burned and used to make wood coal for the nearby Litchfield County Iron Furnaces in Cornwall and other towns. The furnaces later moved closer to the railroads and the more industrial towns, and the lumber was no longer needed. Iron ore was used from the area for a time and there were three water-powered mills in Dudleytown as well. Most of the mills eventually closed because of the long trip down the mountain to deliver their goods.

Despite the outward signs of prosperity, there were strange deaths and bizarre occurrences at Dudleytown from the start. Some historians have attempted to downplay the unusual events in recent years. They will debunk the legends of the town by first stating how few people there ever were who lived here and then will try and downplay the disappearances, cases of insanity and weird deaths, as if such things happen all of the time. And perhaps they do—but why so many unusual happenings in such an isolated area with so few people living in it? The number of deaths that have occurred here would not be such a high number in a larger town but in this small community, one can't help but wonder what exactly was taking place. There are also, I believe, an inordinate number of people who went insane in this area, as well as people who simply vanished that are in addition to those who are documented here. It's no wonder—bogus or not—that a story started about a Dudleytown curse.

Three of the Dudleys moved out of the region and lived long and full lives, dying of natural causes and forever diminishing any possibilities of a curse. Only Abiel Dudley remained in town and after a series of reverses, lost his entire fortune—and his mind. Abiel died in 1799 at the age of 90 and when he was no longer able to pay his debts, the town took his property, sold it and then made him a ward of the town. Toward the end, Abiel was senile and insane and would not be the last to suffer from this affliction.

In 1792, seven years before Abiel Dudley passed away, his good friend and neighbor, Gershon Hollister, was killed while building a barn at the home of William Tanner, Abiel's closest neighbor. Tanner was also said to have gone insane, although likely from old age and senility rather than from supernatural influences. He lived to the age of 104 and according to records was "slightly demented" at the time of his death. There have been stories that have circulated claiming that Tanner told other villages of "strange creatures" that came out of the woods at night. If this is true, there is no way for us to know if these creatures were products of the unexplained or products of Tanner's feeble mind.

The Nathaniel Carter family moved to Dudleytown in 1759 and lived in a house once owned by Abiel Dudley before he was made a ward of the town. A mysterious plague swept through Dudleytown and Cornwall and took the lives of the Adoniram Carter family, relatives of Nathaniel, and saddened by the loss, they moved to Binghampton, New York from Dudleytown in 1763. Those who believe in the curse say that the taint of Dudleytown followed after them but their tragic fate was actually far too common during the early days of the frontier. The Carters moved to the Delaware wilderness, in the heart of Indian territory, and during an attack, Indians slaughtered Nathaniel, his wife and an infant child. The Carters' other three children were abducted and taken to Canada, where two daughters were ransomed. The son, David Carter, remained with his captors, married an Indian girl and later returned to the United States for his education. He went on to edit a newspaper and became a justice on the Supreme Court.

Another bizarre tragedy affected one of the most famous residents of the region, General Herman Swift, who had served in the Revolutionary War under George Washington. In 1804, his wife, Sarah Faye, was struck by lightning while standing on the front porch of their home near Dudleytown. She was killed instantly. The General went insane and died soon after. Many have dismissed this incident as not being connected to the other unusual events, saying that Swift did not actually live in Dudleytown but on Bald Mountain Road (where his house remains today) and that he only went insane when he became old and senile. But in an area this sparsely populated, the records indicated three people to have gone insane in the space of less than a half century—could this be mere coincidence? And does a person being struck by lightning while standing on their front porch qualify as being unusual? I would say that it does and our story is not yet complete.

Another famous personage allegedly connected to Dudleytown was Horace Greeley, the editor and founder of the *New York Tribune*—or so the stories of the curse go. In this case, the story deserves to be debunked. Greeley married a young woman named Mary Young Cheney, who the stories of the curse say was born in Dudleytown. In truth, Mary was born and raised in nearby Litchfield and never lived in Dudleytown. She left the area as early as 1833 and went to live in a vegetarian boarding house that was owned by Dr. Graham (of Graham Cracker fame) and became involved in the popular wellness movement of the time. While there, she met and later married Horace Greeley. In 1872, Greeley ran for president against Ulysses S. Grant and lost the election. A short time before it, Mary suffered from an attack of lung disease and died. Her death occurred in New York City with her husband and two daughters, Ida and Gabrielle, in attendance. She was buried in Greenwood Cemetery. The legends claim that she committed suicide but this was not the case. Greeley himself died one month later and the electoral votes that he received in the election were distributed to minor candidates.

After the Civil War, Dudleytown began to die and many of the villagers simply packed up and moved away. The demise of the town itself is hardly surprising, whether you believe in the so-called curse or not. Its geographical location was foolhardy at best. Surrounded by hills and at elevations of more than 1500 feet, there was little chance that a good crop would ever grow and sustain life in the village. The winters were harsh here and even the hardy apple trees were stunted from months of cold. As mentioned already, the soil was rocky and the area was plagued by almost too much water. It pooled into tepid swamps and seeped into the earth, creating a damp morass.

But even if you overlook the idea of an actual curse and admit that the location of the town must have had a hand in its undoing, the sheer number of unusual deaths (leaving out that of Mary Greeley) and mental conditions in such an isolated area more than suggests that something out of the ordinary was occurring in the little town. And no matter how hard the debunkers try to disregard the next mysterious event to occur in Dudleytown, their efforts fall short.

This event occurred in 1901, at a time when the population of Dudleytown had dwindled away to almost nothing. One of the last residents of the town was a man named John Patrick Brophy. Tragedy visited swiftly and in several blows. First, his wife died of consumption, which was not uncommon in those days and there was nothing strange about her ailment, as she had been suffering from it for years. This did not lessen Brophy's grief however, but he was soon further stricken when his two children vanished into the forest just a short time after the funeral. And while their disappearance could have been voluntary (they had been accused of stealing sleigh blankets, a minor offense), there is nothing to indicate that it was. They vanished and were never found. Shortly after, the Brophy's house burned to the ground in an unexplained fire and not long after, Brophy himself vanished into the forest. He was never seen again.

By the early 1900s, Dudleytown was completely deserted. The remaining homes began to fall into disrepair and ruin, and soon, the forest began to reclaim the village that had been carved out of it. But there was still one other death that proponents of the curse have connected to Dudleytown and while the curse may be unlikely, it does mark one additional case of insanity for an isolated region that was already riddled with them.

Around 1900, Dr. William Clarke came to Cornwall and fell in love with the forest and the quiet country life. Clarke had been born in 1877 and grew up on a farm in Tenafly, New Jersey. He later became a professor of surgery and taught at Columbia College of Physicians and Surgeons, as well as earning a reputation as the leading cancer specialist in New York. He purchased 1,000 acres of land in the wilds of Connecticut, which included Dudleytown, and began construction of a summer and vacation home here. Over the next number of years, he and his wife, Harriet Bank Clarke, visited the house on weekends and during the summer until it was completed. After that, it became mostly a holiday house for short trips in the summer and for Thanksgiving. Together, they maintained an idyllic second life near Dudleytown until 1918.

One summer weekend, Dr. Clarke was called away to New York on an emergency. His wife stayed behind and according to the story, he returned 36 hours later to find that she had gone insane, just as a number of previous residents of the village had done. The story also claims that she told of strange creatures that came out of the forest and attacked her. She committed suicide soon after. But how much truth is there to this tale? Perhaps more than some would like you to believe. It has been recorded that for several years before her suicide, Mrs. Clarke suffered from a chronic illness. There is nothing to indicate what this ailment might have been or whether it was a physical or mental one. I think that it is safe to say though that mentally stable individuals do not ordinarily take their own lives. As far as whether or not she saw "strange creatures in the woods"—well, we will never really know for sure but even if we disregard this, we still have one more suicide that occurred to a resident of the nearly nonexistent village of Dudleytown.

While undoubtedly shattered by his wife's suicide, Dr. Clarke continued to maintain his house in Dudleytown and continued to visit. A number of years later, he remarried and returned to stay at his summer house until a larger home was completed nearby in 1930. In 1924, he and his wife, Carita, as well as other doctors, friends and interested landowners formed the Dark Entry Forest Association. It was designed to act as forest preserve so that the land around Dudleytown would remain "forever wild." They held their first meeting in 1926 with 41 members. Dr. Clarke died in Cornwall Bridge in February 1943 and Carita passed away five years later. A number of their children and family members still reside in the area.

Today, Dudleytown is mostly deserted, except for the curiosi-ty-seekers and tourists, who come looking for thrills. The Dark Forest Entry Association still owns most of the land the village once stood on. There are a group of homes on Bald Mountain Road that are very secluded from the main roads and they belong to the closest residents. These locals maintain that nothing supernatural takes place in this region and perhaps they are right. It seems unlikely that the curse on Dudleytown ever really existed but on the other hand, there is something strange about such a small area with so many disappearances, unusual deaths, suicides and cases of insanity. The stories of a curse had to have gotten started for some reason and perhaps this was why.

As far as we know, the ghostly tales began to surface in the 1940s. It was at this time that visitors to the ruins of the village began to speak of strange incidents and wispy apparitions in the woods. Even today, those who have visited the place boast of para-normal photographs, overwhelming feelings of terror, mysterious lights, sights and sounds and even of being touched, pushed and scratched by unseen hands. Some researchers refer to the area as a "negative power spot," or a place where entities enter this world from the other side. They say this may explain the strange events in Dudleytown's history, like the eerie reports, the strange creatures and perhaps even the outbreaks of insanity and madness. The place is often thought of as tainted in some way, as if the ground has somehow spoiled here, or perhaps was sour all along.

Some historians and debunkers dismiss such reports and theories and maintain that because the so-called Curse of Dudleytown doesn't exist, then nothing strange has ever occurred here either. However, an open-minded look at some of the things that have happened do seem to show this is a strange place and one that has been an enigma from the earliest days of its history. Whether or not there is any truth to the accounts of people who have come here since the days when the village was abandoned is up to the reader to decide.

I should warn you though that trying to visit Dudleytown today can be hazardous—and not because of ghosts. It should be noted that the planners for the Dark Forest Entry Association have forbidden trespassing on their property. In 1999, they announced that they would no longer allow hikers on the land. In spite of this, many still go—now daring not only the spirits, but the authorities as well. Unfortunately, the ruins of Dudleytown have been vandalized in recent years and the constant streams of trespassers have had a negative effect on the ecology of the area. Just as unfortunate is the fact that the forbidden quality of Dudleytown is what brings so many curiosity-seekers to the vicinity. However, this author advises readers to refrain from visiting this area until methods can be devised to better preserve the wilderness here and until this unsettled corner of New England has been opened to the public again.

THE STRATFORD KNOCKINGS

The Mystery of the Phelps Mansion

On a late winter morning in March 1850, strangeness came to the peaceful New England town of Stratford, Connecticut. It came quietly and without fanfare but its arrival would shake the community to its core—and would create a mystery that remains unsolved even more than a century and a half later.

Reverend Eliakim Phelps came to Stratford in February 1848 and bought a sprawling mansion on Elm Street that had once belonged to a sea captain named George R. Dowell. The house was as eccentric as its builder was. For instance, the captain had constructed the main hallway of the house to be 70 feet long and 12 feet wide, with twin staircases that met at each end of the second-floor landing. The odd design replicated the layout of Captain Dowell's clipper ship.

The seaman sold the house and retired, passing ownership to Dr. Phelps, who soon planned to retire in the new home. However, he would find the place anything but peaceful!

Dr. Phelps had been born in Belchertown, Massachusetts to an old and respected New England family. He was a graduate of the Union and Andover Seminaries and had been in charge of congregations in both Geneva and Huntington, New York. He had been widowed in his late 50s but his children were all grown and had moved from home by then. He was well known in religious circles and was seen as somewhat unusual in his thinking, often expressing an interest in mysticism, mesmerism and later, in the growing Spiritualist movement in America. He devoted most of his time to reading and exploring his unique interests. Phelps was definitely outside of the norm when it came to Presbyterian clergymen.

Then, at 59 years of age, Phelps began to make some changes in his life. Not only did he relocate from Philadelphia to Stratford, but he also married again. His new bride was many years younger and already had three children: Anna, 16, Henry, 11 and another girl, who was 6. Together, they had a son, who was three-years-old when the strange happenings on Elm Street began.

Despite what seemed to be a blissful life, some accounts state that the family was not entirely happy. Apparently, Mrs. Phelps did not care for Stratford and did not like her neighbors. She was constantly tired and upset and it was said that her daughter, Anna, suffered from a nervous disposition. The stress carried by these two women is worth noting during the pages to come.

It began on Sunday, March 10, 1850. The entire Phelps family returned from church services that morning to find the doors of their house standing wide open. Dr. Phelps was shocked by this! As the maid was away, he had been sure to secure the entire house, locking not only the exterior doors and windows, but the interior ones as well. The only keys were in his pocket. But now, they discovered that all of them had been flung open, both inside and out.

Dr. Phelps cautiously entered the house, unsure of what he might find. What he discovered was chaos. Someone had ransacked the place, knocking over furniture, smashing dishes, scattering books, papers and clothing. Yet strangely, they had not apparently been robbed. Phelps found that his gold watch, the family silver and his loose cash were in plain sight, but had been left alone. He wondered if perhaps an unlocked window had provided the thieves means to escape when the family returned from church and caught them by surprise.

Phelps summoned his family and they went upstairs to inspect the bedrooms. Here, they found no burglars hidden away but something even more unnerving. In one of the bedrooms, someone had spread a sheet over the bed and had placed one of Mrs. Phelps' nightgowns on top of it. Stockings had then been placed at the bottom of it to suggest feet and the arms of the gown had been folded over the chest as though crossed in preparation for a funeral. What sort of message had the thieves, or more likely vandals, been trying to send?

The family attempted to restore some order to the house before returning to the church for the afternoon services. When the clock struck past noon, Mrs. Phelps and the children departed, but Dr. Phelps remained at the house, hoping to catch the burglars when they returned. He hid in his study, armed with a pistol, and waited in silence. A few hours passed and he heard no sounds but that of the house creaking in the wind. No doors opened or closed, no footsteps fell in the rooms or the corridors.

Eventually, he left his hiding place and wandered about the lower floor. He opened the door to the dining room and got a shocking discovery! The previously empty room was now filled with a crowd of women! They had entered the house without sound and now stood silent and still, standing and kneeling in positions of religious devotion. Several of them held bibles, others bowed so low that their foreheads nearly brushed the floor, and all of them seemed to be centered around a small, demonic figure that was suspended in the center of the room.

It was several moments before Dr. Phelps realized that the women in the room were incredibly lifelike effigies that had been fashioned from the family's clothing. The dresses had been filled with rags, muffs and other materials from around the house. The dummies had somehow been created and positioned during the short time that Mrs. Phelps and the children had been away from the house.. and while Dr. Phelps had been so vigilantly standing guard! How could it have been done? And more importantly, what did it mean?

Notably, this would not be the last time that the effigies would appear without explanation in the house. Over the months to come, these eleven "women" would be joined by nearly 20 more. They would appear without warning and with no clue as to how they were constructed so quickly or so secretly. On March 10, the family would not know that this incredible event was only the beginning!

Some time later, the events on that Sunday morning would be connected to an almost forgotten incident that had taken place a few days before. Some would suggest that perhaps the spirits that came to the Phelps mansion came there by invitation.

In 1850, the Spiritualism movement was just starting to capture the attention of America. Two years before, in 1848, the Fox sisters of New York had received national attention with their spirit rappings and Americans were becoming intrigued by communication with the dead.

On March 4, an old friend of Dr. Phelps had come to Stratford for a visit. Knowing of the minister's interest in unusual things, they began discussing Spiritualism and the possibilities of contacting the spirit world. One thing led to another and the two men decided to try their hand at a séance. In reply to their questions, the men reported some disorganized knocking and rapping sounds, but neither of them considered it very extraordinary. But did they summon up something that night which would come back to plague the house later?

By March 10, the séance was undoubtedly forgotten in the confusion over the vandalized house and the mysterious effigies. After that, things got even worse! Activity became more frantic the following day as objects began to move about the house. An umbrella jumped into the air and traveled nearly 25 feet; forks, spoons, knives, books, pens and assorted small objects launched from places where no one had been standing; pillows, sheets and blankets were pulled from beds and fluttered into the air. This continued all day long and finally, by evening, the activity seemed to be exhausted and the house fell silent.

But the next morning though, it started all over again. Mrs. Phelps pleaded with her husband to call someone for help. So Phelps contacted Reverend John Mitchell, a friend and a retired minister. Mitchell listened to the story and quickly suggested the most obvious solution, that the maid or the older children were playing tricks. He took the suspects away from the house and sequestered them nearby, but the activity continued. He still suspected some natural explanation though, until he actually saw some of the objects move for himself. He soon became convinced that the events were unexplainable.

On March 14, the haunting took another turn. During the morning meal, a potato literally dropped from nowhere and landed on the breakfast table. This was just the beginning too. Throughout the rest of the day, Dr. and Mrs. Phelps, along with Reverend Mitchell, witnessed 46 objects appear and drop out of the air in the locked parlor. Most of the items were articles of clothing that had been somehow transported from the upstairs closets.

In the weeks to come, observers, friends and the curious witnessed objects appearing and flying through the air at the Phelps home. Most of these items would move at abnormally slow speeds and they would touch down on the floor as if carefully placed there. Phelps and others also claimed to see the objects change course while in flight.

There were many accusations of trickery toward the Phelps family but with each, Dr. Phelps invited the skeptics to see the house for themselves. He was hospitable to reporters, investigators, and even mere curiosity-seekers, and he permitted them to come to the house and to stay as long as they liked. Many of them would witness the disturbances first hand.

Finally, after reading accounts of the haunting in newspapers, Dr. Phelps' son, Austin, journeyed to Stratford to get to the bottom of the matter. His uncle, Abner Phelps, a well-known Boston doctor and Massachusetts legislator, accompanied him. Austin himself was a professor at Andover Theological Seminary. Neither of the men was pleased with the family's growing notoriety and neither of them had approved of Dr. Phelps' marriage to his young wife either. They were sure that they would discover a trickster among the family.

During their first night, they heard a loud pounding noise that they surmised was coming from the knocker on the front door. They took turns pulling it open and guarding the door, but each time they expected to pounce on the prankster, they found the doorstep to be deserted. Finally, they stood on both sides of the door, Austin on the outside and his uncle inside. The loud knocking continued, but the source was a mystery.

The men were also disturbed by rapping noises upstairs. On the second night, they determined the noise was coming from Anna's room, the daughter with the nervous condition. The hammering seemed to be coming from the inside panel of the door. They burst into the room, thinking to catch her in the act, but she was far from the door when they entered. Austin later wrote: "The young lady was in bed, covered up and out of reach of the door. We examined the panel and found dents where it had been struck."

The two men would depart from the house believing that whatever phenomenon was being experienced there, it was genuine.

The haunting continued, becoming both a physical and psychological attack on the entire family. The night time hours were filled with rapping, knockings, voices, screams and bizarre sounds, while the daylight hours saw objects sailing about through the rooms. Silverware bent and twisted, windows broke, papers scattered and tables and chairs danced across the floor as if they had come to life. And of course, the strange effigies continued to appear. It was reported in the *New Haven Journal* that: "In a short space of time so many figures were constructed that it would not have been possible for a half a dozen women, working steadily for several hours, to have completed their design, and arrange the picturesque tableau. Yet these things happened in short space of time, with the whole house on the watch. In all, about 30 figures were constructed during this period."

Author Joseph Citro wrote that one of the kneeling figures, wearing a dress belonging to Mrs. Phelps, was so realistic that when the youngest child walked into a room with his sister and saw the effigy, he whispered to her: "Be still, Ma is saying prayers."

Unfortunately, the haunting was not limited to the destruction of items in the house. Daughter Anna soon became a target for the spirit's wrath, as did young Henry. A reporter from the *New York*

Sun wrote that he visited the house at the end of April 1850 and was present in a room with Anna and Mrs. Phelps and was able to observe them at all times. At one point, he saw Anna's arm jerk and twitch and she announced that she had just been pinched. The reporter rolled back her sleeve and stated that her arm bore several savage-looking red marks.

At other times, Anna was slapped by unseen hands. Those present sometimes only saw the girl shake or jerk her head, but reported hearing the sound of a slap. They often saw red marks and welts appear on her skin. Once, while she was asleep, a pillow was reportedly pressed over her head and then tied around her neck with tape. According to the editor of the *Bridgeport Standard*, she nearly died.

But Henry was tortured even further. He was beaten, pinched, struck and occasionally rendered unconscious and abducted. Once, in the presence of Dr. Phelps, he was hit with a flurry of small stones. A newspaper reporter claimed that he once saw the boy carried from this bed by an invisible force and dumped on the floor. In front of a number of witnesses, he was once lifted into the air so high that his hair brushed the ceiling of the room. One day, he vanished and would later be found outside, tied up and suspended from a tree. He had no idea how he had gotten there.

The young boy was also burned, thrown into a cistern of water and his clothing torn apart in front of visiting clergymen. He was discovered missing again one afternoon and he was later discovered shoved onto a closet shelf with a rope around his neck.

Numerous theories were put forth (and continue to be today) as to just what was going on in the Phelps house. Many believed that the house had been invaded by intelligent spirits, bound and determined to wreak havoc with the family. But why? Locals stated that the haunting was caused by the ghost of a Goody Bassett, who was hanged near the house for witchcraft in 1651. However, there was no evidence to support this piece of fanciful lore.

While the charges of the skeptics about trickery seemed to be mostly answered by more displays of incredible happenings, the question still remains as to whether the haunting could have been the work of unconscious or involuntary psycho-kinesis. The poltergeist-like events that occurred could have been the unknowing manipulations of Anna (she of the nervous condition) or even perhaps Mrs. Phelps, who was bitter and unhappy in her new home. Nearly all of the phenomena could be explained in this matter, save for the eerie and mysterious effigies that appeared in locked rooms.

It would be these figures, along with the knocking and rapping sounds, that would convince Dr. Phelps and some of the other clergymen that the force in the house was clearly a demonic one. Reverend John Mitchell, who spent the most time in the house as an investigator, even managed to engage the spirits in conversation using a primitive alphabet code of raps and replies. However, the foul answers that he received to his questions had him believing Phelps' insistence that the force was an evil one.

And the communication continued beyond mere knocks and raps. On one occasion, Dr. Phelps was in his study alone, writing at his desk. He turned away for a moment and when he turned back he found that his sheet of paper, which had been blank, was now covered with strange-looking writing. The ink on the paper was still wet.

In the days that followed, other family members and friends would experience the same thing and would find papers with writing on them. The letters sometimes appeared from thin air, floating down over the dinner table or appearing in a sealed box. None of the messages were very revealing and, unfortunately, they were all disposed of as Dr. Phelps felt they were missives from an evil source.

Now, desperate for information that the spirits had been unwilling to provide, Dr. Phelps agreed reluctantly to perform another séance in the house. This time, communication was easily resolved and the spirit claimed to be a soul in hell, enduring torment for the sins he had committed in life. Dr. Phelps asked the spirit what he could do to help and using the knocking code, the ghost asked that Phelps bring him a piece of pumpkin pie. Thinking that he had been misunderstood, he asked again and this time the spirit asked for a glass of gin.

Finally, Phelps asked why the spirit was causing such a disturbance in the house and the spirit replied: "For fun."

Then, the spirit further detailed its history, claiming to be a law clerk who had done some financial work for Mrs. Phelps. He confessed that he had committed fraud and had been sent to hell when he died. He did not explain why he was haunting the Phelps home though. Eerily, Dr. Phelps later made a visit to the Philadelphia law firm where the spirit claimed to have been employed and he examined the papers in question. It turned out that a fraud had been committed and that it had been serious enough to warrant the man's prosecution, had he lived until his arrest and trial.

Later on though, Phelps would change his position about the identity of the ghost and would feel that he had been tricked using the fraudulent papers. It is unknown what made him change from his original position. He simply stated that: "I am convinced that the communications are wholly worthless, in that they are frequently false, contradictory and nonsensical." The Phelps family had gone through just about all they could take.

After months of madness in the house, they decided to abandon the place and move back to Philadelphia. They would at least winter there and see how things looked in the spring. Following this decision, Dr. Phelps was in his office one night and a paper suddenly came from nowhere and fluttered down onto his desk. The message asked how soon the family would be leaving the house? On a nearby paper, Dr. Phelps scratched the words "October 1" and by that day, they had departed. Phelps sent his wife and family ahead of him to Philadelphia and he remained briefly in Stratford to put his affairs in order. During this period, the house was quiet and still. The spirits had apparently departed with the Phelps family. However, they did not accompany them to

Philadelphia. The haunting seemed to be over at last. But was it?

The Phelps family spent the winter and spring in the city and they returned to Stratford in the early summer days of 1851. The house was calm and still and over the course of the next eight years, nothing out of the ordinary occurred there. The supernatural forces, whether spiritual or man-made, seemed to have resolved themselves. In 1859, the house was sold to Moses Y. Beach, the founder of the *New York Sun*.

The Beach family remained in the house into the early 1900s. Moses' son, Alfred Beach, lived in the house for many years after. As the longtime editor of *Scientific American* magazine, Beach turned part of the mansion into the Stratford Institute, a private school for the children of wealthy city families. He remodeled and renovated the house for this purpose in 1907.

Several other owners followed the Beach family until the 1940s. It was then purchased by Mrs. Maude Thompson, who converted the house into a residence for senior citizens. In 1947, Carl Caserta and his wife, both registered nurses, bought the house and converted it into the Restmore Convalescent Home until the late 1960s.

It was during this period that the ghosts of the Phelps Mansion are said to have reared their ugly heads again! The Caserta's occupied a third-floor apartment in the house and the elderly patients lived on the lower two floors. Shortly after they moved in, Mrs. Caserta put her infant son, Gary, to bed one night. She placed a blanket over one of the wall light fixtures so that it wouldn't disturb his sleep. She needed to leave it on so that she could see when she came upstairs later that night. The baby was left alone sleeping as Mr. Caserta was away for the evening.

Years earlier, a series of electric buzzers had been installed throughout the mansion to summon household help to the various floors. They had largely been forgotten by this time and they were certainly not on Mrs. Caserta's mind as she went downstairs to the basement to finish some work with other staff members. However, just a few minutes after she arrived there, the basement buzzer

The Phelps Mansion as it looked in the days not long before it burned down. Vandals nearly destroyed the house and the fire did the rest.

Soldiers at Fort Warren in during the Civil War.

blared to life! Mrs. Caserta and her two assistants ran upstairs to find the source of the alarm. None of the patients on the lower two floors were even capable of reaching the buzzers from their beds.

Still frantic, Mrs. Caserta hurried up to the third floor. Just as she reached the stairs, she smelled smoke and she heard her baby crying. As she ran into the apartment, she saw that the blanket that had been placed over the light fixture was smoldering. Small holes had been burned in the material and it was moments away from bursting into flames. She threw the blanket into the bathtub and snatched up Gary from his crib. The child wasn't old enough to have reached the alarm and no one else could have done it. Oddly enough, another alarm buzzer warning would save Gary again a few years later when he almost took what would have been a fatal fall.

The Casertas began to realize that the house was haunted. In their opinion though, the spirit was a benevolent one, much different than what was experienced by the Phelps family. Was the lost soul not trying to atone for the things that he had done?

In some cases, this may have been true, but despite the rescues of Gary, most of the activity that was reported in the house during this period was still weird and unsettling. The peaceful lives of the patients in the house began to be disrupted by odd noises, tapping from inside of the walls, voices and frightening cries in the night. A series of investigations was never able to get to the bottom of the problem. Eventually, the Casertas sold the house and moved away.

The new owners, the Alliance of Medical Inns, Inc., a New England company that operated rest homes all over the northeast, began making plans for the house. They wanted to build a large hospital adjacent to the property and use the mansion as office space. Sadly though, financial problems prevented the plans from being completed and the house was boarded up and abandoned. Within a short time, vandals nearly destroyed the house and put the owners into a situation where renovation would be too costly.

Author Joseph Citro recalled a time when a Stratford police officer was dispatched to the house on a vandalism call. He and his partner entered the building and both later remarked that the interior was unusually cold. They heard loud noises on the third floor and both men, thinking that the perpetrator was trapped up there, ran up the stairs. As they rounded a corner, they saw a dark figure that vaguely resembled a nun. The figure ran away from them and darted into a bedroom. The officers arrived just in time to see the person duck into a closet. Believing the vandal was trapped, one of them flung open the closet door. The shadowed interior was empty!

The Phelps Mansion was destroyed by fire in the early 1970s and no trace of it remains today. The knockings, the weird reports, the bizarre effigies and the later events all remain unexplained. The spirits who came here are gone, apparently having returned from whence they came. Of course, where that place might be is as puzzling as what these creatures were in the first place. Ghosts? Demons? Who knows? The answer is unlikely to ever be revealed.

THE LADY IN BLACK

The Ghost of Boston's Fort Warren

One of the greatest ghost stories of the Northeast is that of the spectral woman in black who haunts Fort Warren in the Boston harbor. During the years when this was an active military post, the Lady in Black was allegedly the cause of several court-martial cases. It was said that men who were on duty and saw the specter, then fired at her, were called to account for shooting at nothing! In one noted case, a sentry deserted his post, which is an unforgivable act. In his defense, he testified that the Lady in Black chased him away.

But who is this strange character and why does she haunt the fort? To answer that, we have to take a journey back to the time of America's bloodiest conflict, the Civil War.

Andrew Lanier was a young Confederate soldier from Crawfordsville, Georgia. When the call came for men to serve in the southern armies, Lanier answered the charge and enlisted. Just hours before he was to leave home though, he went to his intended bride and asked for her hand in marriage. It was granted and the two married, only spending a single night together as husband and wife. As he rode away, his new wife (known in the lore as Melanie) knew that he might not return for the duration of the conflict. She saw him last on June 28, 1861.

A few months later, Lanier was captured and sent with many other Confederate soldiers to the prison in Boston harbor known as Fort Warren. The fort was located on George's Island, seven miles off the shore from the city of Boston, and had a prison known as the Corridor of Dungeons. The fort had originally been designed to defend the harbor, although it was known for the fact that it always lacked in guns and strength. Luckily for the people of Boston, its readiness was never put to the test.

Over the course of the war, thousands of Confederate soldiers were held here, but not one made a successful escape. As prisons go though, it was not a bad place, especially in comparison to some of the dreaded Civil War era prison camps like Point Lookout and Andersonville. The food was tolerable, the weather was usually mild and the health of the men didn't suffer too much. The biggest complaint among the men was about the rats. From the earliest days at Fort Warren, the rats had laid claim to the fort's darkest corners. One southerner later wrote that their tails were as "thick as fingers."

The prisoners who suffered the least were the wealthy officers. Their loved ones were allowed to send packages of food and liquor and most played backgammon, cards and drank whiskey punch. Even the poor soldiers ate decently and for pleasure, played poker or climbed atop the walls to enjoy pleasant evening views of the harbor. A great deal of singing and music could be heard within the walls, from both the Confederate and Federal soldiers. The great marching song of the Union troops, "John Brown's Body," was composed at Fort Warren. Even the fort's commander, Colonel Justin E. Dimmock, was admired by the men on both sides. He was liked by his own troops and respected by the Confederates for his fairness and humanity.

While life was endurable for most of the Confederate prisoners, it was intolerable for Andrew Lanier. He spent each day within the confines of the Corridor of Dungeons pining away for his lost love in Georgia. After a week passed, he decided to write a letter to his wife and he told her of his capture, the location of his prison and then ended the letter with endearing words of romance and terrible loneliness.

The letter somehow made it through the battle lines and some weeks later, Melanie received it. She wept over the heartfelt sentiment and the horrible fate that had befallen her husband. She soon became determined to leave her home and travel to Massachusetts. A plan was beginning to form that would take the young woman within the walls of Fort Warren, where she would somehow, some way, free her husband from his captors.

Melanie contacted a blockade runner, who agreed to take her up the coast. She then obtained a man's suit of clothing and cut off all of her long and luxuriant hair. Into her coat pocket, she tucked an old pepperbox pistol. Thus prepared, the "young man" set sail for Boston, arriving in Cape Cod just over two months later. She managed to get in touch with Southern sympathizers that she knew through her family and moved from home to home, eventually landing in Hull, Massachusetts, less than one mile away from George's Island.

Over the next few days, Melanie studied the prison through a telescope and familiarized herself with the coastline, the walls and the section of the fort where the prisoners were housed. She planned and prepared and soon, her fate was sealed.

On January 15, 1862, a terrible storm blew into Boston Harbor. The rain fell in sheets and prevented anyone from seeing more than a few feet in front of them, especially after darkness fell. Melanie's host agreed to help her and he rowed her in a small boat to the island and he left her on the beach. He then returned to the mainland, his boat tossing dangerously in the violent sea.

Melanie carefully crossed the beach, passing two rain-soaked sentries as she ducked behind tumbles of rock. She carried with her a small bundle, which contained her pistol and a short-handled pick. The sentries made another round and then Melanie ran from her hiding place and scrambled up to the outside edge of the building where her husband was imprisoned. Standing there alone, drenched and shivering, she recalled a tune that she and her husband had used to signal each other when they were courting. She began to whistle it, softly at first and then louder. There was no answer. Finally, against her better judgment, she gave a final, piercing whistle and then ducked down out of sight. Finally, an answering whistle came from within the fort!

As Melanie looked up, she saw a rope of cloth emerge from one of the narrow windows high above her. It came lower and lower until she was able to take hold of it and begin climbing up the wall. From inside the prison, strong arms lifted her into the air and then helped her to ease through the seven-inch opening in the stone wall. In moments, she was in the arms of her husband.

The other Confederates were thrilled to see a Southern woman among them and perhaps more excited to see the pistol and the pick that she had brought along with her. They soon came up with a bold plan. They would not simply escape. Instead, they planned to tunnel from one of the dungeons and rather than escape to the beach, they would dig toward the inner part of the fort. They planned to come up under the parade ground, break into the arsenal, capture weapons and then seize the fort! They would then turn the fort's guns against Boston and besiege the city. They managed to convince themselves that their small uprising could change the entire course of the war!

Weeks passed and the tunnel began to grow. The dirt was pushed out of the hole and then carried and spread by prisoners using their shirts and coats as containers. Melanie remained carefully concealed among the men. Her clothing was fastened to hide the fact that she was a woman.

At last, the night came when the tunnel would be completed. Only a short thrust would be needed to open the hole into the parade ground, they believed. The men who had engineered the project believed that the passage had reached its proper length. In the early morning hours, a young lieutenant mightily swung the pick against the top of the tunnel. The pick went through the earth and smashed against the stone wall of the prison. The planners had miscalculated the distance!

Unfortunately, one of the sentries guarding the parade ground heard the metal tip strike the rock and suspected what was happening. He shouted a warning and soon the entire fort was on alert. When word reached Colonel Dimmock, he immediately headed for the dungeons and made a surprise inspection of the prisoners. He walked in to find several of the men scattering loose dirt outside of the walls. He quickly ordered the men into formation and the prisoners were removed and marched outside until the dungeons were seemingly empty. A head count was taken and it was realized that eleven of the Confederates were missing. An examination of the corner dungeon revealed the entrance to the tunnel.

Dimmock shouted down into the shaft and he ordered the men to come out. One by one, the unhappy southerners crawled out of the hole, all except Andrew Lanier and his wife. Her plan was for her husband to crawl out and surrender and she would stay behind. Once all of the prisoners were counted, and found to be all present, the guards would not be looking for anyone else. She would then emerge from hiding and surprise the guards, taking them prisoner with her pistol.

Lanier knew that it was a desperate plan, but he agreed. He slipped out of the tunnel, throwing up his hands in surrender. The guards pushed him into line and once again counted all of the prisoners. Dimmock shook his head and stated that the tunnel would be filled in the morning with cement and for tonight, the men who had been incarcerated here would use other quarters. He began to lead the way out of the dungeon when Melanie suddenly appeared from the mouth of the tunnel!

"Throw up your hands!" she ordered the Federal guards and officers. "I have a pistol and I know how to use it!"

Colonel Dimmock thought quickly. He raised his hands but slowly advanced toward the girl. Carefully, his men followed him, forming a circle around the young woman. Then, moving quickly, he knocked the gun from her hand, just as she fired it. The bullet erupted from the gun and tragically, it stuck her husband in the head, killing him instantly!

Andrew Lanier's lifeless body was buried in the desolate cemetery at the fort and Melanie was sentenced to be executed as a spy.

On the morning of February 2, 1862, the guards asked the young woman if she had any final requests. "Yes," she replied, "I am tired of wearing men's clothing and I would like to wear a gown once more before I die."

A search was carried out of the entire fort and just as Colonel Dimmock was going to send a man ashore for a suitable dress, a soldier uncovered a black robe that had been used during one of the fort's theatrical performances, given by the First Corps of Cadets. It was in this costume that Melanie was hanged just a few hours later. He body was then cut down and she was carefully buried in a grave next to her husband.

But Melanie Lanier, determined in life, would return in death.

Time passed, the war ended and the prisoners and guards at the fort were shipped out. Young recruits came to take their place. Several of the men however stayed on. One of them, Richard Cassidy, was a private at the time of the execution of Melanie Lanier and later, it was his duty each night to patrol the area where she had been hanged. The other men joked with him and warned him to watch out for the Lady in Black. He laughed along with his friends, but he was never too pleased with the duty.

One night, Cassidy came running toward the guard house, screaming at the top of his lungs. After a few moments, he calmed down enough to explain to the other men what had happened. He had been patrolling his post and began thinking back to the day of the execution. Suddenly, two hands fastened onto his neck from behind! He gasped for breath and spun around to see who was attacking him. It was none other than Melanie Lanier, he swore, dressed in the black robes that she had been hanged and buried in! Her face was a pale and frightful mask and her eyes blazed with anger. Then, Cassidy summoned all of his strength, broke away from her and ran for his life.

The other guards roared with laughter, but it was no laughing matter to Cassidy. He never forgot the incident and even after being detained for 30 days in the guard house for deserting his post, he swore that he would never patrol that area after dark again.

The Lady in Black has been said to walk the night ever since. In the winter of 1891, four officers were walking out through the massive sally port and saw fresh tracks in the snow that appeared to have been made by a woman's slipper. No woman was present on the island at that time and legends blamed the Lady in Black.

During World War II, it has been recorded that one sentry suffered a nervous breakdown while patrolling the area where Melanie was hanged. He was placed in the island hospital to recover but was never able to fully explain what happened to him. He was later institutionalized and never was the same again.

In 1947, Captain Charles Norris of Towson, Maryland was on the island alone one night and was reading in the library of his home. He distinctly felt someone tap him on the shoulder but when he turned, there was no one in the room. The strange incident was repeated several times and then moments later, the upstairs telephone rang. He placed his book on the chair and climbed the stairs to answer it. He picked up the telephone and a man's voice said: "Operator speaking, what number please?"

Norris replied that the telephone had been ringing and he had picked it up. He was not dialing out because someone had called him. The operator agreed but then added that it had been a previous call and that the Captain's "wife answered and took the message, sir."

Needless to say, Norris was startled by this. Neither his wife, nor any other woman, was on the island!

Since 1946, thousands of visitors have come to Fort Warren as the island has been restored and preserved as a military post. Like the history and lore, the ghost of Melanie Lanier remains here. Should you ever get the chance, I recommend a visit to Fort Warren and George's Island; you never know who might still be waiting there to greet you!

OCEAN-BORN MARY

A Classic Tale of Haunted New England

The year was 1720 and the place was Londonderry, Ireland. A small sailing vessel called Wolf departed from the port, bound for the New World. Here, weary passengers and immigrants would have the chance to reunite with relatives from another Londonderry, this one in New Hampshire. But fate was not kind to these travelers, for as they neared the coast of New England, the ship was overtaken by a band of Spanish pirates. They scrambled aboard the crippled vessel, seized jewelry and valuables and then, at the command of their captain, a buccaneer named Don Pedro, they prepared to murder everyone on board.

Just as the pirates raised cutlass and pistol, Don Pedro ordered his men to stand down. Beyond the terrified screams of the passengers, he heard another sound, the unmistakable wail of a baby. He ordered the captain, James Wilson, to bring the infant and mother to the deck. This must have taken incredible courage on his part, as the baby was his own. She had been born at sea.

After a long moment, Captain Wilson turned and went below. Soon, Elizabeth Wilson stood on the deck at his side, holding a tiny baby in her arms. Don Pedro looked down into the face of the infant and sheathed his sword. Although he was a killer, he also knew that killing this child would bring him bad luck for the rest of his days. It was a superstition of the sea. He turned and ordered one of his men back to the pirate ship. When he returned, he handed his captain a package. Don Pedro unwrapped it and revealed a bolt of beautiful, sea-green brocaded silk.

He held it out to Elizabeth. "*Por favor, Senora*," he spoke to her softly. "If you name your daughter Maria, Mary…after my mother, and accept this silk for her wedding dress, I will spare the lives of all aboard." Elizabeth tearfully took the cloth from his hands and Don Pedro and his men departed. Captain Wilson managed to bring the Wolf into Portsmouth harbor a few days later.

Mary Wilson grew up to be a tall Irish beauty with flaming red hair and fiery green eyes. In August 1742, she married Thomas Wallace, her childhood sweetheart and her wedding dress was made from a sea-green silk that her mother had carefully stored for more than two decades. The radiant bride soon settled into her happy marriage, but her happiness was short-lived. In 1760, Thomas died and left her with four sons to raise.

At about the same time, the golden age of piracy came to an end and Don Pedro retired from his exploits on the high seas. Although he had not thought of Mary in more than twenty years, he sought her out and learned that she lived in New Hampshire. Using money that he had plundered over the years, he purchased 6,000 acres of land in New Hampshire and aided by ship's carpenters and slaves, he built a mansion on a hilltop south of Henniker. It was an awesome ten-room house with six fireplaces and it was said to be one of the largest homes in the state. When he settled in, he called on Ocean-Born Mary and he invited her to come and live with him. He told her that the house was hers but asked that she care for him in his old age.

Mary accepted and she and her sons moved into the house. Don Pedro made sure that she never wanted for anything, showering her with fine clothing and jewels and buying her a black and gold carriage that was drawn by a four-horse team. Mary happily entertained townspeople and distinguished guests at the elegant mansion and lived in comfort for the next ten years.

Death came to Ocean Born Mary again a short time later. Don Pedro returned late one night from the coast and Mary heard the murmur of voices in the field behind the house. She looked out and saw the old pirate and a large, swarthy man burying a large trunk in a rocky hole beneath the trees. When she asked Don Pedro about it, he brushed her off and refused to answer. Time passed, but Mary never forgot the strange incident and soon, it would come back to haunt her.

A year passed and one afternoon Mary returned home from town. When she arrived, she found no stable boy waiting to greet her. In fact, there was no one around at all. She soon found the slaves huddled in a garden shed, too afraid to come out. Moments later, she found Don Pedro lying facedown in the orchard. A cutlass had been plunged into his back, pinning his body to the bloody ground. He had been dead for hours.

In keeping with his final request, Mary instructed her slaves to bury the pirate beneath the large hearthstone in the kitchen fireplace. Rumors spread about who the "fine Spanish gentleman" really was and stories began about a fortune in pirate gold that was hidden on the property. From time to time, gangs of men trespassed on the ground, searching for gold and buried loot, but Mary never stopped them and soon interest waned.

Mary stayed on the house for the rest of her days. Her sons went off to fight in the War for Independence, married and started families of their own. Mary lived until 1814, when she passed away at the age of 94. For the next 100 years, the house remained in the Wallace family. It was rented out but never sold. However, few of the renters ever stayed very long and none of them explained their hasty departures. Regardless, stories began to spread that the house was haunted.

The stories grew more credible by 1910, when the house really began to look like a haunted old mansion. It stood empty and dilapidated, with broken windows and sagging steps. No one lived in the place anymore, but this didn't stop people from reporting lights in the window at midnight and hearing strange cries echoing in the darkness. A few who were brave enough to peer into the windows claimed to see a tall woman coming down the staircase. Others stated that they had seen, or had heard, a horse-drawn coach pulling into the driveway.

In 1918, a Mrs. Flora Roy and her bachelor son, Louis (known as Gus), from LaCrosse, Wisconsin moved into the house. They had bought the place two years earlier and had hired workmen to restore the old mansion and to make it livable again. Even after they moved in though, there was still cleaning to do. One day, they were cleaning out the kitchen cupboards and burning the trash in the kitchen stove. Mrs. Roy had gotten a hot fire going there and was passing papers and refuse to Gus to throw into it. She handed him a paper bag and he went into the kitchen to add it to the fire. But something stopped Gus from doing it. He said that it was like an invisible hand drawing him back away from the stove. He suddenly opened the bag and found that it was filled with gunpowder!

In 1938, a hurricane devastated the Atlantic Seaboard. When the storm hit New England, it turned inland and wreaked even more havoc. The day before it hit Henniker, it rained hard all day and Gus decided to check the condition of the road before trying to take his car into town. Luckily he did, because beyond the driveway, there was no road, only a sea of mud and wet debris. When Gus managed to get back up the drive to the house, he noticed that the garage he had built was swaying. If it went down, it would crush his new car! He quickly found a few long poles and propped up the building the best that he could.

He was drenched to the skin when he went back into the house. He saw this mother had been watching from the window. "Who was helping you shore up the garage?" she asked him when he came inside. When he replied that there had been no one out there with him, she insisted that there had been. In fact, she described this person as a tall lady in a white dress. When Gus had started back to the house, the lady seemed to vanish.

At that point, Flora and Gus began to wonder if the stories they had heard about the house were true. They didn't doubt it any longer when they also began to see Mary inside of the house too. Gus saw her first and described a woman on the staircase with long, flowing auburn hair. Flora also began to see her too and they both believed that Ocean-Born Mary was there, watching over them and protecting her house.

Gus would later state that even though they were convinced the place was haunted, they were never frightened. They learned to ignore the strange sounds that came from the cellar because it seemed that whenever the house, or the family, was in trouble, something would happen to avert the danger. Gus claimed to have suffered 17 near-fatal accidents while living in the house and always survived them!

As stories of the haunting spread, journalists from all over the country came to the house and wrote of the experiences had by Flora and Gus. The tales of Ocean-Born Mary were spread far and wide and appeared in books, magazines and later on television. Gus charged an admission for people to come and tour the house and grounds, using the money he raised to support himself and his mother and for upkeep on the mansion. Every Halloween night, cars would be lined up bumper-to-bumper as people came to see the house and hoped to catch a glimpse of Mary herself.

From 1960 to 1978, the house was owned by David and Corrine Russell, who had once worked for Gus Roy and had cared for him in his final illness before he died. Even though they contacted author Hans Holzer for his 1963 book *Yankee Ghosts* and told him about the haunting in the place, including their own supernatural experiences, they soon began to deny the stories. They claimed that the house was not haunted and had never been haunted. In an interview with author Susy Smith for her book *Prominent American Ghosts*, the Russells claimed that stories of the house being haunted had been invented by Gus Roy so that people would come to see the house. When Smith then asked them about the stories they told to Hans Holzer, she received only a letter from their attorney in reply. The house was not haunted, it said.

In addition, stories and rumors remain today that say Mary never lived in this house at all. They say the story is nothing more than a folk legend that draws upon old tales of England and confusion over just who did live in the house. Despite this, the legend continues to be told today!

So, what was the truth? Who knows? Ocean-Born Mary's house still stands today, as magnificent as ever, although it is a private residence now. Mary's grave can be found in Henniker at the Centre Cemetery, and her ghost? Well, if the Russells are to be believed, she never existed at all. If that's true though, then who was the tall, red-headed woman that was seen floating alongside the roadway by two New Hampshire state troopers a few years ago? Was it Ocean-Born Mary, or a startling coincidence?

THE GHOST OF EDITH WHARTON

The Haunting of the Mount

While author Edith Wharton is best remembered today as the novelist of such classic titles as *The House of Mirth* and *Ethan Frome*, she is also considered to be one the greatest of the American ghost story writers. Her ghostly tales span the entire length of her career from 1904 to 1937 and some might even say that she was obsessed with supernatural terror.

And while the author created more than her share of ghosts and hauntings of the literary sort, there are many believe that she may not have departed this mortal coil at the time of her death in 1937. Some believe she haunts her former home in Massachusetts, now a spectral character from one of the many stories that she penned!

Edith Wharton was born in 1862 as Edith Jones, a member of a prominent New York society family, much like the ones that she wrote so scathingly about in her novels. Her first brush with ghosts came at the age of nine when she was suffering from a near-fatal attack of typhoid fever. Sequestered in her room, she was given a children's book of ghost stories to keep her entertained. She later stated that the stories so frightened her that she suffered a relapse of her disease and was hurled into "a world haunted by nameless horrors." From that time on, she was terrified by the supernatural. In fact, until she was 28 years old, she was unable to sleep in a room that might contain a ghost story book!

Fortunately for the reader, she decided to try and exorcize her terrors by writing about them. In 1904, she wrote her first ghost story, "The Lady Maid's Bell," and the rest is history.

Her stories of supernatural dread made her a master of the ghost story, although she never claimed to believe in the spirit world. Instead, she simply stated: "No, I don't believe in ghosts, but I'm afraid of them."

Perhaps the fact that Wharton wrote so prolifically about ghosts, and yet never claimed to believe in them, is what makes the story of the Mount such an ironic one.

Wharton's professional name came from her marriage to Edward Wharton, a fellow New York socialite who was often described as "charming, but a bit dim." She eventually divorced him, preferring the excesses of the literati to her wealthy, but conventional, husband. Prior to this though, Edward Wharton constructed a country retreat for his wife in the Berkshire Hills of western Massachusetts. Set on an estate of over a hundred acres, the house boasted servant's quarters and exquisite gardens. Edith often entertained here and played host to many of her literary friends, especially Henry James, whose own ghost story, *The Turn of the Screw*, is considered a classic today.

The house was built between 1900 and 1902 but Edith only remained in residence until 1908. She then moved to Paris and sold the house in 1912. However, according to the legends, she left a lasting impression on the place.

The Mount passed to the ownership of a number of private individuals after 1912, one of them being the well-known journalist Carr van Anda, managing editor of the *New York Times*. The property was later sold to Foxhollow School and they in turn sold it several years later to a developer, who renovated the school buildings and campus into an expensive resort. In 1978, an acting troupe called Shakespeare & Company moved into the Mount.

Before they arrived though, the house already had a reputation for being haunted. During the years of the girl's school, Foxhollow, rumors of ghosts and strange incidents abounded. After the acting company, which was headed by an eminent Shakespearean actress from England named Tina Packer, took up residence in the house, they realized quickly that they were not alone.

Dennis Krausnick, a former Jesuit priest turned actor and director, was one of the founders of the company. He was one of the first to enter the building, coming one day to the boarded-up house to measure rooms and look things over. As he worked alone in the place, he constantly heard footsteps upstairs and in other rooms. He searched the place, but found it deserted. This was just the beginning though, and soon, other members of the troupe began to have their own unexplainable experiences. The identity of the ghosts was a mystery, but few of the actors had any doubt that they were there!

Tina Packer had her own bizarre experience one night during a thunderstorm. She had been living at the Mount for almost four years at the time, sleeping in one of the larger bedrooms that has been dubbed the Henry James Room. She had a lot of difficulty sleeping and woke that night to find someone standing at the end of her bed. "I woke up," she said, "and I could see and feel that there was somebody in my room. I could see the outline of a man who was standing in the center of the room with his back to me."

Tina at first thought the figure was the man that she lived with, but when he turned around she saw that it was not. Suddenly realizing that he was a ghost, she did what many of us might do; she pulled the bed covers over her head! She waited a few moments and looked again, only to find the man was still standing there. He turned and looked at her and she immediately ducked beneath the covers again! When she looked again a few moments later, he was gone.

Perhaps the most famous ghost of the house (and most famous former resident) was encountered by Andrea Haring, an actress and voice teacher, in the winter of 1979. One night, a meeting was going on in her bedroom and so she went upstairs to Edith Wharton's old writing room to get some sleep. She went to bed around midnight, only to be awakened a few hours later by the cold in the room and the unmistakable feeling that someone else was present.

She looked up and saw three figures in the room and where the room had been bare of furniture before, there was now a small divan and a desk with a chair. Andrea was sure that she was dreaming and so she literally pinched herself to be sure that she was awake. She was, and that's when she realized that she must be seeing ghosts!

"One of them was Edith Wharton," she stated, recognizing the author from a biography that she had read. "I could see the details in her dress and in her face and the way that her hair was done, even though it was dark outside."

One of the other men she described as having muttonchops sideburns and writing at the desk. He said nothing but appeared to be making gestures to the other two, as though carrying on a conversation that Haring was unable to hear. The third figure stood back with his arms folded and the actress recognized him as Edward Wharton.

"I thought to myself, I wonder if I can leave?" Haring went on. "The minute that thought crossed my mind, all three of them turned and looked at me. I looked from one to the other...Edith Wharton gave me kind of a short, dignified nod. Teddy Wharton gave me a kind of brusque acknowledgement, with a nod."

The man at the desk, who Haring believed appeared to be taking dictation, beamed at her and nodded his head vigorously. After that, all three of them returned to what they had been doing and Haring was apparently forgotten.

She immediately left the room and returned to her own bedroom for a few moments. She then returned to the writing room to discover that the ghosts were gone. The room that had been freezing was now warm and all traces of the strange scene had vanished.

She later told others about her odd experience and a friend showed her a book about Wharton and she was able to identify the third man in the room as a secretary of the author. She recalled details from her experience that she never could have known in advance.

Haring also found that others had experienced the ghosts. One of them, Josephine Abady, had never told anyone because she feared that they would not believe her. Abady was a well-known figure in American theater and at the time of her ghost sighting, she was the head of the theater department at Hampshire College. The Mount had been in such a state of disrepair when the Shakespeare troupe moved in that Abady had led a group of students from Smith, Hampshire, Amherst, Mount Holyoke and the University of Massachusetts to help renovate the place.

She was living on the top floor of the Mount, in one of the servant's rooms, when she encountered a ghost. She walked into a hallway and saw the figure of a woman in an antique dress. The woman abruptly vanished!

"A couple of weeks went by and I saw it again," she recalled, "standing in the hall with a man. The woman looked very much like Edith Wharton and the man looked like Henry James. I found out later that James had indeed spent a lot of time at the Mount. I didn't know this when I saw the figure."

Other members of the troupe and their guests, including Abady, have also heard a number of unusual things in the house. Some have recalled hearing the rustling of fabric pass by them in the halls and rooms. It sounds just like someone in a long dress passing by.

Dennis Krausnick also tells of hearing voices that come from the outside of the house. "They would always be on the side of the house I wasn't," he said. "I would look and there would be nothing. The sound would always stop when I looked out the window. There were never tracks in the snow or anything like that."

Could the voices belong to the young girls of Foxhollow School? Perhaps, but even when they were in residence, the school was regarded as haunted. Former students and staff members admitted that they had also encountered Edith Wharton, although one alumnus, Dorothy Carpenter, always disregarded the stories. Later on, she would change her mind.

After the school closed down, the Mount fell on hard times. Carpenter however, hated to see the place fall apart and she wanted to preserve the ornate ceiling of the ballroom. She returned to the school by herself in the early 1970s to work on it. She lived in the place for two months and while she was there, she saw a ghost standing on the terrace.

"It was during the day," she later remembered, "and the ghost looked like somebody in an off-white summer dress, sort of maybe lace but not real gauzy. I think it was Edith Wharton."

The phantom walked back and forth on the terrace and then eventually she vanished. Carpenter didn't tell anyone about her experience for a long time, always guessing that she simply inhaled too much plaster dust during the restoration of the ceiling. The encounters that followed her own seem to shed a different light on the matter though!

Today, the Mount is undergoing a long-term and intensive restoration project that is scheduled to be completed on the 100th anniversary of the house. Edith Wharton Restoration, Inc., was established in 1980 to preserve and restore The Mount, and to establish it as a cultural and educational center dedicated to the study and promotion of Edith Wharton and to recognize and celebrate women of achievement. Remarkably, only a few of America's National Historic Landmarks are dedicated to women and the Mount is one of them. The house is open for guided tours during the summer months.

And while I would never assure the reader that he might encounter the ghost of Edith Wharton on one of these tours; you might bring along your copy of *House of Mirth* to be autographed just in case!

THE VILLAGE OF VOICES

The Mystery of Bara-Hack

There is a haunted village in New England, but it's not a village that you will find on any map. You see, even today, in places that are as populated as Connecticut, it is still possible for towns to become lost. One such town, called Bara-Hack, is in a place that is so remote and mysterious that only the strange stories told about the place keep it from being lost altogether.

The lost village of Bara-Hack is located deep in the northeastern woods of Connecticut, close to Abington Four Corners and in the Pomfret township. It can only be found by following a seldom-used trail that runs alongside Mashomoquet Brook. If you ask most people in the region, they will have never heard of Bara-Hack but ask them about the Village of Voices and you are much more likely to get a positive response. You see, unlike Dudleytown, Connecticut's more infamous lost village, there is nothing demonic about Bara-Hack, but the things that are said to happen here remain just as unexplained.

Two Welsh families settled the isolated village around 1780 and the name of the place, Bara-Hack, is actually Welsh for "breaking bread." Legend has it that one of the first settlers was Obadiah Higginbotham, a deserter from the British army. He was accompanied by his friend, Jonathan Randall, and his family, and both men came to the Connecticut wilderness from Rhode Island.

The Randall family brought slaves with them to the new settlement and according to the stories, the slaves were the first to notice that the village was becoming haunted. As the first of the populace began to die, the slaves claimed that their ghosts returned to the local cemetery. They reportedly saw them reclining in the branches of the graveyard trees at dusk. These were the first ghost stories of Bara-Hack, but they would not be the last ones.

Obadiah Higginbotham started a small factory called Higginbotham Linen Wheels and the mill made spinning wheels and looms until the time of the Civil War. The factory failed after the war and the residents began to slowly drift away from the area. By 1890, the last date recorded on a stone in the graveyard, the village was completely abandoned.

However, travelers and passersby still came through the area and almost immediately after the town died, people began to report strange things were going on in the remains of Bara-Hack. It was not ghosts that they saw though; it was the ghosts that they heard. According to stories and reports, those who came to the ruins of Bara-Hack, and the local graveyard, could still hear a town that was alive with noise! Although nothing would be visible, they could hear the talk of men and women, the laughter of children, wagon wheels passing on the gravel road, farm animals and more. The stories continued and now, more than a century after the town was abandoned, the sounds are still being heard!

A little more than thirty years after it vanished, naturalist Odell Shephard documented the village's anomalies. Although not a writer on the supernatural, Bara-Hack was mentioned in his 1927 book, *The Harvest of a Quiet Eye*. He wrote:

> Here had been there houses, represented today by a few gaping cellar holes out of which tall trees were growing; but here is the Village of Voices. For the place is peopled still....Although there is not human habitation for a long

distance round about and no one goes there except for the few who go to listen, yet there is always a hum and stir of human life…They hear the laughter of children at play…the voices of mothers who have long been dust calling their children into homes that are now mere holes in the earth. They hear vague snatches of song…and the rumble of heavy wagons along an obliterated road. It is as though sounds were able in this place to get round that incomprehensible corner, to pierce that mysterious soundproof wall that we call Time.

Over the years, many people have visited Bara-Hack, although it remains a fairly unknown place in New England lore. Few people have ever written about it and even fewer have ever investigated the claims made by generations of curiosity-seekers. Perhaps the most extensive investigations were carried out by college students in 1971 and 1972. The group was led by then student Paul F. Eno, who wrote about their adventures in *Fate* magazine in 1985 and in his book *Faces in the Window* (1998). The group was escorted to the site by Harry Chase, a local man who had a long interest in the history of the area and in the mysteries of the vanished village. Chase had documented his own explorations of the town with photographs that dated back to 1948. The blurs and misty shapes that appeared in some of the photos have been deemed unsettling to say the least.

According to Eno, the groups of students documented many bits of puzzling phenomena. Although the village site was isolated, well over a mile from the nearest house, the students often heard the barking of dogs, cattle lowing and even human voices coming from the dense woods. They also reported the frequent sound of children's laughter coming from the Bara-Hack graveyard.

It was here that the group had their most unnerving encounters. Eno wrote that for more than seven minutes his group "watched a bearded face suspended in the air over the cemetery's western wall, while in an elm tree over the northern wall we clearly saw a baby-like figure reclining on a branch."

One member of the group claimed that his hat was pulled off and was tossed up into a tree here. In addition, another member, who was a middle-aged man that had come along as an advisor on cameras and equipment and quite definitely a skeptic, was physically restrained by an unseen force. He could move, he said, but not in the direction of the cemetery. He could not explain what had happened to him, other than to say that he felt as though he had been possessed.

Finally, just as Eno's group was departing, they claimed to hear the sounds of a rumbling wagon and a teamster shouting commands to his animals. The sounds began at the cemetery and then moved away, fading off into the dense and mysterious forest.

Chapter Two

MID-ATLANTIC MYSTERIES

The Jersey Devil

The historic states along America's Atlantic Seaboard have given birth to hundreds of ghostly tales and unusual stories over the years. One of the strangest is undoubtedly that of the Jersey Devil, a creature that is believed by some to be a mythical creature and by others, a real-life monster of flesh and blood. Its origins date back to when New Jersey was still a British colony.

According to the legend, Mrs. Jane Leeds came from a poor family who eked out an existence in the Pine Barrens of Jersey, a rugged place with vast forests, sandy soil and patches of swamp. In 1735, Mrs. Leeds discovered that she was pregnant with her 13th child. She complained to her friends and relatives that the "Devil can take the next one," and he did. When the baby was born, he was a monster! He immediately took on a grotesque appearance and grew to more than 20 feet long, with a reptilian body, a horse's head, bat wings and a long, forked tail. He thrashed about the Leeds home for a bit and then vanished up the chimney. The creature, or the Jersey Devil as he was dubbed, began haunting the Pine Barrens.

As the story spread, even grown men declined to venture out at night. It was said that the beast carried off large dogs, geese, cats, small livestock and even occasional children. The children were never seen again, but the animal remains were often found. The Devil was also said to dry up the milk of cows by breathing on them and to kill off the fish in the streams, threatening the livelihood of the entire region.

In 1740, the frightened residents begged a local minister to exorcize the creature and the stories stated that the exorcism would last 100 years, however the Devil returned to the Pine Barrens on at least two occasions before the century was over. Legend has it that naval hero Commodore Stephen Decatur visited the Hanover Iron Works in the Barrens in 1800 to test the plant's cannonballs. One day on the firing range, he noticed a strange creature winging overhead. Taking aim, he fired at the monster and while some say that his shot struck it, the Devil continued on its path.

The second sighting took place a few years later and this time the Devil was seen by another respected witness. Joseph Bonaparte, the former king of Spain and the brother of Napoleon, leased a country house near Bordertown from 1816 to 1839. He reported seeing the Jersey Devil while hunting game one day in the Pine Barrens.

In 1840, as the minister warned, the Devil returned and brought terror to the region once again. It snatched sheep from their pens and preyed on children who lingered outside after sunset. People all across South Jersey locked their doors and hung a lantern on the doorstep, hoping to keep the creature away.

The stories continued to be told and the lore of the Devil was recalled throughout the 1800s, although actual sightings of the creature were few. Then, in 1909, the Jersey Devil returned again and literally thousands of people spotted the monster or saw his footprints. It became so bad that schools closed and people refused to go outside. A police officer named James Sackville spotted the monster while walking his beat one night. He was passing along a dark alley when a winged creature hopped into the street and let out a horrific scream. Sackville fired his revolver at the beast but it spread its wings and vanished into the air.

Sightings continued. On January 19, 1909, Mr. and Mrs. Nelson Evans were awakened in the early morning by the sound of a large animal on the roof of their shed. They described it as: "about three and a half feet high, with a face like a collie and a head like a horse. It had a long neck, wings about two feet long and its back legs were like those of a crane and it had horse's hooves. It walked on its back legs and held up two short front legs with paws on them."

One afternoon of that same week, a Mrs. J.H, White was taking clothes off her line when she noticed a strange creature huddled in the corner of her yard. She screamed and fainted and her husband rushed out the back door to find his wife on the ground and the Devil close by, "spurting flames." He chased the monster with a clothesline prop and it leapt over the fence and vanished.

A short time later, the creature struck again. This time, it attacked a dog belonging to Mrs. Mary Sorbinski in south Camden. When she heard the cry of her pet in the darkness, she dashed outside and drove the Devil away with a broom. The creature fled, but not before tearing a chunk of flesh from the dog. Mrs. Sorbinski carried her wounded pet inside and immediately called the police. By the time that patrolmen arrived, a crowd of more than 100 people was gathered at the house. The crowd was witness to the piercing screams that suddenly erupted from nearby. The police officers emptied their revolvers at the shadow that loomed against the night sky, but the Devil escaped once again.

Eyewitness accounts of the Devil filled the newspapers, as well as photos and reports of cloven footprints that had been found in yards, woods and parking lots. The Philadelphia Zoo offered a

$10,000 reward for the capture of the Devil, but there were no takers. Then, as suddenly as it had come, the Devil vanished again.

The creature did not return again until 1927. A cab driver was changing a tire one night while headed for Salem. He had just finished when his car began shaking violently. He looked up to see a gigantic, winged figure pounding on the roof of his car. The driver, leaving his jack and flat tire behind, jumped into the car and quickly drove away. He reported the encounter to the Salem police.

In August 1930, berry pickers at Leeds Point and Mays Landing reported seeing the Devil, crashing through the fields and devouring blueberries and cranberries. It was reported again two weeks later to the north and then it disappeared again.

Sightings continued here and there for years and then peaked once more in 1960 when bloodcurdling cries terrorized a group of people near Mays Landing. State officials tried to calm the nervous residents but no explanation could be found for the weird sounds. Policemen nailed signs and posters everywhere stating that the Jersey Devil was a hoax, but curiosity-seekers flooded into the area anyway. Harry Hunt, who owned the Hunt Brothers Circus, offered $100,000 for the capture of the beast, hoping to add it to his sideshow attractions. Needless to say, the monster was never snared.

Today, there are only a few, isolated sightings of the Jersey Devil. It seems as though the paved roads, electric lights and modern conventions that have come to the region over the course of two and a half centuries have driven the monster so far into hiding that it has vanished altogether. The lack of proof of the monster's existence in these modern times leads many to believe the Devil was nothing more than a creation of New Jersey folklore. But was it really?

If it was merely a myth, then how do we explain the sightings of the creature and the witness accounts from reliable persons liked businessmen, police officers and even public officials? They are not easy to dismiss as hearsay or the result of heavy drinking. Could the Jersey Devil have been real after all?

A dime museum ad from the Philadelphia Ledger about a fake "devil" they had on display!

HAUNTED GETTYSBURG

America's Most Haunted Battlefield

Most Civil War enthusiasts would say the battle that was fought near the small Pennsylvania town of Gettysburg in 1863 was the greatest battle of the war. At the very least, it is considered the turning point that led to the fall of the Confederacy. For ghost hunters, the mere mention of Gettysburg conjures up images of haunted buildings, strange battlefield encounters and restless ghosts.

The Guns of Gettysburg

By early summer of 1863, the war in the east was going well for the Confederacy. Lee, confident after his victories at Fredericksburg and Chancellorsville, urged President Davis to once again take the war to the north. By doing so, this would take the fighting out of Virginia and relieve the pressure being felt by the government in Richmond. It would also ease the load on the Confederate supply lines because if the invasion could be pushed far enough to the north, it would allow the soldiers to live off the land. In addition, Lee's invasion would also draw attention away from Grant's siege of Vicksburg, plus—if the Confederates could capture any northern towns, it just might push the war-weary citizens of the north to the discussion of a settlement between the two nations.

It seemed as though the outlook for a northern invasion was completely positive and if a downside existed, Lee couldn't find it. So, moving in secret, Lee began his northern thrust on June 3, 1863. He marched his troops into the Shenandoah Valley and pushed them on, using the mountains as a shield. After the death of Stonewall Jackson a short time before, the Army of Northern Virginia had been re-organized into three corps, each commanded by A.P. Hill, Richard S. Ewell and James Longstreet. The cavalry was commanded by the magnificent J.E.B. Stuart.

Although unaware of Lee's plans, the Army of the Potomac, under the command of Joseph Hooker, realized that a major enemy troop movement was underway, following a cavalry engagement at Brandy Station on June 9. Hooker then cautiously followed Lee's march to the north, keeping his army east of the mountains and between Washington and the Confederates. On June 15, Lee overwhelmed a Union force at Winchester and then continued northward. By June 28, all of the Confederate troops had crossed over into Union territory. They were still widely scattered, but all were converging on the Pennsylvania capital of Harrisburg.

Meanwhile, tension between Washington and General Hooker was increasing. Once again, Lincoln was disappointed by the inaction of one of his generals and on June 28, he appointed George Meade to replace Hooker as the head of the Army of the Potomac.

Coincidentally, on this same day, General Lee received a message that the Union Army was on the move, heading toward his new location. This came as a shock to Lee, as he had been depending on Stuart to keep him aware of all enemy activity. Although no one knew it at the time, Stuart had seemingly vanished. He was involved in a daring raid east of the Federal army and all communications with the main Confederate force had been cut off.

Lee's information came from a shadowy figure that has been remembered throughout history only as the spy Harrison, a man who worked for Longstreet but who disappeared after the battle. He informed Lee that Meade was now in charge of the Union Army and was marching north to meet the Confederates.

With the news that the Federal Army was aware of his plans, Lee sent out an order to concentrate the Confederate forces at Cashtown, a small village between Chambersburg and Gettysburg. Here, Lee would prepare to confront the Federal advance troops. The Confederate Army was now in place to the north and west of Gettysburg, while Meade pushed the Federal Army from the south, moving northward from the area around Frederick and Emmitsburg, Maryland.

Both armies were in the dark as to the whereabouts of the other on June 30, the day that cavalry units under the command of General John Buford rode into Gettysburg.

Before this time, there was nothing to set Gettysburg apart from hundreds of other small communities in America. The population of the small town was of about 2,400 people and aside from a thriving carriage industry, its only claims to fame were its two colleges, the Lutheran Theological Seminary and Pennsylvania College (Gettysburg College). It was nothing more than a sleepy little Pennsylvania town in 1863, but all that was about to change.

Buford's cavalry rode into town on June 30 and established a picket line on the other side of the Lutheran Seminary to guard approaches to the town from the west. By coincidence, a brigade of Confederate Infantry under General John Pettigrew, of A.P. Hill's Corps, had been sent to Gettysburg from Cashtown to scout out the area that same day. Legend has it that the Confederates were looking for shoes, but they were actually on a reconnaissance mission. For whatever reason the two groups bumped into each other, it seems likely, with two large armies in such close proximity of each other, they were bound to run into each other at some point. However, once the Confederates spotted the Union pickets, they rode to the west to report the enemy's presence.

Gettysburg: Day One

Early in the morning of July 1, two Confederate brigades were sent to investigate the Federal presence in Gettysburg. Within a short time of the Confederate arrival, a skirmish had broken out between the Rebels and Buford's men. Although Buford knew that he was greatly outnumbered, and in a bad position, he chose to stand his ground and send for help from two Union corps that were a short distance to the south. The Confederates also sent for reinforcements and soon, both armies were headed toward Gettysburg.

Prior to this chance encounter, neither Lee nor Meade had planned to fight at Gettysburg.

For the next two hours, Buford's men, fighting dismounted, managed to hold off a number of Confederate attacks from the area known as McPherson's farm. Buford was later relieved by the arrival of General John Reynolds' corps. One division crossed an unfinished railroad cut to the north of the Chambersburg Pike and formed a battle line. Another Confederate brigade was at the same time attacking McPherson's Woods, which lay to the south of the Pike. General Reynolds himself led the Federal Iron Brigade into the woods, where he was killed instantly by enemy fire. Reynolds was the second in command to the Army of the Potomac and would be the highest-ranking officer to perish during the three days of fighting at Gettysburg.

Around the middle of the day, the fighting broke off and the field was fairly quiet until the middle of the afternoon. The corps commanded by Hill and Ewell advanced against the Federals along a two-mile stretch that ran between the western and northern approaches to Gettysburg. Confederate reinforcements continued to arrive throughout the afternoon and around four, General Jubal Early's division struck the right flank of the Union's XI Corps, which was under command of General Francis Barlow. The attack caused Howard's entire line to begin to crumble.

The corps began retreating into Gettysburg, where they almost collided with retreating Federal troops, who at the same moment had collapsed to Confederate pressure near the McPherson farm. Falling back from two different directions, the Union troops became confused and disoriented in the small town and stumbled along to the shelter of Cemetery Hill, a reserve position located on the southern outskirts of Gettysburg. Here, Union General Winfield Scott Hancock rallied the men into defensive positions on the hill, and along nearby Culp's Hill as well.

Needless to say, the elated Confederates followed and not only captured the entire town, but over 2,500 Unions soldiers as well.

And here they halted; strangely, Lee's forces made no attempt to storm Cemetery Hill that night. One has to wonder what may have been the outcome of the battle if they had. Instead, Lee had given orders to Ewell to renew the attack before nightfall "if practicable." Unfortunately, Ewell took Lee's courteous order as having a choice of whether to fight or to retire from the field. He chose incorrectly. Ewell decided his men needed rest instead and the first day's fighting came to an end.

Lee arrived in Gettysburg that afternoon and established his headquarters in a house along the Chambersburg Pike. Here, he began to make plans for the following day. Even though he was in poor health and suffering from diarrhea, Lee remained confident about the Confederate chances in the battle ahead. He felt the Union Army was weakened by its recent defeats at Fredericksburg and Chancellorsville and by yet another change in command. If he pressed hard enough, the Federals would break.

Gettysburg: Day Two

Throughout the night, the two armies continued to gather and by morning about 65,000 Confederate troops faced a Union force of around 85,000. The northern lines had assumed what has become known as the fishhook formation. Cemetery Hill, became the curve of the fishhook, while Culp's Hill, located just to the east, became the hook, and right flank, of the Union line. Hancock's corps occupied the shank of the formation and they stretched south through the open fields to Cemetery Ridge. The Union left was defended by troops under General Daniel Sickles, a former politician who was best known for killing his wife's lover before the war. Secretary of War Edwin Stanton had been his attorney and had gotten him off by using the first plea of temporary insanity.

Sickles spent the entire morning of July 2 disobeying orders. He had shifted his corps position on lower Cemetery Ridge out into the Peach Orchard, which stood on a flat-topped ridge about a half-mile in front of the Union line. This managed to leave the hills known as Little Round Top and Big Round Top, and the Union's left flank, completely undefended. When Meade got wind of this, he angrily ordered him back into position, but before the corps could be moved, Longstreet had begun his attack.

As Lee studied the Union formation on the field that morning, he noted that the Federal fishhook was overlooked by hills on both ends. Culp's Hill and Cemetery Hill stood above the right and the Big and Little Round Tops loomed over the left. Lee's plan called for the Confederates to take the hills, sending Ewell to attack Culp's Hill and Longstreet the Round Tops.

Little fighting took place during the morning and afternoon, aside from scattered fire from skirmishes. Lee's plan called for attack on both Union flanks at the same time, but the assault was delayed for several hours as Longstreet shifted his two corps into position on the southern edge of Seminary Ridge.

At the same time, Sickles was shifting his own line to the more forward position. By the time Longstreet was ready to attack, Sickle's new line extended northwestward from the tangle of boulders at Devil's Den, through Rose Woods and the Wheat Field, and then sharply to the northeast where it crossed the Peach Orchard and continued along the Emmitsburg Road. The new position was nearly impossible to defend and not only did it not connect its right flank to the left flank of II Corps, but it also left Little Round Top completely unoccupied.

The Confederate attack against the left Union flank began just after four in the afternoon. One of the first points to be struck was the Devil's Den, which fell to Hood's men after a bitter struggle that lasted for several hours. In waves, Longstreet's brigades swept over the Rose Woods and the Wheat Field and then advanced on the Federal positions at the Peach Orchard and along the Emmitsburg Road.

The fighting continued on through the afternoon and while Sickle's beaten line was reinforced by troops under George Sykes, Sickles himself was severely wounded near his headquarters at the Trostle Farm. The Confederates were relentless and after four hours of battle, all of the Union positions along Sickle's line were overrun.

Meanwhile, during the initial attack, the 15th Alabama managed to make it to the summit of Big Round Top. From here, Colonel William C. Oates realized that the summit of Little Round Top was virtually undefended. If he could haul guns to the top of the hill, he would be directly above the Federal lines and could destroy them.

As luck would have it, Little Round Top had also come under the scrutiny of the Union command. Meade had dispatched the army's chief engineer, General Gouverner Warren, and a lieutenant of engineers named Washington Roebling to the summit of Little Round Top to bring back a report of the state of the battle. They found only a handful of Union signalmen on the hill and one look around sent them into shock. Warren quickly realized what was going to happen as he saw Sickles corps pinned down below and Confederate troops coming up the ravine that separated the Little and Big Round Tops.

He sent for reinforcements at once and the last of the four regiments ordered to the hill was the 20th Maine, under the command of Colonel Joshua Lawrence Chamberlain, a professor of rhetoric and languages at Maine's Bowdoin College. The colonel's orders were to hold Little Round Top "at all hazards" and with 350 men, he started up the south slope and they took shelter behind rocks and trees. Fortunately, at the last moment, Chamberlain sent a company of men across the hollow between the hills to bolster the left flank of the defense. Less than ten minutes later, Oates and his Confederates had arrived, attacking before the company could take shelter on the left. The Rebels opened fire and Chamberlain later stated that he assumed his men had been wiped out with the first volley of fire.

The Maine men attacked but the Confederates regrouped and charged again and again, slowly gaining ground and swinging around to Chamberlain's left. He ordered that portion of his line to drop back, forming again at right angles to the rest of the regiment. The men dropped back, continuing to fire as they regrouped.

In less than an hour, over 40,000 rounds had been fired on Little Round Top and still the Federals held firm. The Rebels had driven them from their position five times and yet each time, Chamberlain's men fought their way back again. He would lose 130 of his 386 men, a loss of nearly one-third of his force. He would describe the conflict by saying that: "at times I saw around me more of the enemy than my own men; gaps opening, swallowing; closing again…and all around, a strange, mingled roar."

The sounds of battle behind Chamberlain grew louder and he assumed they had been surrounded. His men had finally run out of ammunition and the only choices that remained were to surrender or die. Instead, Chamberlain ordered his men to fix bayonets. Then, while the right corner of the regiment stood firm, the men were told to wheel around like a great hinge toward the right.

The attacking Confederates were so stunned by the maniacal charge of the Federals that many of them actually dropped their weapons and surrendered. Others began to run, only to get another, more gruesome surprise—the company of men that Chamberlain had sent over to guard the left flank had not been killed by the initial Confederate attack. They suddenly appeared from behind a stone wall and opened fire on the retreating Rebels.

The remaining Confederates broke and ran. Colonel Oates would later admit that "we ran like a herd of wild cattle." The Confederate dead literally covered the ground and while fighting continued on other parts of the slope, the summit of Little Round Top was secure.

Joshua Lawrence Chamberlain would go on to receive the Congressional Medal of Honor for his actions that day.

While the heroics of the men from Maine had saved Little Round Top, things were not going as well on other parts of the Union front. Sickle's corps was in desperate straits as the Confederates continued to attack. A Confederate artillery blast removed the lower portion of General Sickle's leg and he was carried from the field, still calmly smoking a cigar.

Union reinforcements began to arrive and fighting raged through the Devil's Den and the Valley of Death. The Federal troops, as they crossed the Wheat Field, opened a gap on Cemetery Ridge and a Confederate brigade began a drive toward it. Hancock spotted the opening and ordered a single, small regiment, the 1st Minnesota, to countercharge and hold the gap. The Minnesota regiment, made up of only 262 men, raced toward the opening with fixed bayonets and came face-to-face with 1,600 Confederates. The stunned Rebels fell back and the gap in the lines was closed, although only 47 members of the 1st Minnesota came through the skirmish unhurt. They had lost 82 percent of their men in less than five minutes.

By the end of the day, the lack of coordination in Lee's attacks cost them the fight. Despite Longstreet's limited success against Sickles, the Confederate offensive had only worked in some locations and the plan of attacking both flanks at the same time had not worked at all. In fact, it was almost sundown before two divisions of Ewell's corps even began their assault on the hook and curve of the Union's right flank.

The Confederates had clashed with Union troops on the eastern slopes of the hill, which had previously been fortified with earthworks, strengthened by felled trees and rocks. The Federals, although badly outnumbered, used the works to their advantage and the Rebels failed to dislodge them from the hill.

Meanwhile, two brigades under Jubal Early met with even less luck in their attempt to capture Cemetery Hill. The Confederates initially managed to break through the Federal lines at the northern base of the hill in the early evening but soon suffered a devastating blow from Union artillery on Steven's Knoll. The fighting on the hill became hand-to-hand combat but with no reinforcements from the Confederate infantry units on the south edge of Gettysburg, the Rebels soon retreated.

At the end of the second day of battle, Meade's fishhook remained intact.

Gettysburg: Day Three

The third day of battle began badly for the Confederates, further adding to the belief that Lee had created during the night that he must attack the Federal forces at the center. The failure of his attempts to crush the Union flanks suggested that Meade had fortified these areas at the expense of the center. By midday of July 3, Lee decided that the Confederates would take one last shot. It would be a direct frontal assault against Cemetery Ridge. Lee's plan called for an artillery bombardment to weaken the Union line on the ridge, followed by an infantry attack.

During the morning hours, even Jeb Stuart had suffered at the hands of the Yankees. The cavalry commander had arrived in Gettysburg the afternoon before to be greeted by Lee's anger. One officer recalled later that Lee had even raised a hand as if to strike Stuart, as one would discipline an errant child, which perhaps was how Lee saw his relationship with the younger man. "I have not heard from you in days, and you the eyes and ears of my army," he was said to have chastised the cavalryman.

But Lee's anger quickly passed and on the morning of the third day, he put Stuart's men to work, launching an attack on the Federal rear. But the once weak Union cavalry stopped him, thanks to a series of reckless charges led by a 23-year-old general named George Armstrong Custer.

Now, everything depended on the success of Longstreet's assault on the Union center. Longstreet opposed attacking in this manner, knowing what his own rebel gunners had accomplished at Fredericksburg when Union troops had advanced across an open expanse.

But Lee disagreed and ordered Longstreet to prepare the advance. "The enemy is there," he reportedly told the General," and I am going to strike him." The man that Lee chose to lead the advance was a friend and compatriot of Longstreet, General George Pickett, a rather peculiar, but well-liked officer with a beard and long, curly hair. Pickett's men waited in the wood on the opposite side of a long field from the Union center. They passed the time by throwing green apples at each other. They laughed and joked, knowing that what faced them was a nearly impossible task.

At just after one in the afternoon, the Confederate artillery assault on Cemetery Ridge began. The earth shook as the cannons pounded the ridge, trying to weaken the Union line. General Meade had just left his commanders at the lunch table when the barrage started. As an orderly was serving butter, a shell literally tore him in two.

The top of the hill seemed to be tearing apart. Great mounds of earth were catapulted into the air and shells furrowed into the hillside, destroying grave markers and upending stones. Soon, the Union guns began to return fire and the casualty rate began to climb for the Confederate infantry, who were waiting in the woods for the signal to advance. But after about an hour, Meade ordered the Federal guns to silence, hoping to conserve ammunition for the fight that he was sure was coming. And also to lure the Confederates out into the open field.

Pickett came to Longstreet and asked if his men should go forward. The Federal guns had been destroyed and nothing lay between the Confederates and the destruction of the Federal center but Union infantry. The time was now ripe for an attack.

Longstreet was unable to speak and he merely nodded his head, convinced that he was sending his friend to his death. Pickett hurriedly scribbled a note to his teen-aged fiancée and handed it to Longstreet to mail, then, with his usual flair for dramatics, gave the order to attack.

Three divisions, numbering about 13,000 men, started out of the woods and towards the stone wall at the edge of Cemetery Ridge. Although history remembers this advance as Pickett's Charge, it was hardly a quick attack. The men walked at a brisk pace, covering only about 100 yards of the open field by the minute.

"It was," one northern officer recalled, "the most beautiful thing I ever saw."

Union cannons on Cemetery Ridge and Little Round Top began to sound, opening fire on the right side of the advancing line. Men were killed with every shot but the Confederates still kept coming. Behind the stone wall, Union troops waited, holding their fire until the Rebels came closer. Finally, the order was given by General Alexander Hays and 11 cannon and 1,700 muskets went off at once.

Hundreds died in the first volley but the rest continued to come. The Confederates reached the line at just one place, a crook in the wall that has become known as the Angle. They were led by General Lewis A. Armistead, who jumped the wall and managed to capture a Union battery before he was shot down. All of the other Confederates who breached the wall were captured, killed or wounded. Soon, those Confederates remaining on the field broke and ran or gave themselves up as prisoners.

The assault was over—a complete and utter failure.

As the Confederates staggered back to Seminary Ridge, Lee rode out among them, urging them to regroup. "It was all my fault," he was said to have told them, "Get together and let us do the best we can towards saving what is left of us."

Pickett had watched the advance with disbelief. Half of his men, over 6,500, had been killed or captured; 16 of his 17 field officers were gone, along with three brigadier generals and eight colonels. When Lee ordered him to rally his division for possible counterattack by the Federals, Pickett replied, "General Lee, I have no division now."

In the years to come, Pickett would never forgive Lee for what happened that day, always believing that his commander had sent his men into the field to be needlessly slaughtered.

By the end of the third day, the Battle of Gettysburg was over. The fighting had spilled across the hills and through the forests and even into the streets of Gettysburg itself.

The next day, July 4, both armies remained on the battlefield, with Meade and Lee each waiting for the other to move. When nothing of significance occurred that day, Lee realized that his invasion of the north had come to an end. He was now far from his supply line and was running low on ammunition, not to mention the fact that the Confederacy could not afford the over 28,000 casualties they had sustained. It was time to return home. That afternoon, Lee began his long retreat back to Virginia while Meade, despite urgings from Washington, declined to attack the retreating force.

Behind them, the streets and fields of Gettysburg were littered with the bodies of the dead, slowly decaying in the heat of the Pennsylvania summer. The people of the town were also left with thousands of the wounded to attend to and homes and businesses were quickly turned into field hospitals. "Wounded men were brought into our houses and laid side-by-side in our halls and rooms," one local woman recalled. "Carpets were so saturated with blood as to be unfit for further use. Wall were bloodstained, as well as books that were used as pillows."

The dead also lined the streets and walkways, rotting in the summer sun. "Corpses, swollen to twice their original size," wrote a Federal soldier, "actually burst asunder…several human, or inhuman, corpses sat upright against a fence, with arms extended in the air and faces hideous with something very like a fixed leer."

In terms of significance, Gettysburg will always be remembered as one of the greatest battles in American history. It was the turning point in the war and it was probably not a coincidence (in the greater scheme of things, at least) that the day after the battle ended also marked the fall of Vicksburg to General Grant. The war had just taken a darker turn for the Confederacy.

The battle would have a lingering effect on the country, not only for the armies of the Civil War, but for the America itself, an effect that still lingers today.

It goes without saying that the Battle of Gettysburg left a tremendous mark on the small town and on the fields where the fighting actually took place. Few are surprised to learn that many of the buildings in Gettysburg and many locations on the battlefield are now believed to be haunted. In places where so much death and destruction took place, the stories of ghosts and spirits often follow. And in Gettysburg, such spirits make themselves known more strongly than just about anywhere else.

The Farnsworth House

This quaint inn on Baltimore Street has a long, and some say haunted, history in Gettysburg. The original part of this structure, which today boasts an excellent restaurant and inn, was built in 1810 and a brick portion was added later in 1833, constructed by John McFarland. During the battle, the house was occupied by the Sweney family and was eventually opened as an inn by the George Black family in the early 1900s.

Today, the house is a showcase of history and it retains the original walls, flooring and rafters; and some believe it also retains a few of the occupants who passed through the house years ago.

During the battle, the house was occupied by Confederate sharpshooters, who used the garret (attic) of the house as a vantage point to fire at the Union troops on Cemetery Hill, just a few hundred yards away. According to the legends, a sharpshooter was taking aim at a door on a house a short distance away, between the Sweney House and the Federal lines. He was using the doorknob as a target to see just how hard the wind was blowing. He fired and when he did, the bullet pierced the wooden door and struck and killed a woman named Jennie Wade, who was in the kitchen kneading dough. She became the only civilian who was killed during the battle.

It has been said that the deeds and the presence of these sharpshooters have left an indelible mark on the Farnsworth House. According to the ghostly traditions of the place, the sound of a jew's-harp has been heard drifting down from the attic when no one is present there, a musical instrument commonly played by soldiers during the Civil War. And if these soldiers still linger here; they do not do so alone.

After the battle, the house was used as a Federal headquarters, further adding to the history. The battle itself also left a mark on the place in the form of more than 100 bullet holes which can be seen on the south side of the house. Most of these marks still remain, even after all of these years, and many of the bullets removed from the wall are on display inside.

In 1972, the house was purchased by the Loring Shultz family, who began restoring the place to the way it looked in 1863. The inn and restaurant are operated today by the Shultz family who run the place and operate not only a theater for ghost stories but also organize the inn's popular ghost tours.

The owners and staff members are a veritable treasure chest of stories relating to hauntings at the Farnsworth House, from the spectral sharpshooters to tales of guests who have heard phantom footsteps on the stairs, have detected unexplained noises, have felt invisible intruders sitting on the ends of their bed, and many more.

Staff members have reported seeing movement out of the corner of the eye, only to turn and find nothing there. Some have also reported seeing shadows moving through the dining room at night, after everyone else has gone home, only to find the place is deserted. There are also a number of reports of footsteps pacing through the main floor at night, and of employees hearing these footsteps following behind them, only to turn and see no one is there. On other occasions, staff members have been tapped on the shoulder, or touched, by unseen hands.

On one occasion, two different waitresses reported a similar experience. One summer evening, a waitress in period costume rushed into the kitchen and claimed that her long apron had been roughly yanked by something she could not see. The force of the pull had literally spun her completely around. This occurred in an outdoor dining area, adjacent to the Farnsworth courtyard. It had also taken place in front of a table of understandably surprised patrons, who also witnessed the apron being forcibly yanked.

On another occasion, two staff members were standing and talking in the inn's tavern. As they chatted, they were facing the back hallway that ran between the kitchen and the tavern. Suddenly, one of the women realized they were no longer standing there alone. Down the hallway, she spotted an older woman in what looked like a period costume. The strange woman seemed to be looking at items stored on the shelves there. The staff member glanced away for a moment and when she looked back, the older lady was gone.

Concerned now that a customer may have wandered into a staff area, because she knew that she was certainly not an employee, she went into the kitchen to see if the woman had returned in that direction. No one had seen her come inside, even though the kitchen was the only place the old lady could have gone.

One Valentine's Day, which is a busy night during a normally slow winter season, the restaurant was packed with people and all of the extra work made it so that several staff members had to stay until the early hours of the morning to get things cleaned up. Just before they were ready to go home, an employee went to put away the last tray of clean silverware in the pantry off the dining room. Moments later, there was a loud crash in the pantry and a groan from the staff member who had just walked in there.

According to her story, she had just placed the tray where it was supposed to go, and was walking away, when the tray suddenly raised up under its own power, flew several feet and then dumped into the middle of the floor, showering the pantry with pieces of silverware. Needless to say, the normally welcome spirits were very unwelcome that night, as the staff angrily had to re-wash the tray of silverware.

If this is not one of the most haunted buildings in Gettysburg, then it must be near the top of the list.

Pennsylvania Hall

Located within the boundaries of the town is Gettysburg College, or as it was known in 1863, Pennsylvania College. This small, attractive campus seems a quiet place today and anyone who visits here would probably be surprised to learn that during the battle, the college was in the midst of the fighting. At the time, the college consisted of only three brick buildings, which provided lodging and classrooms for little more than 100 students. When the battle erupted, the campus was thrown into the midst of the fight, providing shelter for the wounded and dying as a field hospital.

Not surprisingly, the college is said to still bear the marks of not only the physical effects of the battle, but the spiritual effects as well.

One of the most haunted buildings on campus is said to be Pennsylvania Hall, a large building with stately white columns. It once served as a dormitory for students and now houses the campus administrative offices. The hall was constructed in 1837 and is often referred to as Old Dorm. The large structure was taken over by the Confederates during the battle, not only for use as a field hospital, but as a lookout post as well. A number of officers, including General Lee, used the cupola of the Old Dorm to keep an eye on the progress of the battle.

It has been said that on certain nights, students and staff members of the college have reported seeing the figures of soldiers pacing back and forth in the cupola of the building. The descriptions of the men vary but it is believed they may be sentries who were placed on duty there to guard the safety of Lee, or to deliver messages to the battlefield.

One student reported that he and his roommate, who lived in a dorm about 50 yards away from Pennsylvania Hall, saw a shadowy figure in the tower over a period of several nights. On another occasion, a figure was seen to be gesturing wildly, apparently to a student below. When the student called out to him, believing that perhaps someone was trapped in the tower, the figure vanished. An investigation by campus security found the building to be empty.

It is believed to be the terrible conditions of the field hospital however, which have left the strongest impressions on the building. According to the records of the time, blood sprayed the walls and floors of the rooms as doctors operated without anesthetic, dealing with bullet wounds by the preferred treatment of the time: amputation. Outside of the operating rooms was an area where those who could not be saved were left to die. There is no way that we can even imagine the horrible wails, groans and cries that echoed in this area.

Perhaps the most famous story connected to the time of the battle was related by author Mark Nesbitt. He told of two college administrators who were working on the fourth floor of the building one night. As they were leaving, they stepped into the elevator and punched the button for the first floor. Instead of taking them to their destination, the elevator mysteriously passed it and came to a stop on the basement level. The elevator doors then opened to a terrifying scene!

The basement storage room had vanished and in its place was the blood-splattered operating room of 1863. Wounded men were lying prone on the floor and administering to them were doctors and orderlies in bloody clothing. The entire scene was completely silent, although it was obvious that it was one of chaos.

Stunned and horrified, the administrators repeatedly pushed at the elevator button, desperately trying to close the doors and escape the scene that lay before them. Just before the doors closed though, one of the spectral orderlies was said to have looked up, directly at the two administrators, as though asking them for help.

Whatever happened that evening, the two administrators were shaken and frightened by it and needless to say, never forgot their strange experience. However, both of these men continued to work in the building. In small concession to the weird experience though, whenever they had to work at night, they always departed the building by way of the stairs.

Battlefield Hauntings

There are scores of ghostly stories and supernatural incidents that have been recorded and experienced by everyday people across the official confines of the Gettysburg Battlefield. Factor into this number the encounters of those ghost seekers who have purposely traveled to the battlefield in search of spirits, and the number of strange tales becomes an amazing one.

There are a number of once private residences scattered across the battlefield which have reportedly played host to the spirits in the years that have passed since the battle. Most of these homes are now the property of the National Park Service and often they serve as residences to park rangers and personnel who stay in the houses to keep them occupied and in good repair.

Nearly all of the nearby homes were used during the battle as makeshift field hospitals and as shelters for the wounded during the fighting. Many believe that such incidents may be what has caused them to gain reputations for being haunted over the years. Perhaps these traumatic events served as catalysts for the ghostly events that have allegedly followed.

Not surprisingly, as employees of the United States Government, the rangers are usually very reluctant to discuss their supernatural encounters on the battlefield. Those who do speak, usually do so off the record, which nevertheless, creates a fairly impressive documentation of events beyond our understanding.

The George Weikert House is one such odd location on the battlefield. This small house has had a surprising number of different occupants over the years, many of whom have had stories to tell. One of the previous residents of the house spoke of a door on the second floor that refused to stay closed, no matter what they did to it. One ranger even nailed the door shut with a small wire nail, and yet it refused to stay closed.

Possibly connected to this, other tenants reported the sounds of footsteps pacing back and forth in the attic. They would hear the heavy tread cross the area above their heads, and then cross back, as if someone up there were worried or deep in thought. Needless to say, when they would go up to the attic to check for an intruder, they would find the area to be deserted.

The Farnsworth House was occupied by Confederate sharpshooters during the battle of Gettysburg

The haunted tangle of rocks known as "Devil's Den."

Another residence is the Hummelbaugh House, where the stories say the cries of Confederate Brigadier General William Barksdale can still be heard on certain nights. Barksdale was wounded while leading a charge on Seminary Ridge and was brought to the Hummelbaugh House. According to an officer from the 148th Pennsylvania Volunteers, Barksdale was last seen lying in front of the house and a young boy was giving him water with a spoon. The General continued to call for water, as though the boy did not exist, calling over and over again. In the years since, the legends say the sound of Barksdale's voice can still be heard.

And that is not the only story connected to the house, or to Brigadier General Barksdale either. The other story is connected to the days after the battle, when Barksdale's wife journeyed to Gettysburg to have her husband's remains exhumed and returned to their home in Mississippi. She was accompanied on her trip by the General's favorite hunting dog. As the old dog was led to his master's grave, he fell down onto the ground and began to howl. No matter what Mrs. Barksdale did, she was unable to pull the animal away.

All through the night, the faithful dog watched over the grave. The next day, Mrs. Barksdale again tried to lure the dog away, but he refused to budge, even though the General's remains had already been loaded onto a wagon to begin the journey back to Mississippi. Finally, saddened by the dog's pitiful loyalty, she left for home.

For those who lived nearby, the dog became a familiar fixture during the days that followed. He would occasionally let out a heart-breaking howl that could be heard for some distance. Many locals came and tried to lead the dog away, offering him food, water and a good home. The dog refused all of their gestures and eventually, died from hunger and thirst, still stretched out over his master's burial place.

Within a few years, a tale began to circulate that the animal's spirit still lingered at the Hummelbaugh Farm. It has been said that on the night of July 2, the anniversary of Barksdale's death, an unearthly howl echoes into the night, as the faithful hunting dog still grieves from a place beyond this world.

In addition to these former private residences, spirits on the battlefield itself abound. There are numerous reports of apparitions of phantom soldiers seen marching in formation, riding horses, and still seemingly fighting the battle, from various parts of the park. These ghosts haunt the fields where Pickett's Charge took place, the slopes of Little Round Top, the Peach Orchard, the Wheatfield, and many other places.

However, the highest concentration of ghostly sightings and strange experiences seems to be in the area called the Devil's Den, and also in the areas around it. It is in the nearby Triangular Field where electronic equipment and cameras are said to seldom work. It is in the aptly named Valley of Death where the apparitions of soldiers are frequently reported. And it is in the Devil's Den itself where not only are the ghosts of the slain soldiers seen, but they are heard as well. If there is a place on the Gettysburg Battlefield which is more haunted than any other, there is little doubt that such a place would be the Devil's Den.

The Devil's Den: Gettysburg's Most Haunted

The events that created the lore and legend of the Devil's Den is undoubtedly the fighting which took place here on July 2, 1863, the second day of the Battle of Gettysburg. However, stories surrounded the place long before the battle was ever fought.

According to early accounts from the area, the tangled, outcropping of rocks was a Native American hunting ground for centuries and some say that a huge battle was once fought here, called the Battle of the Crows during which many perished. A Gettysburg writer named Emmanuel Bushman wrote in an 1880 article of the "many unnatural and supernatural sights and sounds" that were reported in the area of the Round Tops and what he called the Indian Fields. He wrote that the early settlers had told stories of ghosts that had been seen there and that Indian "war-whoops" could still be heard on certain nights. In addition, he reported that strange Indian ceremonies also took place here.

Also according to local legend, the name Devil's Den was actually in use before the battle took place. How the area got its name though, remains a mystery. Many believe that the strange atmosphere of the area itself may have contributed to the designation. Another legend persists that the Devil's Den was always known for being infested with snakes. The legends say that one gigantic snake in particular eluded the local hunters for many years and they were never able to capture or kill him. He was allegedly nicknamed the Devil and thus, the area of rocks was called his den.

No matter how the area got its name, it was apparently already considered a strange and haunted spot before the battle, at least according to Emmanuel Bushman. In the years that would follow, the Devil's Den would gain an even more fearsome reputation. The fighting here, which took place on the second day of the battle, was especially brutal and bloody.

Control of the rocky area went back and forth between the Confederate and the Federal troops and hundreds were mowed down in the narrow rocky field that has been dubbed the Slaughter Pen.

After hours of bloody fighting the Confederates finally controlled the area. The fight for the Devil's Den may have been the most confusing and intense skirmish on the battlefield that day. The heat of the afternoon and the collapse of the battle lines, thanks to the difficult terrain, had caused the entire chain of events to happen so fast that many of the men were almost stunned to find the battle was over.

Stranger yet were the reports from the men who were ordered to stand guard in the tangle of boulders that night. Many of them later spoke of the macabre and unnerving surroundings and of sharing the space in the looming boulders with the bodies of the dead.

Days later, the Federals would return to the Devil's Den, this time triumphant as the battle had come to an end with a Confederate defeat. As men approached, they were stunned by the scene that greeted them. The hills and boulders were covered in blood and carnage and the dead lay scattered about in every direction. One of the first soldiers to enter the area recalled that some of the dead men "had torn and twisted leaves and grass in their agonies and their mouths filled with soil…they had literally bitten the dust."

Another Federal soldier, A.P. Chase of the 146th New York described a scene of horror that July 4 afternoon. As he climbed the stones, he found "those rocky crevices full of dead Rebel sharpshooters, most of them still grasping their rifles."

That afternoon, the rain began to fall in a heavy downpour that lasted for several hours. The dead men, who were already bloated beyond recognition, were now drenched and beginning to decay. No one knows just how long the Confederate dead remained unburied around the Devil's Den but it could have been days or even a few weeks. And many of the bodies were said to not have been buried at all, but merely tossed into the deep crevices between the rocks.

The sheer number of supernatural incidents said to have taken place here do lend some credence to the belief that the Devil's Den may be haunted. If Emmanuel Bushman was correct, then the forbidding jumble of rocks was already long haunted before the battle was even fought. If this was the case, then what sort of impact did the hundreds who suffered and died here have on the place?

The stories about the Devil's Den being haunted by the battle began not long after the battle itself. Local legend had it that two hunters had wandered onto the battlefield one day and had gotten lost in the woods near the rocky ridge. They had completely lost their way when one of them looked up and saw the dim figure of a man standing atop the boulders. He gestured with one hand as if pointing the way and the hunter realized it was in that direction they needed to travel. He looked back to thank the man —but the apparition had vanished.

Even those who are skeptical about the hauntings at Gettysburg, and who claim that the stories of ghosts here are a recent addition to the battlefield, admit that there have always been tales recalled about supernatural doings at the Devil's Den. While admittedly, most of these stories are of a rather recent vintage, Emmanuel Bushman wrote of "many unnatural and supernatural sights and sounds" back in 1880 and local lore has always included odd happenings in the area.

One afternoon in the early 1970s, a woman was said to have gone into the National Park Service information center to inquire about the possibility of ghosts on the battlefield. One can imagine just how many times this question must come up and, although the official position of the park is to neither confirm nor deny the ghostly tales, the ranger on duty was reported to have asked why the woman wanted to know.

The visitor quickly explained that she had been out on the battlefield that morning, photographing the scenery. She had stopped her car at the Devil's Den and had gotten out to take some photos in the early morning light. The woman stated that she had walked into the field of smaller boulders, which are scattered in front of the Den itself and had paused to take a photo. Just as she raised the camera to her eye, she sensed the uncomfortable feeling of someone standing beside her. When she turned to look, she saw that a man had approached her.

She described this man as looking like a hippie, with long, dirty hair, ragged clothing, a big floppy hat and noticeably, no shoes. The man looked at her and then simply said, "What you are looking for is over there," he said and pointed over behind her.

The woman turned her head to see just what the unkempt fellow was pointing at and when she turned around again, he had vanished. There was no trace of him anywhere.

A month or so later, the same ranger was on duty at the information desk when another photographer had come in and asked almost the same question. He too had been taking photos at the

Devil's Den, only this time, he had taken a photo about a month before in which the image of a man had appeared on the exposed frame...a man who had not been there when the photo was taken!

When asked what the man had looked like, he also described the man as looking like a hippie (remember, this was the early 1970s) and also mentioned his long hair, old clothing and the fact that he was barefoot. Could this have been the same man? And if so, who was he?

During the war, many of the Confederate soldiers, and especially those connected with the fighting at the Devil's Den, were from Texas. At that time, this was America's most remote frontier and most of these men did not receive packages from home containing shoes and clothing as many of the men from states in the immediate vicinity did. Because of this, the "wild" Texas boys were often unkempt and dirty, lacking shoes and new clothing.

Could this reported specter be one of the soldiers from Texas, still haunting the rocks of the Devil's Den? Since those reports from the 1970s, this same soldier (or at least one fitting his description) has been reported several times in and around the rocks of the Devil's Den. According to some of the stories, a number of visitors have mistaken the man for a Civil War re-enactor and have even had their photographs taken with him. The accounts go on to say that when they return home and have their film rolls developed, the man is always missing from the photo.

In addition to this apparition at the Devil's Den, there are also reports of a ghostly rider who has been seen and who in turn vanishes, the sounds of gunfire and men shouting that cannot be unexplained (not unlike Bushman's phantom "Indian whoops" from long ago) and literally dozens of photographs which allege to be evidence of supernatural activity.

So, do the Spirits of Gettysburg still walk the lonely battlefield? As much as I would like to tell you that they do, the answer to that question remains in the hearts and minds of the reader. You'll have to be the judge of that one for yourself!

HAUNTED ELLICOTT CITY

Ghosts of One of the East Coast's Most Haunted Towns

The small town of Ellicott City, Maryland lies just outside of Baltimore and without a doubt is one of the most haunted towns in the entire state. It may even be one of the most ghost-infested spots along America's eastern seaboard. On a past visit to this picturesque town, one of the local residents mentioned to me that "there may be as many ghosts as there are residents in Ellicott City." And he may be right!

Ellicott City was founded as a Quaker community in the 1770s by three brothers named John, Joseph and Andrew Ellicott, who moved here from Bucks County, Pennsylvania. They were looking for a place to build a grist mill and found it along banks of the swiftly moving Patapsco River. In 1772, they established Ellicott Mills and paid about $3 per acre for the land.

They soon began building, starting with a sawmill and then adding a house and store. They eventually built a wooden bridge to span the Patapsco and established several operations for milling flour and for manufacturing iron products.

The city continued to grow, perhaps reaching its peak in 1830 when the Baltimore & Ohio Railroad built the Old Main Line to the town from Baltimore. New hotels and business came to town and an opera house was established, along with a number of fine restaurants and even a girl's school.

Over the years, Ellicott City has seen its share of hardship and tragedy. The area was sharply divided during the Civil War, as most of the residents were Confederate sympathizers, now trapped north of Washington. In 1868, a horrible flood swept through the Patapsco River valley and wiped out much of the town. Before it was over, 13 houses and 36 lives were lost. Perhaps this dark side of the town's history is the reason why the area is so filled with ghosts, legends and lore.

There are a number of places in and around Ellicott City that are reputed to be haunted. Even the Patapsco River itself is said to be haunted by the ghost of a river worker who drowned around 1900.

Another haunted place is a mansion called Avoca, a Native American word that means "vale of tears." Arthur Pue built the stone house in 1800 along what is now Montgomery Road. The legends say that the young son of the family suffered a tragedy when he was blinded and badly injured after a fall from his horse. When his cruel fiancee then refused to marry him, he hanged himself in a fit of despair. His ghost remained behind. Years later, the house was purchased by the Thomas family and on one night, during a party, Miss Emily Thomas announced that she did not believe in ghosts. At that moment, the brass lock on the front door began to shake and gave a loud click. It could not be opened and the guests had to leave by another door that night. Since that time, residents have also reported strange voices, footsteps and a chair that rocks by itself.

Near Ellicott City is a house called Belmont. Caleb Dorsey built it in 1738, just above the banks of the Patapsco River. Dorsey owned a number of mines, which scraped iron ore from inside of the earth. The ore was fired in the local mines and furnaces and it was used to make cannons for the military during the American Revolution. Dorsey was said to have been very strict with his children and one of his daughters angered him by eloping with a man of whom he did not approve. After that, she was forbidden to ever return to his house again. In the years that followed, locals have told of a spectral coach, drawn by four horses, that has been glimpsed on Montgomery Road, not far from Belmont. The legends say that it is Dorsey's daughter, still trying to return home.

The old Ellicott City Fire Station on Main Street is also rumored to harbor at least one ghost. The presence is said to be that of Mr. Harry (B. Harrison Shipley) a former resident of the building and the local fire chief from 1935-1957. He is said to be responsible for the slamming doors, the eerie footsteps and strange sounds that have been experienced here. Televisions have been known to turn on and off and chairs have been seen sliding across the floor. A few new firefighters who were assigned to the building became so unnerved by the events that they sometimes refused to stay in the station alone.

Another local haunt is the gothic Castle Angelo, a miniature fortress that was designed in the shape of a crucifix. No one seems to know for sure who built the place, but credit is given to two different men: Samuel Vaughn, an artist, or Alfred S. Waugh, an architect. Regardless, it was named for the famous artist, Michelangelo. The house changed hands many times over the years and the first person to make the claims that it might be haunted was a Reverend Moore in the middle 1800s. Strangely, the minister also became a part of the house's lore years later when a story developed that a minister who helped slaves escape along the Underground Railroad haunted the place. Allegedly, he was killed and his body was buried in a tunnel that runs under the house. His ghost has been connected to the place ever since.

Ghosts of Lilburn

Lilburn is one of the most beautiful homes in the town of Ellicott City and it is also the most notorious of the town's haunted residences. The unexplained happenings here have given rise to ghost stories that date back more than a century. And they still continue today.

Lilburn was built in 1857 by Henry Richard Hazelhurst, a prosperous business owner who would go on to make a fortune in the iron trade during the Civil War. As the years passed, a series of tragedies struck the family as Hazelhurst lost his wife and several children. One of them, a daughter, was said to have died in childbirth at Lilburn. Hazelhurst outlived most of his family and died in 1900 at the age of 85.

In 1923, the Maginnis family purchased Lilburn and it was during the time in which they lived in the house that the stories of ghostly activity in the mansion began making the rounds in town.

It was said that footsteps were heard by the family in the tower, along with many other strange noises that could not be explained. It was suggested that the ghost might be the daughter of Henry Hazelhurst who had spent her final days in the house before dying when giving birth.

Tragedy almost struck another family at Christmas time that year, when a fire broke out and much of the mansion was ruined. The place was completely rebuilt, except for one minor change. When the tower was reconstructed, Maginnis chose to replace the gothic peaks that had been on it with stone battlements. Apparently, this slight change did not sit well with the ghosts of Lilburn, because paranormal activity began to increase, leading many to wonder if Henry Hazelhurst himself might still be lingering behind.

The stories of ghosts continued for years and the house was owned by several different families. In the 1960s, it was purchased by the Balderson family who had their own share of supernatural tales about the house. The phantom footsteps continued to be heard and the family dog refused to go into a small room on the second floor hallway. On another occasion, a heavy chandelier in the dining room began swinging back and forth during a party, startling a large number of guests.

The windows in the tower refused to stay closed and at one point, Balderson resorted to pulling the windows shut with a heavy rope. By the time he had finished tying the rope and walked outside to see the windows from the exterior of the house, the ropes had already been undone and the windows opened by unseen hands.

A housekeeper for the Baldersons claimed to hear a child crying in the house and also to smell a man's cigar in the library, even though there was no one else in the room. She also claimed to see several apparitions in the house, including the shadowy figure of a man and a girl in a chiffon dress, walking down one of the hallways.

Following the Baldersons tenure in the house, it was purchased by Dr. Eugenia King, who lived there with her son. They also reported problems with the tower windows and a repeat performance of the chandelier in the dining room. An additional occurrence took place when a vase of flowers suddenly turned upside down and emptied itself onto the floor.

In 1983, the house was purchased by another family, who restored the house and made some major renovations. They claimed to have no encounters with the supernatural occupants of the house. And yet by 1988, it was on the market again.

In 1997, a Howard County police officer reported that he had gone to Lilburn a few years before to interview a young woman who had been a witness to a robbery at a nearby shopping mall. She had been quite shaken by the experience, so he offered to interview her in her own home, rather than at the police station. When he arrived at Lilburn, he knocked several times before the young woman opened the door. However, she invited him inside and asked him to take a seat in the living room while she made some coffee.

A few minutes after they began the interview, the officer said that he heard footsteps crossing the floor upstairs. When the woman did not react to them (as she had already told him that no one else was home), he asked her about the sounds. He was stunned by her reply: "Oh, that's just the poltergeist," she said.

She went on to explain that the ghost was not in any way dangerous, but that he was active. He would often open the window on the tower of the house during the winter months and her father had gotten so upset over this that he had finally nailed it closed. Even so, it was not uncommon to find it open again the next morning.

"After I finished the interview, I left hastily," the police officer recalled, "with more than one hair sticking up on the back of my neck!"

Annie's Ghost

Located high atop a hill that overlooks Ellicott City are the ruins of the Patapsco Female Institute. Many years ago, in the days before the Civil War, the structure was one of the most elegant buildings in the area. And today, it is perhaps the most haunted.

The majestic stones of Lilburn

The ruins of the Patapsco Female Institute.

The Patapsco Female Institute is found high above Ellicott City on Church Road. The view from the front lawn of the ruins, once a girl's school, is a commanding one and looks out over the small town, the hills and the river beyond. It is hard to imagine the place as it once looked, although valiant efforts in recent years have ,erased the signs of time and vandals and have restored at least a portion of the old building. It is not hard to imagine that this scenic and beautiful spot may become a little bit spookier once darkness comes to Ellicott City.

The school had the distinction of being one of the first female institutes in the south when it was officially opened in 1839. The walls were constructed of yellow granite and huge columns supported the magnificent porch. The west wing was given over to an immense ballroom and the floors were made from a fine hardwood. The house was decorated with fine tapestries and imported furnishing and fabrics and, needless to say, attracted daughters from the cream of southern society.

Despite the opulent surroundings, life at the institute could be rigid, especially for wealthy girls who were used to be waited on at home. The building was made of stone and could be bitterly cold in the winter. There were no sanitary facilities at the school and so chamber pots were used. Colds and sickness spread among the girls during the wet and cool months, and a number of girls even died from influenza and croup.

One such girl was said to be Annie Van Derlot, the daughter of a rich southern planter. She died from pneumonia during her first winter at the school and her ghost is said to still linger there, roaming the ruins where her classrooms and dormitory used to be.

Annie was said to have resented being sent to the small mill town of Ellicott City to attend school. She sent a number of letters home which protested her incarceration and spoke badly of the school. One has to wonder how happy her spirit must be when wandering the despised building under the light of the moon.

Needless to say, much has changed at the Institute over the years;

but the stories of Annie's ghost remains, through the years of the school, through the occupants after and even up until today. A few years ago, a girl who found herself separated from a group of visitors to the site saw something that she will never forget. She was alone near the front steps of the school when she saw a young woman in a long gown walk out of the front doors, down the stone steps and across the lawn. And then she abruptly vanished! Was it Annie, or was it some other spirit lingering behind at the former institute?

After the Civil War, the lives of the young girls who attended the Patapsco Institute changed drastically. Things were now very different in the south and classes on etiquette and manners did not seem so important anymore. The curriculum at the school made many changes and shortly, its reputation began to suffer. By 1891, the Patapsco Female Institute had closed its doors for good.

Later that same year, James E. Tyson purchased the building and it was turned into a summer hotel. It was during this time that a large porch was added (since destroyed) and a spacious in-ground swimming pool. The pool has survived, although it is now a weed-choked ruin that lies just off of the current property line of the old building.

The building was purchased again 14 years later and named Bern Alwick, after the English ancestral home of the new owner Miss Lilly Tyson. She used the place as a residence for three years before it changed hands again.

This time, in 1917, the school was turned into a 50-bed hospital for wounded servicemen from World War I. It is unknown just how many soldiers may have passed away in the old building but one has to wonder if any of them chose to stay behind in the massive building as time passed on.

In the 1930s, the building became known as the Hilltop Theater for a short time, but it saw its last occupants in the 1940s. The last resident was Mrs. Magnolia Brennan, who later willed the school to her daughter. She, in turn, sold the house to Dr. James J. Whisman, who willed it to his alma mater, the University of

Cincinnati. It was during the time that Dr. Whisman owned the building that he ordered it gutted so that no one would be hurt there. It had become a popular spot for teen-agers to visit but even after the work was done, the local police still received disturbance calls from neighbors.

Today, the site is accessible as a historic park and has been partially restored for events. Tours are sometimes given of the grounds and ghost hunters have roamed the place in search of the elusive spirits of the past.

The Haunting of Mt. Ida

But the ruins themselves are not the only thing connected to the Patapsco Female Institute that is rumored to be haunted. Located a short distance away is a historical mansion called Mt. Ida. It is now home to the offices of the Friends of the Patapsco Female Institute, which looms on the hill above it, and has been restored magnificently to become an Ellicott City showcase. Besides playing host to the restoration group, the house also plays host to one of the former owners of the home, a woman who passed away in the 1920s!

Mt. Ida was designed in the early 1800s by the famous architect N.G. Starkweather, who also designed the chapel that was added onto the Patapsco Female Institute in the 1850s and many homes and buildings in the Baltimore area. In the old photos and prints of Ellicott City, Mt. Ida is depicted as one of the most prominent landmarks of the town. The house was actually built by Charles Timanus (who also built the Patapsco school) for William Ellicott. He was the son of Jonathan and Sarah Ellicott and the grandson of Andrew, the founders of Ellicott Mills. Mt. Ida was the last home to be built by an Ellicott within the town limits. Unfortunately, William died in 1838 at the age of only 43 and he never had the chance to really enjoy his new home.

In the 1850s, the house became the residence of Judge John Snowden Tyson, a member of one of Maryland's most prominent families. He and his wife Rachel lived there until the 1870s and it was from this family that the ghostly legend of the house has sprung.

After the death of the Tysons, the house was left to their children. The eldest son, John, was tragically killed in a boating accident, leaving three maiden sisters behind. All three of them resided in the house until they died. The last to pass away was Miss Ida Tyson and many believe that it is her ghost who maintains a presence in the house. According to many who have lived and worked here over the years, they have heard the peculiar sound of Miss Ida's keys rattling as she roams the house. Apparently, the elder lady kept a ring of keys with her at all times and many claim to have heard these keys on various occasions.

During the last years of her life, Miss Ida was recalled as a lively person who used an ear horn and walked with a cane. She is said to have loved the old house and the spirit that she left behind certainly seems to be a benevolent one.

Mt. Ida has changed little over the years, still looking much as it did more than a century ago. Recent restoration work has dramatically enhanced the house and looks to make it a viable landmark of Ellicott City for many years to come.

The Cooking Ghost of Oak Lawn

While this house may not be easiest place to find in Ellicott City, hidden among the building of the County Courthouse complex, it does play host to perhaps one of the most unique ghosts in this small and very haunted town. This ghost is different because it is not so much seen as it is smelled!

The old Hayden House, or Oak Lawn as the place was called, is a small stone house that was built back in the early 1800s. Once located on its own lot, the house is now surrounded by additions that have been made to the Howard County Courthouse over the years.

The house was built by Edwin Parson Hayden, the first county clerk in Ellicott City, and he lived there with his wife and six children up until the time of his death in 1850. After that, the house saw several different owners, including the Howard County Board of

Education and the District Court. In 1981, the house sat vacant for several years before being taken over by the county law library.

Stories about Oak Lawn and the mysterious events going on there began many years ago and continue today, although they probably peaked during the 1970s, when the house was occupied by the district court and the county office of parole and probation. Clerks and secretaries often reported lights turning on and off by themselves, a coffee pot that would heat up, even when it was unplugged, and the sounds of phantom footsteps echoing through unoccupied parts of the building. There were also stories of a rocking chair that moved by itself and of a staff member who came to work early one morning and saw a man through the glass panes of the front door. A check of the building revealed that no one was inside.

The most commonly reported strange events though were the phantom smells of Oak Lawn—the smells of soup and bacon and eggs that would waft through the building during the day and into the night!

It was not the odors themselves that seemed to disturb the staff but the source of them, or rather the lack of a source. At the time, there were no cooking appliances in the building and no cooking done there at all. Soon, the ghost was dubbed the cooking ghost and the smells of various foods became commonplace.

The smells of food were not the only way the ghost chose to make its presence known however. One staff member, who probably had more strange encounters than any other because of the late and solitary hours he worked, reported a number of events like seeing cloth napkins fold and re-fold themselves before his eyes and hearing a number of noises that he could not explain.

On one occasion, he believed that he actually saw the ghost itself. He was working late one night and was on his way to the second floor when he noticed what appeared to be a "white haze" out of the corner of his eye. He looked quickly and saw the misty ball of vapor hanging in the air. It was very dense but he could still see through it. It hung there for a moment and then vanished!

The Lawn on Lawyer's Hill Road

Not far from Ellicott City is another haunted house with a chilling reputation in the region. Judge George W. Dobbin built the house, dubbed The Lawn, in 1840 as a summer retreat. The beauty and peacefulness of the location, overlooking the Patapsco River, was so impressive that two other judges, friends of Dobbin, also built homes nearby.

In 1951, the last descendant to live in Judge Dobbin's estate, George Dobbin Brown, the judge's grandson and a doctor of English and Philosophy at Princeton, sold The Lawn to two teachers, Joe and May Cobb. The Cobbs were only looking for a modest home with a little land in the area but since none of the houses "had personality," as Mrs. Cobb put it, they were persuaded to look at The Lawn. They were so impressed with the house that they sunk all of their savings into it and moved it. Six months later, the strangeness began.

The first unusual incident occurred when a blue china plate mysteriously flew from the fireplace mantel and landed on the floor. Nothing else on the mantel even shook! When the Cobbs visited Dr. Brown to pay their mortgage, they told him of the event and he explained that the house was haunted. (The reader has to wonder if perhaps he should have mentioned this before the Cobbs bought the place!)

The second incident happened after the Cobbs installed a gate valve for the water system to the main house and to the two tenant houses. One afternoon, the Rolpets, who lived in one of the tenant houses, complained that they hadn't had any water since earlier that day. Upon inspection of the system, Joe Cobb found that the water tanks were full but that the gate valve had been positioned so that water would only go to the main house. This might not have been strange, a mere accident, but the Cobbs had not even been home that afternoon! There was no one who could have changed the valve.

Later, when the Peed family was living in the Rose Cottage,

Mrs. Cobb noticed that entire rolls of wet paper towels were being left in the trash cans. Curious, she spoke to the Peeds and they explained that someone had been removing the toilet paper from the bathroom fixture and dropping the rolls into the toilet every day. They had also been reversing the curtains on the bathroom windows.

Frustrated, Mrs. Peed finally took matters into her own hands. She purchased a Ouija board and attempted to make contact with the otherworldly, and annoying, visitors in the house. The Cobbs were skeptical of the entire process until the Ouija board was able to provide the answer to a bizarre question that Mrs. Peed could not have known. After that, the Cobbs were believers! The board went on to reveal that there were three spirits in the tenant house and 15 of them had taken up residence in The Lawn. Mrs. Peed also requested that the bathroom pranks end and they promptly did.

In an interview, Mrs. Cobb was asked to guess who the spirits in the house might be. She had no idea but surmised that one of them was a strong child who liked to play pranks. She based this on an occurrence when one of the house's heavy basement brass door keys had been twisted into the shape of a corkscrew!

More occurrences took place after the tenant houses were moved to accommodate a new road. While working on one of the relocated houses, Joe put down his pliers to answer the telephone and when he returned, they were gone. The following day, a college student was helping him with some siding. When the siding was moved and ready to be unloaded, the student found Joe's pliers sitting in the truck on top of the siding!

A later incident took place when the Cobbs went to Spain for two weeks on vacation. When they arrived home, they went to get their keys from the tenant who had been watching the house. She wasn't home, so the Cobbs walked over to their home and found the back doors standing wide open. To their relief, they found nothing in the house disturbed. When they caught up with the tenant, she explained that even though she locked the doors, they were always open again the next day. This had happened for the entire two weeks the Cobbs had been gone!

So, who haunts The Lawn? Is it Judge Dobbin himself or a bevy of spirits who have somehow wandered into the place and who have found it hospitable? It's possible that the ghosts come here for the scenery, as many tourists do, and have found the land around Ellicott City to be accepting of ghosts and a haunted, historical place.

THE HAUNTED HIGHLANDER

The Ghost of Fort Ticonderoga

Major Duncan Campbell was an accomplished military man, a laird of Inverawe who came to America with the 42nd Highland Regiment during the dark days of the French and Indian War. The Scottish regiment filled the lines with an army of British regulars and American colonials. In September of 1758, they were marching north to drive the French troops, and their Indian allies, from the region. Campbell's Highland Regiment, which would be known as the Black Watch, was under the command of the British General Abercrombie. Their destination was Fort Carillon, the stronghold of Marquis Louis de Montcalm, located on a stretch of land between the upper end of Lake George and the lower end of Lake Champlain. Montcalm and his allies were greatly outnumbered and had to defend their position against the superior army. It looked like the end for the French forces, but things had not always gone so well for the British.

Along the march by Campbell's men, they passed by the ruins of Fort William Henry, which had been burned just one year before in August 1757. Nearly 2,000 British soldiers and American militiamen had been forced to surrender the fort after being wracked by disease and pounded by the French guns. Finally, after six days of siege, Colonel Monro had surrendered to Montcalm. The marquis extended generous terms, promising safe conduct for the British to a garrison at Fort Edward, near Glens Falls. However, as soon as the prisoners marched out into the forest, they were attacked by Indians under French command and the troops were massacred. Soldiers and civilians were scalped, decapitated and tortured before the French commanders could restore order and take the survivors to Fort Edward. The story of these bloody events may be known to readers of James Fenimore Cooper's book, *The Last of the Mohicans*.

This was the violence of the land and the period but Duncan Campbell was no stranger to bloodshed and danger. He lived what some would call a "haunted life." For years, he had been plagued by the chilling memory of a visitation that had occurred at his castle in Inverawe, Scotland. It was a ghostly presence that had delivered a fatal warning that now became clearer with each step Campbell took into the American wilderness. He followed an eerie course that had long ago been charted for him by a specter. Now, despite the overwhelming odds in favor of the British and Campbell's own experience as a soldier, he had every reason to believe that he was now marching to his death!

Long before Major Campbell had come to America, he lived in the Scottish Highlands, the laird of his castle at Inverawe. In those days, the rugged land was a place of blood feuds, duels and deadly battles. And on one dark night, violence came to the door of Campbell's own castle.

The household was awakened that night by a mad pounding on the outer gate. Campbell opened it himself to admit a wild-eyed man in torn clothing that was smeared with blood. He claimed that he had been involved in a brawl in which he had killed a man in a fair fight. Now, he was being hunted by the dead man's friends. He asked for refuge and Campbell granted it, hiding the man in the castle. Then, he found out who the dead man was!

A short time later, searchers came to the castle, looking for the man that Campbell had hidden away. The searchers were members of Campbell's own family, for the man who had been killed by the stranger was Donald Campbell, Duncan's own cousin! They were searching for their kinsman's killer, but Campbell could not help them. He had given his sacred oath to the fugitive and he was forced to send the searcher's away. Duncan Campbell was a man who would never go back on his word, no matter how tragic the circumstances might be.

Campbell slept poorly that night, not only because he was hiding his cousin's killer, but because of a visitation from the ghost of his cousin as well! In the early morning hours, he was pulled from his sleep to find a ghostly, wraithlike figure standing next to his bed. The specter was said to have cried out: "Inverawe! Inverawe! Blood has been shed! Shield not the murderer!"

Shaken by the horrible vision, Campbell slept no more that night. The following morning, he told the fugitive that he would have to leave the house. When the man protested, saying that Campbell had given his word, Duncan compromised and took him to a secure cave that was hidden in the mountains.

But even with the killer removed from the house, Donald Campbell's spirit was not satisfied. The ghost appeared once more and repeated his warning, urging his cousin not to shield his killer. When dawn came, Campbell went to the cave but discovered that the man was gone. The killer had fled the region.

Campbell believed then that the matter was over. He would finally be left in peace. Unfortunately though, this was not to be the case. That night, Donald's ghost appeared once more and spoke to his cousin again: "Farewell, Inverawe! Farewell, till we meet at Ticonderoga!"

With that, the phantom vanished, leaving Campbell both unnerved and bewildered. The warning meant nothing to him, as he had never heard of Ticonderoga. It was an unusual name though and he would not soon forget it.

As the British troops marched on Montcalm's position, they passed through the shadowy forests and along the peaks of the Adirondacks of upper New York. It was in the dark woods that the battle began as an accidental meeting between the British forces and a large French scouting party. The two forces collided with muskets and blades and it became a scene of carnage and confusion. A short time later, the French soldiers were either killed or captured, leading to a small, but splendid victory for the British. Unfortunately, this beginning skirmish would be the highest point of the battle to follow.

Closer to the fort, Montcalm had cut down trees to make an open field and he had filled it with barricades, sharpened stakes and trenches. Such a field would make a frontal assault suicidal. However, a frontal assault was exactly the plan chosen by General Abercrombie.

The thought of a frontal attack on Fort Carillon filled Duncan Campbell with dread, but not for the reasons that most of us might think. As he had marched north towards the fort with the rest of the army, one of the Indian guides had mentioned to him that while the fort was called Carillon by the French, the colonials and the Indians had another name for it: Ticonderoga.

The mere sound of the word chilled Campbell to the bone. After all of these years, he had never forgotten the warning that had been uttered to him by his cousin's ghost. He had a feeling that he was destined to never leave this killing field. He followed the others into battle though, for Duncan Campbell was never a man to shirk his duty, just as he had never been a man to go back on his word of honor either.

To the detriment of the British troops, Donald Campbell's curse was not the only one that plagued them that day. The other curse was that of General Abercrombie, who unbelievably failed to employ the considerable artillery that the British had dragged with them through the forest to Ticonderoga. Instead, he decided to rely on the courage of his soldiers to take the fort and predictably, the brave men were cut to pieces by the French cannons.

Wave after wave of Abercrombie's troops fell in the assault. Some of them reached the earthworks near the fort but were driven back. Almost 2,000 of the British troops were lost that day, compared to just 400 men lost by the French. Even though Abercrombie still had the artillery to annihilate Montcalm, he ordered a retreat instead and the British fled the field.

Duncan Campbell was among those who retreated. As he left the field behind him, he felt a flicker of triumph, as it seemed he would actually avoid the curse placed on him by his dead kinsman. He had not been killed and in fact, had only been wounded. A musket ball had only grazed his arm. However, before he could be treated, the wound became infected and surgeons were forced to amputate Campbell's arm. Tragically, he died just a few days later.

He met his cousin again at Ticonderoga after all and their meeting was the final farewell.

Duncan Campbell was buried in America, in a lonely cemetery not far from Fort Edward. Even so, he did return to his castle in Scotland one last time. According to historian Francis Parkman, who wrote about Campbell in his book *Wolfe and Montcalm* (1884), Duncan visited one of his kinsmen at Inverawe. A letter from James Campbell, the laird of the castle in the 1880s, stated that the kinsmen was "awakened one night by some unaccustomed sound, and behold there was a bright light in the room, and he saw a figure, in full Highland regimentals, cross over the room and stoop down over his father's bed and give him a kiss." In the morning, the son asked the father who the man had been. The father immediately replied, saying that it had been Duncan Campbell returning to tell his kinsmen that he had been killed in America.

According to James Campbell's letter, the spirit had appeared on the same day as the battle at Ticonderoga.

Fort Ticonderoga finally fell to the British in 1759 when French troops under the command of Captain Hebecourt were overwhelmed by a British expedition led by General Amherst. This time, the British moved their artillery into place and literally tore down the walls of the fort. This time, Duncan Campbell's Highlanders marched triumphantly into the fort with the British and American troops.

Duncan Campbell could finally rest in peace. But would he? There are some who believe that Duncan Campbell and his cousin Donald still roam this place still. However, I like to think that they are now at rest, having left the days of violence and death far behind.

SOLITARY CONFINEMENT

Ghosts of Eastern State Penitentiary

When compiling a list of places where ghosts are most frequently found, prisons and jails come in high on the list. The amount of pain, trauma and terror experiences by the men who are incarcerated often leaves a lasting impression behind. The horrible events that occur in some of these places may also cause the spirits of the men who lived and died here to linger behind as well. Jails and prisons can be terrifying places—for those in this world and the next.

America's Prisons

One of the first institutions brought to America by the early settlers was the jail, a place where lawbreakers could be held while they awaited trial and subsequent punishment. There were more than 150 offenses in those days for which the punishment was death and for the rest, there was whipping, branding, beatings or public humiliation. At that time, the jail was not a place where criminals were kept for punishment. In fact, the idea of a prison, or penitentiary, was a purely American institution that would have a profound effect on both this country and around the world.

The first state prison was the notorious Newgate, established in Connecticut in 1773. It was actually an abandoned copper mine where prisoners were chained together and forced into hard labor about 50 feet underground. Newgate became the first "hell hole" of American prisons, but it would not be the last. Almost immediately, social reformers appeared, but it has been questioned whether or not their efforts to achieve humane treatment helped or harmed the prisoners. The first reform was attempted in 1790 at Philadelphia's Walnut Street Jail. It was renovated by the Quakers for the jail was described as being a scene of "universal riot and debauchery…with no separation of those accused but yet untried…from convicts sentenced for the foulest crimes."

The jail was remodeled in 1790 and for the first time, men and women were housed separately in large, clean rooms. Debtors were placed in another part of the jail from those being held for serious offenses and children were removed from the jail entirely. Hardened offenders were placed in solitary confinement in a penitentiary house and prisoners were given work and religious instruction. Within a short time though, the Walnut Street jail became overcrowded and a new institution had to be constructed.

Around this same time, two new prisons were built and would soon become models for the rest of the nation. Eastern Penitentiary was built in Philadelphia in 1829 to further the Quaker's idea of prisoner isolation as a form of punishment. Prisoners were confined in windowless rooms with running water and toilets. They would come into contact with no living persons, save for an occasional guard or a minister who would come to pray with them and offer spiritual advice. This extreme isolation caused many of the prisoners to go insane and it comes as no surprise that the prison is believed to be haunted today.

Also in 1829, a rival system, which gained wider acceptance, was started with the building of a prison in Auburn, New York. Here, the prisoners worked together all day at hard labor and then were isolated at night, as they were at the Eastern Penitentiary.

Even though they worked together, inmates were forbidden to talk to one another and were forced to march from place to place in the prison with their eyes always directed downward. The warden of the prison was Elam Lynds, who believed the purpose of the system was to break the spirit of the prisoners. He personally whipped the men and urged the guards to treat the prisoners with brutality and contempt. One standard punishment was the water cure, which consisted of fastening a prisoner's neck with an iron yoke and then pouring an ice-cold stream of water onto his head. At other times, the man would be chained to a wall and then the water would be turned on him through a high-pressure hose. While the pain was unbearable, it left no marks.

The Auburn system began to be adopted throughout America because it was much cheaper to operate than the Pennsylvania system. The cells were much smaller and money was to be made from the inmate labor. And as the system spread, the treatment of the prisoner became even more imaginative. The striped uniform was first introduced at Sing Sing in New York and floggings, the sweatbox, the straitjackets, the iron yoke, the thumb screws and the stretcher became widely used. The stretcher had a number of variations. A man might be handcuffed to the top of the bars of his cell so that his feet barely touched the floor, then left that way all day—or his feet might be chained the floor and his wrists tied to a pulley on the ceiling. When the rope was pulled, the prisoner was stretched taut.

Sweatboxes were metal chambers that were so small that the prisoner literally had to crawl inside. They might be left in such confinement all day and in some cases, the boxes were moved close to a furnace so that the heat inside of them would be intensified.

The Auburn system was based on cruelty and repression, with the idea that such treatment would reform prisoners and make them change their ways. Instead, it was a failure and led to riots, death and the closure of many of the institutions. Unfortunately, many of the practices have been adopted (in some degree) by modern prisons.

After the Civil War, new ideas began to be experimented with. In 1870, men like Enoch Cobbs Wines, and others who formed the American Prison Association, started the reformatory system. The Elmira Reformatory, the first of the new type, opened in New York in 1876. Although the reformatory plan was originally intended for all ages, prisoners at Elmira were limited to between the ages of 16 and 30. The principle of the plan was reformation, rather than punishment and was hailed as a great advance in humane treatment of prisoners.

By 1900, 11 states had adopted the reformatory system but by 1910, the plan was considered dead. Most guards and wardens were incapable of administering the grading program and fell back on favoritism rather than reformation. Because of this, many of the men who were paroled, and were allegedly reformed, went right back out and committed new crimes. Today, many prisons are still called by the name of reformatory but are merely a part of the general prison system.

Despite some of the claims, there has been little advance in prisons since the introduction of the system in 1829, although thanks to reform wardens like Thomas Mott Osborne and Lewis E. Lawes, much of the outright cruelty and squalor of the earlier prisons has been considerably reduced.

Still, many of the extreme punitive concepts have persisted, as evidenced by the 1930s "super prison" of Alcatraz. This prison, called by some the American Devil's Island, was the worst of the federal prisons and was said to be escape proof. According to some estimates, almost 60 percent of the inmates went stir crazy there. Alcatraz left an extreme mark on the prisoners and on the guards and staff members as well. It soon lost its original purpose of confinement for escape artists and troublemakers and became a place to put inmates who it was deemed deserved harsher treatment, like Al Capone. By 1963, Alcatraz was shut down, having proven to be a failure.

And some would consider the entire American prison system a failure as well. Many critics have charged that the prisons have failed to reform criminals or even to act as a deterrent to crime. Eventually, prisoners are simply released, mostly due to a lack of space, and they go right back out and commit new crimes. Many of the prisons themselves have returned to the status of hell holes as well. The brutal conditions often lead to permanent injury, insanity, trauma and death. Is it any wonder that prisons and jails have become known as such haunted places?

Eastern State Penitentiary

After the changes at the Walnut Street Jail in 1790, the Quakers of Philadelphia began to search for a new method of incarceration for criminals in which penitence would become essential in the punishment of the lawbreaker. (Thus, we have the word *penitentiary*.) The Quaker's concept of such incarceration would involve solitary confinement, a method already popular in Europe with members of monastic orders. It was believed that if monks could achieve peace through solitary confinement and silence, then criminals could eventually be reformed using the same methods.

After years of overcrowding at the Walnut Street jail, a new prison was proposed within the city limits of Philadelphia. Called Eastern State Penitentiary, it was designed to hold 250 prisoners in total solitary confinement and opened in 1829. An architect named John Haviland was hired and he set to work creating an institution in the popular hub and spoke design. It had been used in prisons throughout Europe and was highly effective, allowing for a constant surveillance of the prison from a central rotunda. The original design called for seven cell blocks to radiate outward from the center house and guard post.

Prisoners were confined in windowless rooms that were small, but were equipped with both running water and toilets. This was an amazing innovation for the time period as very few public or private buildings were equipped with indoor facilities. Of course, the reason for this was not for the comfort of the prisoner but to keep him out of contact with other people. The walls were thick and soundproof, so prisoners never saw one another. Each prisoner was also given his own exercise yard, surrounded by a brick wall, furthering the sense of extreme isolation. They would see no other inmate from the time they entered the prison until the time they were released.

Construction began on the prison in May 1822. The site selected for it was an elevated area that had once been a cherry orchard. Because of this, the prison later acquired the nickname of Cherry Hill. As construction began, changes forced John Haviland to create new designs so that the prison could hold an addition 200 prisoners. At that time, the prison was the most expensive single structure ever built but Haviland's design would become so popular that it would be copied for nearly 300 institutions around the world.

Although the prison would not be completed until 1836, it began accepting prisoners in 1829. The first inmate was Charles Williams, who was sentenced to two years for burglary. Like all of the other prisoners who would be incarcerated here, Williams was stripped of his clothing, measured, weighed and given a physical examination. He was also given a number and was not referred to by his name until the day that he was released. A record was made of his height, weight, age, place of birth, age, complexion, color of hair and eyes, length of feet and if he was able to write, the prisoner placed his name on the record.

After the prisoner was examined, he was given a pair of wool trousers, a jacket with a number sewn on it, two handkerchiefs, two pairs of socks and a pair of shoes. Then, a mask that resembled a burlap bag was placed over his head so that he would not be able to see the prison as he was taken to his cells. It was believed that if an inmate were unable to see which direction to go if he slipped out of his cell, it would be harder for him to escape. The masks were eventually discontinued in 1903.

After that, he was taken to his cell. As he entered it, he would be forced to stoop down (as a penitent would) because the doorways were shortened to remind the prisoners of humility. Above him would be the only lighting in the cell, a narrow window in the ceiling that was called the "Eye of God."

Silence had to be maintained at Eastern State at all times. The guards even wore socks over their shoes while they made their rounds. By doing this, they moved in secret around the prison and while the inmates could not hear them, the officers could hear any sounds coming from inside the cells. The prisoners were not allowed any sort of books or reading material and could not communicate with anyone in any way. If they were caught whistling, singing or talking (even to themselves), they were deprived of dinner or were taken to one of the punishment cells. Any prisoners who repeatedly broke the rules were taken to a punishment cell and were restricted to a half-ration of bread and water.

Even though communication was forbidden, most of the prisoners attempted it anyway. The easiest way to do this was to attach a note to a small rock and toss it over the wall into the next exercise yard. It was probably the quietest form of communication and the most popular. Other forms of contact ranged from coded tapping on the walls to whistling softly and even muffled speech. Since there were vents for heat in every cell, a limited amount of contact could be made through the ducts. They could also tap on the vents and be heard by several prisoners at once. However, if they were caught, they knew with certainty that they would be punished.

At first, punishment at Eastern State was mild compared to other institutions. Most prisons used the lash, a leather strap that was administered to the back, but officials at Eastern State believed that solitary confinement in the 8 x 12 stone cells was punishment enough. However, as the prisoners began to repeatedly break the rules, the punishments became more intense—going far beyond the plans that had been conceived by the Quakers. The most common forms of punishment created by the prison staff became the Straitjacket, the Iron Gag, the Water Bath and the Mad Chair.

The straitjacket was commonly used by mental institutions to restrain crazed patients and to keep them from hurting themselves or others. At Eastern State, the jacket was used in a different way. Inmates would be bound into the jacket until their face, hands and neck became numb. Eventually, they would turn black from a lack of blood flow and the inmate would usually pass out. The use of the straitjacket was finally discontinued around 1850.

The Mad Chair was another form of punishment, or restraint, adapted again from mental asylums. Here, the prisoner would be tied to the chair by chains and leather straps and held so firmly that he was unable to move at all. After long periods of time, his limbs would become very painful and swollen. The offending prisoners would often find themselves strapped into the chairs, unable to move a muscle, for periods of time befitting their punishments. These periods could last anywhere from a few hours to days. Prisoners who spent any length of time in the chair would find themselves unable to walk for hours (or even days) afterward. Their limbs were often a bluish-black color, caused by the lack of circulation, and it could take a week or more before they returned to their normal color.

The Water Bath was another punishment that was adapted from treatments at mental hospitals at the time. It involved either dunking, or drenching, a prisoner in ice cold water and then hoisting them up in chains to spend the night attached to the wall. This punishment was especially popular with the more brutal guards during the winter months, when the water would freeze onto the inmate's skin.

The Iron Gag was the most commonly used punishment—and the one most feared by the prisoners. It was a device that was placed over the inmate's tongue while his hands were crossed and tied behind his neck. His arms were then pulled taut and the hands secured just behind the man's neck. The gag was then attached to his tongue and his hands and locked into place. Any movement of the hands would tear at the gag and cause intense pain. The inmate would be bleeding and in agony by the time that he was released from his bonds.

These punishments and tortures had not been planned by the Quakers who devised the penitentiary system. They had been improvised by the guards at Eastern State, with full blessing from prison officials. It's no surprise that these officials were investigated for the first time concerning the inhumane treatment of prisoners in 1834, which was two years before the prison was officially opened. Investigations continued over the years and revealed chilling and horrific punishments that had not been conceived of by even the early guards. For example, Block 13, which was constructed in 1925, contained especially small cells that had no light and no ventilation. Prisoners who broke the rules were incarcerated in these cells but when they were discovered by inspectors years later, authorities were ordered to tear down the walls between them and make them larger chambers. Another dark discovery was made when inspectors uncovered "the hole" under Block 14. It was a pit that had been dug under the cell block that was reserved for especially troublesome inmates. They were often kept for weeks in this black, rectangle of earth, chasing away rats and vermin and subsisting on only one cup of water and one slice of bread each day.

While punishments and seclusion were undoubtedly hard on the health of the prisoners, the diseases within the prison were even worse. During the first few years of the prison, poor planning caused the odor of human waste to constantly invade every part of the building. This was caused by the design of the vents and by the plumbing and heating methods that were used. Water was supplied to every cell for the toilets and for the running water. Since the prisoners were only permitted to bathe every three weeks, they were forced to wash themselves in the basins inside of their cells. To heat the water and the rest of the prison, coal stoves were placed in tunnels underneath the floors. Since the sewer pipes from the toilets ran alongside the pipes for the fresh water, the coal stoves also heated the waste pipes. Because of this, the prison always smelled like human waste. The problem was finally corrected in later years because of the frequency of illnesses among the prisoners and the guards.

But most damaged of all was the mental health of the inmates. The inmates at Eastern State often went insane because of the isolated conditions and so many cases were reported that eventually the prison doctors began to invent other reasons for the outbreaks

of mental illness. It was believed at that time that excessive mas-
turbation could cause insanity. Because of this, the doctor's log
book of the period listed many cases of insanity, always with mas-
turbation as the cause. It was never documented that the total isolation caused any of the men's breakdowns.

Without question, being imprisoned at Eastern was mind-
numbing at best. The prisoner was required to remain in his cell all
day and all night in solitary confinement, thinking of nothing but
their crimes. The system was brutal on the inmates but hard for the
warden and guards as well. The first warden at Eastern was Samuel
Wood and it was up to him to insure that the punishment of total
solitary confinement was carried out. He and his family were
required to reside on the premises of the prison and were not
allowed to leave for periods of more than 18 hours without permission from the prison commission.

One of the biggest problems in the early days at Eastern was
keeping the guards sober. It was so boring making the rounds and
maintaining total silence that the guards often drank to combat the
monotony. At one point, the guards were even given a ration of
alcohol during the workday so that they would not drink too
much. Not surprisingly, they found ways around this and guards
were often found asleep at their posts, passed out from too much
liquor. Eventually, a rule was passed that promised immediate ter-
mination for anyone found intoxicated while on duty.

In time, Eastern State Penitentiary became the most famous
prison in America and tourists came from all over the country to
see it. Some sightseers traveled from even further abroad. Perhaps
the most famous penitentiary tourist was the author Charles
Dickens. He came to the prison during his five-month tour of
America in 1842 and named it as one of his essential destinations,
right after Niagara Falls. Although he came to the prison with the
best of intentions, he really did not believe the officials knew what
damage the isolation was doing to the minds of the prisoners. He
later wrote about his trip to the prison in 1845 and stated that "the

system here is rigid, strict, and hopeless solitary confinement…I believe it, in its effects, to be cruel and wrong." He went on to write about the inhumane treatment of the inmates and after speaking to many of them, came to believe that the solitary conditions were a "torturing of the mind that is much worse that any physical punishment that can be administered."

Dickens wrote about a number of the prisoners that he encountered during his visit, including a man who had turned every inch of the interior of his cell into a breathtaking mural. Dickens was stunned when he saw it and exclaimed that it was one of the most amazing works of art that he had ever seen. He tried to speak to the man who had created it but was shocked when he realized that the prisoner's eyes and expression were totally blank. Although he did not rant, rave or weep hysterically, Dickens knew that the man had gone totally insane.

And this man was just one of the thousands who were incarcerated at the prison during its years of silence. The loneliness, misery and solitude drove many of them to madness. The conditions of the place drove many of the inmates over the brink, leaving little doubt as to why insanity and escape attempts were a major problem at Eastern State Penitentiary throughout the 1800s and beyond.

Although it wasn't easy for a prisoner to escape, there were many that tried. The only way to get out was to scale the wall of the exercise yard and then make to the high wall or the front gate. This had to be done without attracting the attention of the guards and with the added disadvantage of not knowing the prison layout. Each of the inmates had been brought into the prison and marched to their cells with hoods over their heads. This way they could not see their surroundings.

In spite of this, the first escape came in 1832. Prisoner number 94, a prison baker named William Hamilton, was serving dinner in the warden's apartment. The warden stepped out of the room and Hamilton managed to tie several sheets together and lower himself out the window. He was not caught until 1837 and when he was, he was returned to his old cell.

There were other escapes as well, but the most memorable came in 1926. Eight prisoners took turns tunneling under cells 24 and 25. They went down about eight feet and then started digging toward the outer wall. The tunnel had been extended nearly 35 feet before they were caught. A similar tunnel actually succeeded in making it out of the prison in April 1945. A group of prisoners, using wood from the prison shop for reinforcement, managed to dig a shaft under the prison and beyond the wall. After it was completed, the men went out at slightly different times to avoid being noticed. By the time they all reached the tunnel's exit, the guards had realized they were missing and the last two were caught climbing out of the tunnel. The others were apprehended a few blocks away.

The method of total solitary confinement was finally abandoned in the 1870s. It was largely considered a failure in that it was too expensive to manage and had shown little in the way of results. It was decided that Eastern State would become a regular prison. From this point on, being sent to solitary confinement was a punishment and no longer the accepted norm at the prison.

The prisoners were no longer confined to their cells only and a dining hall and athletic field were built. Since the prisoners no longer needed the individual exercise yards, the areas were converted into cells to help with the overcrowding that was starting to affect the prison. Between 1900 and 1908, many of the original cells were also renovated and what had once been a small chamber for one man, became close quarters for as many as five. Along with these changes came new cell blocks, a wood shop, a new boiler room and other buildings where the prisoners could labor. There were also art and educational programs added as the prison system began to try and rehabilitate the inmates rather than merely punish them. The work done by the inmates also helped both the prisoners and the prison itself. No work was contracted out and the goods that were made in the shops were sold and the proceeds helped to pay for the prison's expenses for many years.

Eastern State underwent sweeping reforms in 1913 after the structure overflowed with a population of 1,700. But despite the renovations that followed, talk began to circulate in the 1960s about closing the place down. By this time, it was in terrible shape and the only way to keep it in operation was to renovate it again. The buildings were still overcrowded and walls had crumbled in some locations and in others, ceilings were starting to collapse. The cost of repairing the prison was nearly as high as building a new one.

By 1970, Pennsylvania Governor Shafer announced that four new prisons would be built to replace Eastern State. Most of the men from Eastern State would be transferred to Graterford Prison, which would be located about 25 miles from Philadelphia. Construction began immediately on this institution to help relieve the overcrowding and the concern about the conditions at the old prison. As Graterford was completed in 1971, prisoners began to be sent there.

On April 14, 1971, Eastern State was completely empty. The last of the men were transferred out and the prison was shut down until a short time later, when it became the Center City Detention Center.

Prison riots at the New Jersey State Prison at Trenton later that year forced Eastern State to open its doors once again. Because of the overcrowding and the riots at the New Jersey prison, a number of the inmates had to be relocated. Eastern State was the closest available facility and they were temporarily moved here. The place operated with a skeleton crew for eight months and then was shut down again. Once more, the prison stood empty and silent.

The Haunting of Eastern State Penitentiary

During the early years of the Twentieth Century, when the penitentiary was still in operation, the first rumors of ghosts began to circulate at the prison. The walls of the place had an almost tangible oppressiveness about them and it was not hard to believe that the generations of prisoners who had lived, died and lost their sanity within the penitentiary could still be lingering behind. However, the first real ghost story of Eastern State surrounded not the prison itself but perhaps the most famous (or infamous) prisoner to ever be incarcerated here—Al Capone.

Following the bloody events of the St. Valentine's Day Massacre in Chicago, Capone slipped out of town in May 1929 to avoid the heat that was still coming down from the massacre and to avoid being suspected in the deaths of several of the men believed responsible for the killing of the Moran gang. While in Philadelphia, Capone, along with his trusted bodyguard Frankie Rio, was picked up on charges of carrying a concealed weapon and was sentenced to a year in prison. The men eventually ended up in the Eastern Penitentiary.

Capone continued to conduct business from prison. He was given a private cell and allowed to make long-distance telephone calls from the warden's office and to meet with his lawyers and with Frank Nitti, Jack Guzik and his brother, Ralph, all of whom made frequent trips to Philadelphia. An article in the Philadelphia Public Ledger for August 20, 1929, described Capone's cell: "The whole room was suffused in the glow of a desk lamp which stood on a polished desk....On the once-grim walls of the penal chamber hung tasteful paintings, and the strains of a waltz were being emitted by a powerful cabinet radio receiver of handsome design and fine finish." The place was obviously unlike the cells that were being used by other prisoners of the time! He was released two months early on good behavior and when he returned to Chicago, he found himself branded Public Enemy Number One.

It was while he was incarcerated in Pennsylvania that Capone first began to be haunted by the ghost of James Clark, one of the St. Valentine's Day Massacre victims and the brother-in-law of his rival, George Moran. While in prison, other inmates reported that they could hear Capone screaming in his cell, begging Jimmy to go away and leave him alone. After his release, while living back in

Chicago at the Lexington Hotel, there were many times when his men would hear him begging for the ghost to leave him in peace. On several occasions, bodyguards broke into his rooms, fearing that someone had gotten to their boss. Capone would then tell them of Clark's ghost. Did Capone imagine the whole thing, or was he already showing signs of the psychosis that would haunt him after his release from Alcatraz prison?

Whether the ghost was real or not, Capone certainly believed that he was. The crime boss even went so far as to contact a psychic named Alice Britt to get rid of Clark's angry spirit. Not long after a séance was conducted to try and rid Capone of the vengeful spirit, Hymie Cornish, Capone's personal valet, also believed that he saw the ghost. He entered the lounge of Capone's apartment and spotted a tall man standing near the window. Whoever the man was, he simply vanished. Years later, Capone would state that Clark's vengeful specter followed him from the Eastern State Penitentiary—to the grave.

Whispers and rumors of ghosts had echoed from the prison walls for many years before the penitentiary was actually closed down. By the time the building's last living prisoners were removed though, anyone who had spent any time in the place were certain that something supernatural was taking place at Eastern State. It has been said that when the last guards made their rounds through the prison, this last foray into the darkness caused them to utter chilling stories to one another—and to anyone else who would listen and not think them insane. They spoke of the sounds of footsteps in the corridors, pacing feet in the cells, eerie wails that drifted from the darkest corners of the complex and dark shadows that resembled people flitting past now darkened doorways and past windows and cells. It seemed that the abandoned halls, corridors and chambers were not so empty after all! Those who left the penitentiary on that final day had become convinced that a strange presence had taken over the building and most breathed a sigh of relief to be gone.

But if ghosts lingered in the building, they would soon be sharing the place with a handful of those from among the living. In the middle 1970s, the empty prison was designated as a National Historic Landmark and was eventually purchased by the city of Philadelphia to be used as a tourist attraction. The Pennsylvania Prison Society of Philadelphia was placed in charge of operating and promoting it as a historic site and they continue to conduct tours of the penitentiary today.

And from these tours and forays into the prison, came more tales of ghosts and hauntings. Without question, the prison was designed to be a frightening place and in recent times, it has become even more so. The prison still stands as a ruin of crumbling cellblocks, empty guard towers, rusting doors and vaulted, water-stained ceilings. It is a veritable fortress and an intimidating place for even the most hardened visitors. But does the spooky atmosphere of the place explain the ghostly tales as merely tricks of the imagination? Those who have experienced the spirits of Eastern State say that it does not.

"The idea of staying in this penitentiary alone is just overwhelming...I would not stay here overnight," stated Greta Galuszka, a program coordinator for the prison.

Over the years, volunteers and visitors alike have had some pretty strange experiences in the prison. In Cell Block 12, several independent witnesses have reported the hollow and distant sound of laughter echoing in certain cells. No source can ever be discovered for the noises. Others have reported the presence of shadowy apparitions in the cells and the hallways, as though prisoners from the past can find no escape from this inhuman place. Several volunteers believe that they have seen these ghostly figures in the six block, while others have seen them darting across corridors and vanishing into rooms. Eastern State's Death Row has also been the scene of strange encounters and chilling visitations by the same shadowy figures encountered by others.

A locksmith named Gary Johnson was performing some routine restoration work one day when he had his own odd encounter. "I had this feeling that I was being watched," he recalled, "but I turned and I'm looking down the block and there's nobody there. A couple of seconds later and I get the same feeling...I'm really being watched! I turn around and I look down the block and shoooom...this black shadow just leaped across the block!" Johnson still refers to the prison as a "giant haunted house."

Angel Riugra, who has also worked in the prison, agrees. "You feel kinda jittery walking around because you feel something there, but when you turn around, you don't see anything," he said. "It's kinda weird, it's spooky!"

One of the most commonly reported specters in the prison is encountered by staff members and visitors alike among the older cellblocks. The phantom is always described as being a dark, human-like figure who stands very still and quiet. The figure usually goes unnoticed until the visitor gets too close to him and he darts away. The sightings never last for long but each person who has encountered the apparition state that it gives off a feeling of anger and malevolence. Could this be a prisoner who has remained behind in protest of the inhumane treatment that he and so many others received in this cruel and brutal place? Perhaps—and it's likely that this single spirit does not walk here alone.

Another of the penitentiary's most frequently seen phantoms is a ghost that stands high above the prison walls in a guard tower. It has been assumed for many years that this is the spirit of a former guard who is still standing his post after all of these years. One has to wonder why a guard, who was free to leave this place at the end of the day, would choose to remain behind at the prison. But perhaps he has no choice—we can only speculate as to what dark deeds this lonesome man may have been witness to, or perhaps had taken part in, during his years at the prison. Maybe he is now compelled to spend eternity watching over the walls that held so many prisoners in days gone by.

As intimidating as all of this sounds though, it is the history and the hauntings of the prison that continue to bring people back. Many of the staff members, while unsettled by the strange events that sometimes occur, are nevertheless fiercely protective of the place and are determined to see that it is around for many years to come. Even so, they can't help but feel that forces are at work inside of the prison.

"So much did happen here," Greta Galuszka added, "that there's the potential for a lot of unfinished business to be hanging around. And I think that's my fear—to stumble upon some of that unfinished business."

Chapter Three

SOUTHERN SPIRITS

The Haunted History of the LaLaurie Mansion

Of all of the cities in the American South, there is none so haunted as New Orleans. It has been noted by authors Lyle Saxon, Edward Dreyer and Robert Tallant that New Orleans "has more ghosts than there are wrought-iron balconies in the Vieux Carre" (French Quarter). And this is not surprising given the dark history of the Crescent City, which includes death, murder, war, bloodshed, violence, disease, destruction, fire, slavery and on occasion, downright depravity. New Orleans is certainly a city that stands as a prime example for the deeds of the past creating the hauntings of today!

While there are dozens of famous stories of ghosts in the city, there is no story as famous as that of the mansion of Madame Delphine LaLaurie. For generations, it has been considered the most haunted house in the Vieux Carre and in many early writings of the city, it has been referred to simply as the haunted house. While such a title is more than a little vague, everyone seemed to know exactly what house the storyteller was referring to!

The origins of the ghostly tales centering on 1140 Royal Street began around 1832, when Dr. Louis LaLaurie and his wife, Delphine, moved into the mansion in the French Quarter. The mansion itself was said to be wondrous. According to a *Daily Picayune* newspaper article from March 1892, the house was said to be "grand, even in its decay." The author of the article, Marie L. Puents, wrote: "It towered high above every street in the French Quarter...a large, solid rectangular mass, with its three stories and attic and gray stuccoed front and sides...The walls and ceilings of the deep white portal-way are curiously ornamented by a pair of great gates of open ornamental ironwork...within a marble hallway is a great wide door...and there rises and iron-railed staircase, that winds like a spiral column to the drawing room and sleeping apartments above."

The author also goes on to describe the interior of the house. "The drawing rooms are spacious and the different doors that lead to them, and the great folding doors between, are ornamented with panels beautifully carved in flowers and human faces. All around the walls of these great rooms there extends a frieze covered with railed work representing angels with folded wings and holding palm branches; the lofty ceilings and framework of the doors are beautifully carved with stars and raised garlands of flowers. The fireplaces are high and old-fashioned....the chandeliers are rare and quaint...the windows, high and wide, measure seven feet across, and are set between fluted Corinthian pilasters, and open upon a broad balcony.

"At the end of one of these rooms, there was some years ago a little door with large iron hinges...many strange stories have been connected with this door," the author wrote, "thrilling, bloodcurdling stories!"

Shortly after moving into the mansion, the LaLauries became renowned for their social affairs and were respected for their wealth and prominence. Madame LaLaurie became known as the most influential Creole woman in the city, handling the family's business affairs and carrying herself with great style. Her daughters from her previous marriages were among the finest dressed girls in New Orleans, even though one of them was crippled or suffered from some deformity. She was rarely seen at public or social gatherings.

Madame LaLaurie was considered one of the most intelligent and beautiful women in the city. Those who received her attentions at the wonderful gatherings could not stop talking about her. Guests in her home were pampered as their hostess bustled about the house, seeing to their every need. They dined on European china and danced and rested on Oriental fabrics that had been imported at great expense. One of the things that nearly all of her guests recalled about her was her extraordinary kindness.

But this was the side of Madame LaLaurie the friends and admirers were allowed to see. There was another side. Beneath the delicate and refined exterior was a cruel, cold-blooded and possibly insane woman that some only suspected, but others knew as fact.

The finery of the LaLaurie house was attended to by dozens of slaves. Many guests to her home remembered her sleek, mulatto butler, a handsome man who wore expensive livery and never ventured far from her side. During dinner parties, she always left a sip of wine for him in her glass.

The other slaves that were sometimes seen were not so elegant. In fact, they were surprisingly thin and hollow-chested. It was said they moved around the house like shadows, never raising their eyes. It was concerning these slaves that the rumors about Madame LaLaurie began to circulate. The stories said that she was brutally cruel to them. She kept her cook chained to the fireplace in the kitchen where the sumptuous dinners were prepared and many of the others were treated much worse. In fact, the treatment of them went far beyond cruelty.

It was a neighbor on Royal Street, a M. Montreuil, who first began to suspect something was not quite right in the LaLaurie house. There were whispered conversations about how the LaLaurie slaves seemed to come and go quite often. Parlor maids would be replaced with no explanation or the stable boy would suddenly just disappear—never to be seen again. He made a report to the authorities, but little, if anything, was done about it.

Then, one day another neighbor was climbing her own stairs when she heard a scream and saw Madame LaLaurie chasing a little girl, the Madame's personal servant, across the courtyard with a whip. The neighbor watched the girl being pursued from floor to floor until they at last appeared on the rooftop. The child ran down the steeply pitched roof and then vanished. Moments later, the neighbor heard a horrible thud as the small body struck the flagstones below. The woman also claimed that she later saw the small slave girl buried in a shallow grave beneath the cypress trees in the yard.

A law that prohibited the cruel treatment of slaves in New Orleans caused the authorities to investigate the neighbor's claims. The LaLaurie slaves were impounded and sold at auction. Unfortunately for them, Madame LaLaurie coaxed some relatives into buying them and then selling them back to her in secret. She explained to her friends that the entire incident had been a horrible accident. Some believed her, but many others did not, and the LaLaurie social standing began to slowly decline.

The stories continued about the mistreatment of the LaLaurie slaves and uneasy whispering spread among her former friends. A few party invitations were declined, dinner invitations were ignored and the family was soon politely avoided by other members of the Creole society. Finally, in April of 1834, all of the doubts about Madame LaLaurie were realized.

A terrible fire broke out in the LaLaurie kitchen. Legend has it that it was set by the cook, who could endure no more of Delphine's tortures. She stated that she would rather be burned alive than endure anymore of her master's abuse. Regardless of how it started, the fire swept through the house. Flames began pouring from a window on the side of the house and smoke filled the rooms. The streets outside began filling with people and soon the volunteer fire department was on hand carrying buckets of water. Bystanders began crowding into the house, trying to offer assistance.

Throughout the chaos, Delphine remained calm. She directed the volunteers who carried out the expensive paintings and smaller pieces of furniture. She was intent on saving the house but would not allow panic to overcome her.

Montreuil, the neighbor who had first aroused suspicion about Madame LaLaurie, came to assist during the fire. He asked if the slaves were in danger from the blaze and was then asked by Delphine not to interfere in her family business. Montreuil then appealed to Judge Canonge, a local official who was also present. They began searching for the rest of the servants and were joined by a man named Fernandez and several of the fire fighters.

They made an attempt to reach the upper floor of the house, but found locked doors barring the way. Finally, they discovered a locked wooden door with iron hinges that led to the attic. Dr. LaLaurie refused to open it, so they broke the door down.

What greeted them behind the door is almost beyond human imagination. They found more than a dozen slaves here, chained to the wall in a horrible state. They were both male and female; some were strapped to makeshift operating tables; Some were confined in cages made for dogs; human body parts were scattered around and human organs were placed haphazardly in buckets; grisly souvenirs were stacked on shelves and next to them a collection of whips and paddles. The men were forced back, not only from the terrifying sight, but also from the stench of death and decaying flesh in the confined chamber.

According to the newspaper the *New Orleans Bee,* and the accounts of those who were present that day, all of the victims were naked and the ones not on tables were chained to the wall. Some of the women had their stomachs sliced open and their insides wrapped about their waists. One woman had her mouth stuffed with animal excrement and then her lips had been sewn shut.

The men fled the scene in disgust and doctors were summoned to provide aid for the tortured slaves. It is uncertain just how many slaves were found in Madame LaLaurie's torture chamber. Several of them were dead but there were a few who still clung to life, like a woman whose arms and legs had been removed and another who had been forced into a tiny cage with all of her limbs broken than set again at odd angles. A few of them, and only a few, were strong enough to be able to leave the "chamber of horrors" under their own power.

As the mutilated slaves were carried and led out of the house, the crowd outside gathered around. Only one of two friends remained beside Madame LaLaurie. Even her husband had disappeared. Delphine's mulatto servant acted quickly. He slammed the heavy door that led to the street and quickly locked it. He then hastened to the courtyard and locked the large wooden gates. This effectively sealed the LaLaurie household off from the crowd outside, which was still milling about, waiting to see if any arrests were going to be made. Nothing happened over the course of the several hours that followed.

Needless to say, the horrifying reports from the LaLaurie house were the most hideous things to ever occur in the city and word soon spread about the atrocities. It was believed that Madame LaLaurie alone was responsible for the horror and that her husband turned a blind, but knowing, eye to her activities.

According to the newspapers "at least 2000 people" came to the Cabildo to see the slaves that had been taken from the mansion. Here, they received medical care and those who were conscious were prodded with questions about their captivity and abuse. A long wooden table was filled with instruments of torture that had been brought from the attic. They included whips, shackles, knives and crude medical equipment, some of which was crusted with the red stain of dried blood.

One of the statements taken that day came from a female slave who testified that Madame LaLaurie would sometimes come and inflict torture on the captives while music and parties were going on below. She would come into the attic still clad in her ball gown and lash the slaves as they cowered on the floor. After a few lashes, she would appear to be satisfied and would leave. The mulatto butler would sometimes accompany her. What perverse pleasures she had taken from her medical experiments were not spoken of. One of the women also testified that Delphine once beat her own crippled daughter for bringing food to the starving slaves.

Passionate words swept through New Orleans as curious crowds came to gape at the starving and brutalized slaves. As the wounded creatures gulped down the food that was given to them, Judge Canonge, Montreuil, Fernandez and a Felix Lefebvre all made formal statements to the authorities about their discovery of the attic chamber.

In the meantime, the mob was still waiting outside the gates to the house on Royal Street. They expected to see arrests being made and for the authorities to come and demand entrance to the house. Hours passed though and the police did not arrive. The mob continued to grow. More and more people came and as each hour would pass, they would grow more restless and belligerent. Soon, threats were being shouted at the shuttered windows and calls for vengeance were heard from the street.

Suddenly, late in the afternoon, the gates to the high-walled courtyard burst open and a carriage roared out of the gates. It plowed directly into the mob and men scattered before the angry hooves of the horses. The mulatto servant was atop the box and he lashed his whip at the horses and at the faces of those nearby. The coach pushed through the crowd and disappeared from sight, racing down Hospital Street and down toward the Bayou Road.

It all happened so quickly that everyone was taken by surprise. Someone cried out that the carriage had been only a decoy, that Madame LaLaurie was actually escaping through a rear door. While some went to look, others swore that she had been in the carriage, alone. Dr. LaLaurie was nowhere to be found. Her daughters, it was discovered afterward, had been forced to escape the house by climbing over a balcony and into a house next door.

But it was Delphine who the angry mob was after and she had easily escaped their clutches. The carriage drove furiously along the Bayou Road and it is said that a sailing vessel waited for her there and left at once for Mandeville. Another story claimed that she remained in hiding in New Orleans for several days and only left the city when she realized that public opinion was hopelessly against her. No one knows which of these stories is true, but we do know that she was in Mandeville nearly 10 days later because she signed a power of attorney there that would allow an agent in New Orleans to handle her business affairs for her.

The seething mob that remained behind continued to grow. Her flight had enraged the crowd and they decided to take out their anger on the mansion she had left behind. The *New Orleans Courier* newspaper reported that "doors and windows were broken open, the crowd rushed in, and the work of destruction began."

Feather beds were ripped open and thrown out into the street while curtains were dragged down from the window and pictures torn from the walls. Men carried furniture, pianos, tables, sofas and chairs and hurled them out the windows to see them splinter on the streets below. After destroying nearly every belonging left in the house, the mob, still unsatisfied, began to tear apart the house itself. The mahogany railings were torn away from the staircase, glass was broken, doors were torn from their hinges and worse. The mob was "in the very act of pulling down the walls" when the authorities arrived with a group of armed men and restored order. It was later suggested that the house itself be completely torn down, but cooler heads prevailed and instead the house was closed and sealed. It remained that way for several years, silent, uninhabited and abandoned, or was it?

Madame LaLaurie and her family were never seen again.

Rumors circulated as to what became of them; some said they ran away to France and others claimed they lived in the forest along the north shore of Lake Pontchartrain. According to the author George W. Cable, Madame LaLaurie made her way to Mobile and then went on to Paris. He went on to say that her reputation preceded her to France and when she was confronted and recognized in Paris, she spent her days "skulking about in the provinces under assumed names."

However, this story is disputed by travelers from New Orleans who later visited Paris. They positively asserted that they met Delphine in the city and that she had a handsome establishment there. Her gracious manners and style had made her a guest in the most exclusive circles in Paris. They also said that when the stories of what happened in New Orleans reached the French capitol, they were looked upon simply as a result of her well-known eccentricity and her uncontrollable temper. This temper, some said, almost bordered on insanity.

But whatever became of the LaLaurie family, there is no record that any legal action was ever taken against her and no mention that she was ever seen in New Orleans, or her fine home, again. Of course, the same thing cannot be said for her victims.

The stories of a haunting at 1140 Royal Street began almost as soon as the LaLaurie carriage fled the house. The mansion remained vacant for a few years after its sacking by the mob, falling into a state of ruin and decay. Many people claimed to hear screams of agony coming from the empty house at night and saw the apparitions of slaves walking about on the balconies and in the yards. Some stories even claimed that vagrants who had gone into the house seeking shelter were never heard from again.

The house had been placed on the market by the agent of Madame LaLaurie in 1837 and was purchased by a man who only kept it for three months. He was plagued by strange noises, cries and groans in the night and soon abandoned the place. He tried leasing the rooms for a short time, but the tenants only stayed for a few days at most. Finally, he gave up and the house was abandoned.

Following the Civil War, Reconstruction turned the empty LaLaurie mansion into an integrated high school for "girls of the Lower District" but in 1874, the White League forced the black children to leave the school. A short time later though, a segregationist school board changed things completely and made the school for black children only. This lasted for one year.

In 1882, the mansion once again became a center for New Orleans society when an English teacher turned it into a "conservatory of music and a fashionable dancing school." All went well for some time, as the teacher was well known and attracted students from the finest of the local families; but then things came to a terrible conclusion. A local newspaper apparently printed an accusation against the teacher, claiming some improprieties with female students, just before a grand social event was to take place at the school. Students and guests shunned the place and the school closed the following day.

A few years later, more strange events plagued the house and it became the center for rumors regarding the death of Jules Vigne, the eccentric member of a wealthy New Orleans family. Vigne lived secretly in the house from the later 1880s until his death in 1892. He was found dead on a tattered cot in the mansion, apparently living in filth, while hidden away in the surrounding rooms was a collection of antiques and treasure. A bag containing several hundred dollars was found near his body and another search found several thousand dollars hidden in his mattress. For some time after, rumors of a lost treasure circulated about the mansion, but few dared to go in search of it.

The house was abandoned again until the late 1890s. In this time of great immigration to America, many Italians came to live in New Orleans. Landlords quickly bought up old and abandoned buildings to convert into cheap housing for this new wave of renters. The LaLaurie mansion became just such a house but for many of the tenants, even the low rent was not enough to keep them there.

During the time when the mansion was an apartment house, a number of strange events were whispered of. Among them was an encounter between an occupant and a naked black man in chains who attacked him. The black man abruptly vanished. Others claimed to have animals butchered in the house; children were attacked by a phantom with a whip; strange figures appeared wrapped in shrouds; a young mother was terrified to find a woman in elegant evening clothes bending over her sleeping infant; and of course, the ever-present sounds of screams, groans and cries that would reverberate through the house at night. The sounds, they said, came from the locked and abandoned attic.

It was never easy to keep tenants in the house and finally, after word spread of the strange goings-on there, the mansion was deserted once again.

The house would later become a bar and then a furniture store. The saloon, taking advantage of the building's ghastly history was called the Haunted Saloon. The owner knew many of the building's ghost stories and kept a record of the strange things experienced by patrons.

The furniture store did not fare as well in the former LaLaurie house. The owner first suspected vandals when all of his merchandise was found ruined on several occasions, covered in some sort of dark, stinking liquid. He finally waited one night with a shotgun, hoping the vandals would return. When dawn came, the furniture was all ruined again even though no one, human anyway, had entered the building. The owner closed the place down.

In 1923, the house was renovated and sold to William Warrington, who established the Warrington House, a refuge for poor and homeless men. For the next nine years, the house opened its doors to penniless men who were released from jails and prisons. In 1932, the mansion was sold to the Grand Consistory of Louisiana, an organization like the Freemasons, who kept the place for the next decade. They sold the house in 1942.

In 1969, the mansion was converted into 20 apartments before its current owner, a retired New Orleans doctor, purchased it. He restored the house to its original state with a living area in the front portion and five luxury apartments to the rear. Apparently, tenants are a little easier to keep today than they were one hundred years ago.

Since moving into the place, the owner has reported no supernatural activity and residents who live nearby are unable to recall any recent ghost stories about the mansion. Back in the early 1970s, a tenant named Mrs. Richards claimed to witness a number of strange events in her apartment like water faucets turning on by themselves, doors opening and closing and a number of minor annoyances. Other tenants often spoke of the familiar bizarre noises and the lingering story of a young girl's screams that could be heard in the courtyard at night. Since that time, the house has been quiet, leading many to believe the haunting here has simply faded away with time.

Is the LaLaurie house still haunted? It doesn't seem to be, but one has to wonder if the spirits born from this type of tragedy can ever really rest?

A number of years ago, the owners of the house were in the midst of remodeling when they found a hasty graveyard hidden in the back of the house beneath the wooden floor. The skeletal remains had been dumped unceremoniously into the ground. When officials investigated, they found the remains to be of fairly recent origins. They believed that it was Madame LaLaurie's own private graveyard. She had removed sections of the floor in the house and had hastily buried the bodies to avoid being seen and detected. The discovery of the remains answered one question and unfortunately created another. The mystery of why some of the LaLaurie slaves seemed to just simply disappear was solved at last; but it does make you wonder just how many victims Madame LaLaurie may have claimed? And how many of them may still be lingering behind in our world?

THE WORLD'S LARGEST HAUNTED PLACE!

Ghosts and Hauntings of Mammoth Cave, Kentucky

Mammoth Cave in Kentucky is the largest system of caves in the entire world, with over 330 miles of passages on five different levels. There are thousands of secrets in the dark corridors of the cave and according to some.. there are plenty of ghosts too!

Hidden among the forests and hills of southwest Kentucky is Mammoth Cave National Park. It is the largest cave in the world and impossible to see in one day, or probably even in one week. There are many passages, paths and tunnels that are not open to the general public, thus adding to the mystery of this place. But in addition to the secrets of nature, there is much in the way of legend and lore about the cave. The place has a strange and unusual past and perhaps for this reason, there are those who feel that ghosts would be right at home in Mammoth Cave!

The Haunted History of the Cave

The first people came to Mammoth Cave more than 12,000 years ago, when bison and mastodons still roamed the wilderness of what would someday be called North America. During this period, small groups of nomads wandered the territory and many of them came to Mammoth Cave seeking shelter. No one knows what these primitive people may have called the cave, but modern researchers are sure that it had great value to them. They traveled deep into the cave, seeking mineral deposits of gypsum, mirabilite and selenite. It remains a mystery as to why these people were willing to risk their lives in the depths of the cave for the minerals, but perhaps they believed that they have medicinal or even magical qualities.

Regardless, they did leave signs of their passage and some modern explorers have navigated narrow and nearly impassable crevices only to find that they were not the first to arrive in the deepest chambers of the cave. The naked footprints of aboriginal man have remained unaltered in some of these chambers for centuries.

These early cave explorers also used Mammoth Cave as a burial place for their dead, perhaps believing that it provided some sort of passage to the next world. There have been a number of mummies found in the cave over the years. Some of them have been left behind in former burial postures, while others have been the bodies of early explorers who lost their lives in the cave. All of the remains have been remarkably preserved thanks to the minerals found here.

The most famous of Mammoth Cave's mummies was discovered by two guides in 1935 and dubbed Lost John. The mummy was found more than two miles into the cave and trapped beneath a rock. It was believed that he had been a Native American mineral hunter who had perished in an accident. For many years, the cave mummies were a major tourist attraction for the cave but all have since been buried or removed from display.

In the early 1700s, there were few permanent residents of Kentucky (which was then part of Virginia) although the Shawnee and the Cherokee Indians used the region as a hunting ground. During the French and Indian War of the late 1750s, a British soldier became the first reported European to reach the Mammoth Cave region. By that time, many of the colonists along the eastern seaboard were starting to feel the crush of civilization. The more adventurous among them began crossing the Appalachians for the western territories. They recognized the lure of the wilderness and the frontiersmen often heard from their Native American friends of the natural wealth of "Kain-Tockee."

Despite the skills of these men when it came to living off the land for food and shelter though, they were still at the mercy of other suppliers when it came to gunpowder and a method of preserving food. It was in the discovery of the saltpeter deposits that Mammoth Cave's greatest riches were realized. The saltpeter led to the first legal ownership of the cave.

Valentine Simmons was the first owner of the cave. He claimed

One of the historic entrances to Mammoth Cave. The darkness below only hints at the strange history of this place!

200 acres of land, which included the cave, in 1798. He then sold the cave to the McLean brothers, who began processing the saltpeter deposits. In 1810, the operation was taken over by Charles Wilkins and Fleming Gatewood, who began mass production in the cave.

Prior to buying the rights to Mammoth Cave, Wilkins had already established himself as a saltpeter merchant, supplying the Dupont gunpowder works in Delaware with product from Kentucky. The men were excited at the promise of the cave, already realizing that a fortune was to be made from the increasingly hostile relations between the United States and Britain. The War of 1812 would drive up the cost of saltpeter and production in Mammoth Cave would follow suit.

The war progressed, and Wilkins used more than 70 slaves to work the leaching operation that would remove the saltpeter from the cave. To prepare for the work, square wooden vats were built and wooden pipes were made from long, straight poplar logs. The logs were then bored out with augers and then tapered so that they would fit together end to end. The slaves dug into the soil, placed it into the vats and then saturated it with water that was piped in using the wooden tubes. The water trickled through the soil and the calcium nitrate leached out. The solution was then filtered through ash and then boiled to concentrate the saltpeter. It was bagged and transported to mills in Philadelphia, where it was combined with powdered charcoal and sulfur to make gunpowder.

The business proved to be quite profitable, netting the owners about 21 cents per pound. After the war ended though, the price of saltpeter plummeted and the mills were able to get the product more cheaply from other locations. The operations in Mammoth Cave were closed down for good.

Fortunately though, all was not lost. The fame of Mammoth Cave had started to spread. Numerous newspaper articles had been written about the cave's contribution to the war and they had also discussed its natural wonders and the strange mummies that had been found in the cave. Soon, people began traveling from the east to the Kentucky wilderness and Mammoth Cave began to receive its first tourists.

In 1815, Hyman Gratz became a partner with Charles Wilkins in the ownership of the cave. Gratz was a showman and an entrepreneur and he quickly realized there was money to be made in exhibiting the cave. After Wilkins died in 1828, Gratz continued showing the cave to anyone who was interested and actually stepped up operations to make the place more profitable. He used veterans of the mining operation as guides to accompany curious travelers.

The cave was originally called Flatt's Cave but the name had been gradually changed to Mammoth Cave during the War of 1812. The Rotunda, the first large room that was entered, prompted the name and gave visitors a taste of the massive chambers ahead. At first, the guides rarely ventured any further than the old mining operation and tunnels they were familiar with. As they grew more comfortable with the passages though, they started to venture a little deeper with each excursion. Travelers were then led into what were called the Haunted Chambers and they risked the dangerous, wet and rocky canyons known as the Bottomless Pit and the Crevice Pit.

As the century grew older, the fame of Mammoth Cave grew larger and more widespread. Guidebooks began to boast of the cave's hundreds of miles of passages and word of mouth, combined with newspaper and magazine articles, travelogues and first-person accounts, brought people from all over the world. People came from everywhere to see the marvels of the cave and some said that "more visitors had come from England to see Mammoth Cave than those visitors hailing from Kentucky." Some of celebrity guests of Mammoth Cave included historic personages like Jenny Lind, Edwin Booth, Charles Dickens, Ralph Waldo Emerson, Prince Alexis of Russia and many more. People from all walks of life came to the cave however, not just the wealthy and famous. None of them walked away from it unimpressed!

While the list of early visitors is indeed impressive, it is hard for us to appreciate just how dangerous the cave could be at that time. These intrepid visitors were forced to brave slick floors, narrow passages and dangerous pathways. The greatest challenge though was lighting. Throughout the 1800s, a variety of lights were used in the cave. Visitors carried open-flame lanterns, fueled by refined lard oil on occasion, but the most popular method of light was the full flame torch. The guides would wrap wooden poles with oiled rags and set them ablaze. Then, to show off the wonders of the cave and their own skills, they would fling the torches onto ledges and into narrow gaps in a way that few could duplicate today.

The visitors of the 1800s were also fond of smoking their names onto the smooth, white ceilings of the cave. Today, you can still see names and dates, carefully scripted with fire, that were left behind by visitors more than a century and a half ago.

The Early Cave Guides

Mammoth Cave had many early guides, as the first flood of visitors began arriving here in 1818. The cave was famous by that time, thanks to a number of writers and authors who were already beginning to spread the word about the place, but the lack of decent and accessible roads discouraged many of the tourists. Stagecoaches stopped miles from the entrance, at Bell's Tavern, and the remaining distance had to be covered by way of a narrow, rugged trail.

There was an inn of sorts at the cave, but it was as bad as the roads were. It was simply a log building with two rooms on the ground floor and so most overnight visitors preferred to eat and sleep at Bell's.

In 1838, the cave was purchased by Franklin Gorin, an attorney from Glasgow, Kentucky who envisioned great things for Mammoth Cave. Not only did he plan to improve the roads and accommodations, but he brought in skilled guides as well. He became the most important man in the cave's early history. He improved the inn, enlarging it to sleep up to 40 people, added fences and stables and introduced a young slave to the cave named Stephen Bishop. This young man, who was just 16 years old at the time, would become a legend in his own lifetime. Bishop would go on to live the rest of his life in and among the passageways of Mammoth Cave, becoming the first man to explore and map the cave system.

During that first summer of 1838, Bishop familiarized himself with every room, corridor and passageway known to the previous guides. In addition, he began to explore parts of the cave that had been untouched before. He found confusing mazes, dead ends and hidden wonders. One of the passages led to a deep hole that had always been known as the Bottomless Pit. On October 20, Bishop placed a rickety wooden ladder over the pit and carefully made his way across, becoming the first man to do so. It was soon spanned with a bridge and Bishop began leading visitors to share in the wonders on the other side. Bishop also became the first to discover the cave's underground water system and the strange, eyeless fish that lived in the caverns.

Reports of these discoveries brought even more visitors to the cave, so in 1839, Gorin hired two slaves from Thomas Branford of Nashville, Tennessee. He paid Branford the annual sum of $100. The new guides were brothers, Mat and Nick, and they have taken on the last names of their master in writings of the cave. They became known as the Branfords and along with Stephen Bishop, they became the leading explorers and guides of Mammoth Cave. The three of them would continue leading cave tours until the 1870s and their offspring would continue a tradition here for more than 107 years.

Time marched on and the Civil War brought unrest and trouble to southern Kentucky. However, the manager of the cave, a staunch supporter of the Union, continued to conduct tours throughout the years of the war. Stories that have been passed down tell of encounters within the cave between northern and southern soldiers, each taking a moment from the war to marvel at the natural wonders of the cave.

After the war ended, some of the former slaves in the Mammoth Cave community left the area to find new homes. Others, like the Branfords, chose to stay on. They, like Stephen Bishop, had been offered their freedom years before in return for their services in the cave. They had refused to leave though and they stayed on at Mammoth Cave. Stephen Bishop had died shortly before 1860, but his wife, Charlotte, and son, Thomas, remained at the cave.

Another Bishop, Ed, became one of the cave's greatest explorers. Accompanied by a German cartographer named Max Kaemper, Bishop climbed and slid through a collapse of rock and dirt that had previously been thought of as the end of Mammoth Cave. The exploration, and the map that came from it in 1908, is still thought of as the most important accomplishment in the cave's history.

Bishop's discovery led to the realization that Mammoth Cave is actually several different caves that all connect in some way underground. No one knew this for many years and different people owned separate caves. It was so confusing that some people owned different parts of the same cave, with different entrances, on different parcels of land. In the early part of the 1900s, as automobile vacations became popular in America, the ownership of the caves would have strong consequences in southern Kentucky. And sometimes this would have dire results!

The Croghans of Mammoth Cave

William Croghan and his wife, Lucy, built their brick home called Locust Grove in 1790 in what was then wilderness near Louisville, Kentucky. Their first child, John, was born that same year. He grew up at Locust Grove, spending many hours enthralled with the stories told to him by his famous adventurer uncle, George Rogers Clark.

After graduating from Priestley's Seminary in Danville, Kentucky and from the College of William and Mary in Virginia,

John studied medicine and received a doctorate from the University of Pennsylvania in 1813. He then returned to Kentucky and opened a medical practice in Louisville, taking an active part in the establishment of the Louisville Marine Hospital.

After the death of his father in 1822, John inherited Locust Grove and a large plantation, which he farmed and used to produce salt. In time though, John gained his own taste for adventure, perhaps remembering the stories told to him by his famous uncle, and he went abroad to tour the world. In 1839, he returned home and visited Mammoth Cave. He walked the passages with his guide and was amazed by the size of the rooms and the chambers they found.

While in London, John had heard much of Mammoth Cave and he agreed with the current owner's plans for publicizing the cave in the east and in Europe. He also understood the difficulties of getting tourists to the cave and then finding them suitable lodging once they arrived. He believed that not only should a grand hotel be built at the entrance to the cave, but underground in the cave as well! He envisioned a carriage road leading into the cave, a dining room, a library and a grand ballroom. Croghan quickly purchased the cave from Franklin Gorin (which included Stephen Bishop and the Branford brothers) and set about turning his dreams into reality.

Mammoth Cave prospered under Croghan's ownership, although the underground hotel was never realized. He did however construct the spacious Mammoth Cave Hotel, a large inn constructed from two log buildings. It was equipped with rooms to sleep several dozen visitors, a dining hall and a ballroom. It would continue to serve travelers until it burned down in 1916. Croghan also spent huge amounts of money on advertising and continued to attract visitors from all over the world. He established a reputation for the cave as an international showplace.

At Croghan's own expense, he began building public roads to the cave. The first road was opened from Cave City to the Mammoth Cave Hotel and then continued on across Green River to connect to a road at Grayson Springs. Another road began at the

Louisville and Nashville Turnpike near Rowletts Station and led to the hotel before continuing on to the southwest, where it connected with another turnpike. This was said to be an excellent road in those rugged times and also became the shortest route between Louisville and Nashville. It also just happened to pass the Mammoth Cave Hotel and bypassed Bell's Tavern completely.

Croghan not only saw the cave as a tourist attraction, he also saw medical benefits to it. As a doctor, he had read of underground hospitals in Europe in which those suffering from consumption (tuberculosis) had been cured. He believed that Mammoth Cave just might have the same curative powers. He and many other doctors believed that the moist air and the constant temperature of the cave might slow, or even reverse, the ravages of the disease.

In 1842, Croghan directed Bishop and the Branfords to construct wood and stone huts within the cave and then he invited 15 tuberculosis patients to participate in his experiment. Unfortunately, several of the patients died in the cave and the trial was considered a failure. The surviving patients were sent home and the huts were abandoned. They still exist though and can be seen in the cave today. Several of the patients who died were buried in the Old Guide's Cemetery near the cave entrance.

Ironically, Croghan also contracted tuberculosis and he died in 1849. Being a bachelor, he left the cave in trust for his nieces and nephews. In this way, his death began more than 70 years of tenants and resident managers at Mammoth Cave. The years that followed were strange ones for the cave, with no clear-cut route to follow. Mammoth Cave enjoyed success for most of these years, only slowing down after the Civil War.

David Graves of Lebanon, Kentucky leased the cave in the 1870s. His time at Mammoth Cave is best remembered for the fine food that he served and the billiard hall that he operated inside of the cave. He finally left Mammoth Cave after a number of legal disputes with the owners of the cave and with a competitive stage line that was used to ferry passengers to the cave.

At that time, stage lines were the best methods of bringing tourists to Mammoth Cave. But stagecoach travel was not without danger. One evening in 1880, a group of visitors were returning from the cave when they were stopped by bandits at the Little Hope Cemetery. The robbers took more than $1000 and many personal items from the travelers, including a fine gold watch that was engraved with the name of Judge R.H. Rountree of Lebanon. Later, a newspaper article reported that the same watch was found in the possession of Jesse James after his death. Was this famous outlaw responsible for the Mammoth Cave stage robbery?

In 1886, Francis Klett brought a mushroom farm to the cave but more importantly, W.C. Comstock established the Mammoth Cave Railroad and greatly improved travel for cave visitors. The railroad connected to the L & N line at Glasgow Junction. The rail cars were pulled by an engine called Hercules and the little train served Mammoth Cave and the surrounding communities until 1929, when automobiles made it obsolete. All that remains of the train today is an overgrown spur line, the engine, a single coach car and mostly forgotten memories of a bygone era.

The Cave Wars

The Twentieth Century did not come quietly to the cave country of southern Kentucky. The rivalry that flared up between David Graves and a rival stage line in the 1870s was only the beginning. As it turned out, there would be two realizations that brought about what has been called the Cave Wars of the early 1900s.

The first was that cave tourism could actually be profitable and that it was also very popular. The attention given to various caves in the area had been substantial already, but as the new century dawned, it became obvious that it was no passing fad. With this realization in southern Kentucky, it became necessary for the locals to simply get in on the idea.

The second event was the beginning of the automobile vacation era. More and more people in America were buying cars and they were using them to travel to places where they had never been before. To folks in the surrounding states, Mammoth Cave became a natural destination point. Soon, this type of travel would gain the attention of the entire country and historic monuments like Route 66 would be born. Unfortunately though, the interstates would bypass the small highways and regional attractions in later years and many of them would die and fade away.

The area around Mammoth Cave today is like a time capsule of the past. The boom years of the 1920s through the early 1970s had a lasting effect on the region in the attractions and motor hotels, most of which barely eke out an existence in these modern times. There are faded signs here that depict the wonders of caves and petting zoos that have been closed down for years.

But it wasn't always this way. Around 1920, the Cave Wars were in full swing. The local people who lived and owned land around the already established Mammoth Cave wanted desperately to get into cave promotion. Soon, they began advertising and conducting tours of their own caves, located on their own property. As the years passed, and Mammoth Cave became a national park, many of these caves were absorbed into the park system. Most of these smaller caves merely made up portions of the much larger one.

At that time however, people either didn't suspect this, or just didn't care. If a person had an entrance to a cave on his property, then he had his own cave. The caves were advertised and marketed wildly and each owner would extol the virtues of his cave above all of the others in the area. Each would post as many signs as possible between major roads and the entrance to Mammoth Cave, hoping to lure travelers away from the most popular attraction.

Some of the caves of this period included Diamond Cave, Proctor Cave, Dossy Cave, Ganter Cave, Colossal Cave, Great Onyx Cave and Floyd Collins' Crystal Cave, among others.

Sometimes the competition between the operating caves became more than just who did the most advertising. On many occasions, violence and vandalism marred the countryside. Signs were torn down and destroyed, fires were set and even shots were occasionally fired. Word of mouth was sometimes just as destructive. The owners of caves often told visitors who came to see them that they shouldn't visit another nearby attraction for a variety of reasons, ranging from poison gases in the rival cave to a tourist being killed there in an accident.

On a few occasions, the visitors themselves even got into the act. One incident involved rival caves that were located right next to one another. A fence separated the two entrances and as visitors filed into each cave for a tour, the owners encouraged them to throw rocks at the opposite tour group!

The ultimate high point in the Cave Wars came with the death and the strange odyssey of Floyd Collins, which began in 1925. More on that later on!

The Mammoth Cave National Park

In the early 1920s, a group was formed called the Mammoth Cave National Park Association for the purpose of trying to get the government to grant national park status to the cave. By this time, many were starting to realize that the numerous caves in the area were most likely connected. By turning the underground system into a national park, it would protect the entire region for future generations.

Most of those who started the association were businessmen and politicians, not the people who owned smaller caves in the area and who made their living from guiding tours through the attractions. Obviously, these people were opposed to the government coming in and taking over their property, but they lacked both the funding and the political clout to do anything about it. In 1926, legislation was passed that officially authorized the preparation of Mammoth Cave as a national park. Congress authorized the cave to receive National Park status that same year, however it was not made official until President Franklin D. Roosevelt signed the papers in July 1941.

The delay was caused by the refusal of the local people to sell their land. The national park was slated to absorb all of the land, both above and below ground, where the cave was located. This created a huge parcel of land to be sold to the government. It was the duty of the Kentucky National Park Commission, formed in 1928, to acquire the land but they met with nothing but opposition.

The acquisition became a heated subject in southern Kentucky. While some sold their homes and land willingly, others were forced out by eminent domain. It did not make for a pleasant climate in the area and not surprisingly, there are hard feelings that still linger in the area more than 70 years later.

Many things have changed at Mammoth Cave over the years. In 1981, it was named as a World Heritage Site and nearly 2 million people come here each year to canoe, camp, hike and, of course, to explore the passages of Mammoth Cave.

Other changes have not just been in the services offered in the park, but in the cave itself. At every moment, monumental changes are taking place underground that will have an impact on the future of Mammoth Cave. The underground rivers continue their journey through the rock, the calcium droplets of water slowly slide lower and lower, creating artistic fixtures of stone and cave formations growing in size that can only be measured by the eye over a span of hundreds of years.

In every moment, time marches on and brings changes here. However, some things remain the same, remaining lost and forgotten with time. They are the ghosts and spirits of Mammoth Cave.

Haunted Mammoth Cave

There have been many stories of ghosts at Mammoth Cave, spanning several generations of visitors, guides and service personnel. This isn't surprising considering that caves can be very spooky places, filled with dark corners, shadowed crevices and odd noises. But are the stories of Mammoth Cave merely figments of overactive imaginations? That remains to be seen, although we should take into account that ghostly tales have been told about the place almost from the time when the first cave tours roamed the darkened corridors with only a small lantern to guide the way.

These eerie stories tell of unexplained sounds, strange lights, bizarre noises, disembodied footsteps and of course, apparitions and spirits. However skeptics maintain there are explanations for these things. A person's imagination can play tricks on them in the dark and footsteps and voices can seem ghostly when there are echoes from other parts of the cave. They also state that stories of encounters with ghosts in Mammoth Cave are told by tourists and visitors who have no previous experience with caves and with the natural phenomena that accompanies them.

But there are others who would say that this isn't true! While many of the stories are indeed accounts told by visitors to the cave, others are not so easy to explain away. Many of the tales are experiences shared by park rangers, cave explorers, spelunkers and even geologists who are fully aware of what strange things a cave can do.

Believers in the resident ghosts can cite a number of reasons why the cave might be haunted. The long history of the place includes accidents from the days of the saltpeter operations, Native Americans who wandered into the cave and never found their way out, stranded travelers, missing cave explorers, tragic tuberculosis victims and even those who loved the place so much that they have never left, or so the stories go. I will allow the reader to judge for himself.

I have visited Mammoth Cave many times in years past and while collecting ghost stories, I have had the opportunity to talk with many of the people who work here. I have also been able to find other accounts from those who have gone on the record about the resident haunts in years past. In my own experience, I have found most of the park rangers reluctant to talk about ghost stories, although I have found a few who don't laugh off the odd tales and who will share their own strange experiences.

One such ranger has often served as a guide in the cave. She told me that weird things often happen along the route leading

from the historic entrance to the cave. One day, she had been leading a tour group into the cave and had stopped to point out a site
along the passage. She stopped to wait for everyone to catch up and
noticed a man in the back who was lingering behind the rest. He
was wearing a striped shirt, denim pants and suspenders, but that
was all she remembered. After her discussion, the group moved
further along the passage and she looked for the man again, but he
was gone. There was no one else in the tour group who matched
the description of this man, so she sent another guide back a little
way to look for him. The man was never found!

Another story, told by an experienced tour guide named Joy
Lyons, tells of a tour that was taken a few years ago in the company of a large group and two guides. When they reached a point on
the trail called the Methodist Church, they usually turned out all of
the lights so that visitors could experience what it was like in pitch
blackness. She was standing at the back of the group when the lights
went out and she could hear the lead ranger talking about the experience. Then, she felt a strong shove against her shoulder. The shove
was hard enough that she had to step forward to keep from falling
over. She turned to another ranger, who was supposed to be standing next to her and she whispered to him to stop clowning around.
A moment later, the lead ranger ignited the wick on a lantern and
she saw that the other ranger, she had thought was close to her, was
actually about 70 feet away. There was no way that he could have
shoved her and then walked so far in complete darkness!

"There was no one near me," she said, "but it was a playful
shove. There are a number of us who feel things in various parts of
the cave. It's not frightening, but it's something else."

Another account was passed along to author Arthur Myers by
Larry Purcell, a science teacher from Bowling Green, Kentucky.
He worked as summer guide at the cave for number of years and
had some strange experiences of his own.

The strangest episode seemed to be connected to the ghost of
Stephen Bishop, the cave's most famous guide. Bishop so loved the

cave that he was once offered his freedom from slavery but refused to take it because if he did, it meant leaving Mammoth Cave. Purcell's encounter with what may have been his ghost suggests that he may still be exploring the cave today.

Purcell was on a tour one day and happened to be by himself as another guide was speaking to the group. The lights were all off and it was Purcell's job to turn them back on again. He said: "I was walking along and I saw a black man with a woman and two children. The man had on white pants, a dark shirt, a white vest and a white Panama hat. They were real enough so that I walked around them. I went and turned on the lights and there were no people there…and there were no black people on that trip!"

And Purcell is not the only one to allegedly see Stephen Bishop. There have been a number of visitors who have reported seeing a man of the former slave's description and have assumed him to be part of a historic tour, perhaps playing the part of Stephen Bishop. When they have asked about the man, or have looked for him again, he is gone.

"I can tell you this," said one veteran ranger, who has guided literally hundreds of tours through Mammoth Cave. "I came here as a non-believer in ghosts. I've gotten a lot more open-minded about the subject as time's gone by."

An additional story comes from Charlie Hanion, a former cave guide who became a nature writer. He and a friend were leading a Lantern Tour of the cave (a historic tour designed to give the visitor an idea of how early tourists saw the cave) and as his friend was talking to the assembled group, a girl of about 14 years-old turned to Hanion and asked who the man standing near the rocks was.

Hanion looked about 40 feet away and saw a man in old-fashioned, formal attire. He was dressed in a fashion that tourists from decades past would have dressed to tour the cave. The man quickly vanished!

"But the really weird part came the following week when we were on the same tour," Hanion added.

As the tour group reached the same point in the cave, a guide asked if there were any questions. A woman raised her hand and asked if strange things were ever seen in this part of the cave? The woman was a tourist and claimed to be a psychic. She pointed over to the place in the rocks where Hanion had seen the man the week before and she asked who that person was.

"It was the same spot where we'd seen it before. I didn't see it at all that time," Hanion recalled. He also admitted that while he hadn't seen anything, the entire experience gave him chills to think about.

Based on these accounts, it would seem that apparitions are fairly common at Mammoth Cave and this is especially true when it comes to the most famous ghost connected to the cave. It is said to be a fictional account but many wonder if the story might contain elements of the truth, especially those who believe they may have encountered the main character in the story.

In February 1858, an article appeared in *Knickerbocker Magazine* called "A Tragedy in Mammoth Cave." The story tells of a girl named Melissa, who confessed the entire tale on her deathbed, having succumbed to tuberculosis. Melissa was a southern girl who lived in the vicinity of Mammoth Cave and she had fallen in love with her tutor from Boston, a young man named Beverleigh. The tutor had ignored Melissa's affections and began courting a neighbor girl instead. Melissa plotted her revenge.

Having grown up in the area, she knew well the twists and turns of Mammoth Cave and with careful planning, she lured Mr. Beverleigh to the cave. She conducted him on a tour to the depths of the cave and to a place called Echo River. Here, she vanished into a side passage and left the poor man to find his own way out.

Days passed and Beverleigh did not return. Melissa had only meant the whole thing as a cruel joke and so in despair, she went back to the cave to look for him. She made daily treks underground, searching and calling out to him; but Beverleigh was never seen again.

Melissa was later diagnosed with consumption and died a short time later, never recovering from her guilt over the tutor's death. Many believe that her ghost is still seen and heard in Mammoth Cave, desperately searching for the missing man. While the story sounds incredibly melodramatic, the reader is warned not to dismiss it too quickly. According to Gary Bremer, a former Mammoth Cave guide, there may just be something to the tale.

Several years ago, Bremer and four others were in a boat on Echo River, an underground stream that lies deep in the cave. One of the men had left to get another paddle for the boat. Bremer remembered what happened next: "The three of us in the boat all heard a woman calling out. It wasn't screaming but it was as though she was looking for someone."

The next day, they asked some of the other guides if anyone else had ever had such an experience. One of the older guides told him about a murder that was supposed to have taken place in that area and told him the story about Melissa. Bremer had never heard the story before that time.

Strangely, it would not be his last encounter here either. A short time later, he was again on the Echo River, this time with a new employee who had never seen the river before. She suddenly turned and grabbed his shoulder. "Did you hear a woman cough?" she asked him. Bremer felt a cold chill. Melissa had died of tuberculosis, he remembered.

The other employee would later verify Bremer's version of their experience and would also add that she had also heard garbled voices in the cave and on one night, believed that she heard someone whisper her name.

Not all of the accounts of Mammoth Cave come from parts of the cave that are accessible to the public. Many of the strangest tales come from Crystal Cave, which was once believed to be a separate cave and was once operated as a private attraction. This cave is located along Flint Ridge, now well within the boundaries of the national park. It is not, at this time, open to the public and yet the stories that surround this portion of the cave are too mysterious to not be included here.

Most of these legends involve the ghost of a man named Floyd Collins, the former owner of Crystal Cave. Collins was not only an avid cave explorer but an established businessman too, always on the lookout for new caves that could be developed and put into service as a moneymaking enterprise.

In the winter of 1925, Collins was exploring nearby Sand Cave (also located in the Flint Ridge) and he became wedged under a rock overhang about 60 feet underground. The story of Collins' rescue attempt became front-page news across the country. For 16 days, the attempts to rescue Floyd Collins dominated newspapers and radio. The press descended on the Mammoth Cave area and turned the region upside-down. People all over America were riveted to the story, a story that ended tragically with Collins' death in Sand Cave. Three months later, his lifeless body was removed from the cave and buried near his family home, close to Crystal Cave.

The tragedy brought national attention to the Kentucky cave country, but it also created a backlash, leading many to wonder if the caves were safe. The tourist trade was temporarily affected, with the small commercial caves suffering the most. This was at the height of the previously mentioned Cave Wars and now the smaller caves were fighting one another for an even smaller piece of the pie. Even Crystal Cave, which should have still managed to draw business thanks to the Floyd Collins name, was hurt by the slump. As a result, Floyd's father, Lee Collins, was anxious to sell the place.

In 1927, he accepted an offer from Dr. Harry B. Thomas, a local dentist, to take Crystal Cave off his hands for $10,000. Dr. Thomas already owned two other commercial caves in the area, Hidden River Cave and Mammoth Onyx Cave. In the transfer of property, Thomas was authorized to move Floyd Collins' body from its resting place and re-locate it in Crystal Cave, where it would be given a new burial spot. The Collins family, of course, objected to this, but it was too late. Lee Collins had already signed the deal.

Thomas wanted to move Floyd's body because he was sure that it would be a huge moneymaker for Crystal Cave. He had the body exhumed and then placed it in a glass-covered, bronzed metal coffin, opening it for public viewing in June 1927. It was placed in the middle of the tourist trail leading to Crystal Cave's main concourse. Here, visitors could pass by and look at him as they walked deeper into the cave. He had a large granite tombstone placed at Floyd's head that read:

William Floyd Collins
Born July 20, 1887
Buried April 26, 1925
Trapped in Sand Cave Jan. 30, 1925
Discovered Crystal Cave Jan. 18, 1917
Greatest Cave Explorer Ever Known

Granted, the stunt was ghoulish but it worked. Hundreds flocked to see Floyd's body and in his death, he became the cave's greatest advertisement. The guides would lecture solemnly about the exploits of the "world's greatest cave explorer" while the tourists gawked at the white, waxed face of the man in the coffin.

The Collins family sued Thomas and the case was battled out in court for several years. In 1929, the courts ruled (hopefully reluctantly) that Collins' body could stay where it was. Dr. Thomas had the legal right to the macabre display. Floyd would stay where he was in Crystal Cave. Or at least that was the general idea.

At some point on the night of March 18, 1929, Floyd's body was stolen from its glass coffin and spirited out of the cave. The theft was discovered the next morning and authorities from three counties were enlisted to help in the search. The casket was dusted for fingerprints and bloodhounds, after being given Floyd's scent, scoured the surrounding area. Before the day was over, the missing body was discovered (minus the left leg), about 800 yards from the cave's entrance. It had been wrapped in burlap bags and hidden in the brush along the Green River.

The cadaver was back in its coffin the following day, a little worse for wear, although the missing leg was never found. The identity of the thieves was also never discovered, although many of the local folks had their suspicions.

The prime suspect was Dr. Thomas himself. Although he maintained that he could not guess the motives of the body-snatchers, there were those who believed that he had stolen the body himself in an effort to boost business at Crystal Cave (which it did). Others, however, blamed competing cave owners, jealous over Thomas' newfound success, and some believed that the Collins family had nabbed the corpse, or had hired somebody, and they had lost the body before they could get away.

Regardless, after the attempted theft, the casket was covered each night with a metal lid and was securely locked. As time passed, the body was shown infrequently, although tourists were still asked to pause at the casket and listen to a short spiel offered in memory of the fallen cave explorer. The body continued to be displayed on occasion as late as 1952, although it remained in the cave for years after, long after it was closed to the public.

Many years after his actual death, Floyd Collins was finally buried at the Baptist Church cemetery up on Flint Ridge Road. His grave can easily be found here today. The last time that I visited here, I found a plastic bag that had been left behind on his tombstone with a note that was inscribed "To Floyd." Inside of the waterproof bag was a handful of matches and a candle, the best friends of an old-time cave explorer.

Even after all of this time, Floyd Collins has not been forgotten. Could that be because his ghost is still around?

Over the past several years, Crystal Cave has not been accessible to the public, although it has been charted and explored by national park employees and by a limited number of spelunkers. The fact that these veteran cave explorers have encountered weird phenomena in the cave dismisses the idea that the ghost stories here are merely the result of the overactive imaginations of tourists who are unfamiliar with the ordinary happenings in a cave.

A few years back, a group of Mammoth Cave employees were on an after-hours excursion in Crystal Cave and they noticed an old whiskey bottle that was resting on a rock ledge. One of the men in the group picked it up and looked at it and then placed it back on the ledge where he had found it. The group walked on deeper into the cave.

Later on in the evening, one of the men was walking back toward the cave entrance and was just passing by the old whiskey bottle when he heard a strange sound. "It was just behind my ear," he stated. "I heard a sound as though someone had flicked a finger against glass…a clink. I turned around just in time to see the bottle hit the ground."

Another man who was with him jumped back in shock. He claimed that the whiskey bottle had not just fallen, but that it had come straight out from the wall and had just dropped! "The little clink was loud enough to make me look back toward the ledge," he remembered, "and as I did, the bottle actually came out and then went right down in front of me. It was very bizarre."

Could the ghostly activity in the cave be attributed to the ghost of Floyd Collins? If there were an identity to be given to this ghost, he would certainly be everyone's first choice.

Another tale from Crystal Cave is attributed to a former employee named George Wood, who filed it as a report back in 1976. He wrote that he and another employee, Bill Cobb, had spent a day in June checking springs for a study on groundwater flow in central Kentucky. They didn't make it to the last spring until after dark and it was located near the old and abandoned Floyd Collins house on Flint Ridge.

Cobb went to the spring while Wood waited near the truck. After a few moments, he heard the sound of a man crying out in the darkness. At first, he thought it was his friend calling for help, but the voice seemed too high-pitched. It was also so faint that he had to listen carefully to hear what it was saying.

The voice cried: "Help me! Help me! Help me, I'm trapped! Johnny, help me!" It called out over and over again.

As he stood there on the edge of the dark road, he felt a cold chill run down his back. He vividly recalled hearing and reading about Floyd Collins and how he was trapped in Sand Cave, which was located just a short distance from where he was standing!

A few minutes later, Cobb returned and Wood asked him if he had been calling for him. The other man had heard nothing while at the spring, but after hearing Wood's account, admitted that he was spooked. In fact, they both were and didn't waste any time in getting back in the truck and driving off.

Could the spectral voice have really belonged to Floyd Collins? And if so, could the Johnny that was heard in the mysterious cry have referred to Johnny Gerald, a friend of Floyd's and the last person to speak with him before a cave collapse sealed him off from rescue? Is his spirit still trapped in the cave, or could the sound have been merely an eerie echo of yesterday?

The Cave Research Foundation (CRF) is an organization of highly educated and highly trained cave explorers that was founded in 1957. The members investigate and chart caves all over the country but Mammoth Cave is normally their base of operations.

Mel Park, a neurophysicist at the University of Tennessee and the operations manager for the CRF in the 1980s, stated in an interview conducted in the early 1990s that he was not a believer in ghosts. In spite of this, he did say that strange things often occurred in the cave that he could not explain. "You hear sounds sometimes," he said, "like conversations. Sometimes it sounds like a very active cocktail party...but it's probably just a waterfall."

Other members of the CRF have also reported odd happenings over the years, although their explanations for the events are not quite so mundane as Park's.

A geologist named Greer Price worked at Mammoth Cave a

number of years ago and he stayed at the Floyd Collins home on Flint Ridge, as it was leased by the CRF. Across the road from this house was the former home of Bill Austin, who owned Crystal Cave in the 1950s. The CRF had moved into the houses around 1970 and the Austin house was used as a headquarters and the Collins house for sleeping rooms.

Price moved into the house in the middle 1970s as the care-taker, working part-time for the park service and part-time for the CRF. He lived there during the dead of winter and was very iso-lated during the cold weather months. He had to walk a mile from the gate to even reach the house and he was the only person who had the keys to the site. Needless to say, he didn't get a lot of visi-tors—at least living ones anyway.

"Some of the old time guides would look at me and say I was crazy," Price recalled years later. "They wouldn't live out there for anything."

In front of the house was a small shed that Bill Austin had once used as a ticket office for the cave. The first strange thing that Price noticed about the property was that the light in the ticket shed would often turn on by itself. He would sometimes get out of bed late at night and see the soft glow of the light from inside shining in the darkness. He wondered if the fact that the main chamber of Crystal Cave was located directly beneath the shed had anything to do with the odd goings-on. To make matters worse, the casket where Floyd Collins body still lay was located right under the house where Price slept at night. Even though the cave was closed to the public, it was still a thought that would give anyone the creeps.

Price also heard stories of rangers who had seen Floyd Collins, or at least an apparition who looked like him, inside of the cave. The figure wore a shirt from the 1920s and overalls and had a ten-dency to vanish whenever anyone came close to him.

He was also told about a CRF member who was listening to the radio in the Austin house one night when suddenly the regular broadcast cut out and a static-filled report came through, describing the attempts to rescue Floyd Collins. The next day, when the man asked others about the report, he was told that no such radio show had been playing on the station that night!

Price had other odd experiences at the Austin house, aside from the light in the shed. He explained: "One night, I was sitting up reading and I heard footsteps outside of the house. I know it was not my imagination because both of my cats raised their heads and looked toward the door. I hadn't heard a car drive up and there was no access to the place. I sat there for a few minutes and the footsteps stopped. The next morning, I went out and found footprints in the snow around the house and up to the door, but then they disappeared. There were no footprints going down the steps, and there was no evidence of a car having been driven in."

Dr. Arthur Palmer, a professor in the department of Earth Science at New York State University at Oneonta, was a long-time member of the CRF when he did an interview about ghostly happenings at the cave. "I'm a scientist," he said, "and I'm not susceptible to this type of thing. We weren't looking for ghosts but some of these accounts are fairly well documented, as documentable as these things get."

He spoke of an incident in 1973 when he and his wife visited Crystal Cave. "Collins' body was at that time in a casket in the entrance room. We had to walk past it. We were in a part of the cave that nobody for hundreds of miles knew how to get to, a totally uninhabited part of the park. Access was strictly controlled, so there was no possibility of anyone else being in the cave at that time."

Palmer was setting up his camera equipment to take photographs of some of the geologic features of the cave when he heard a sound from deeper in the cavern. It was the sound of banging, a very rhythmic sound that he described like someone taking a hammer and pounding on a slab of rock. It came about once each second, not random at all, but very steady.

"It was a very insistent, continuous pounding," he stated. "It was not a shifting of rocks, which would be a random clattering."

The scientist decided to make a quick retreat from the cave and as time passed, he wondered what he had heard there. "It was not until a couple of years later that it occurred to me that the noise was coming from the place where Floyd Collins used to come down and eat, and he would flatten his bean cans with a rock...some of those flattened cans are still down there."

Dr. Will White, a CRF member and a professor of geochemistry at Pennsylvania State University, also had some odd experiences in connection with the cave.

Back in the days when Crystal Cave was open for business, there was an old army field telephone in the cave. It had once been used to alert guides that customers were coming to the cave from the ticket office.

"I was with a fellow CRF member, George Deike," White recalled, "and as we were going by the phone, it rang. We looked at each other, wondering what was going on, but we continued walking."

They walked about 100 feet deeper into the cave when the telephone rang again. White recounted what happened next: "We ran back and I picked it up and answered. It was one of those old-fashioned army phones with sort of a butterfly switch on it. What I heard sounded like a phone sounds when it's off the hook and there are people in the room. You can hear the sound of voices but you can't hear what they're saying. I said hello, or something like that, and on the other end there's this startled gasp and that was all...no one responded. The line was now dead."

White and Deike went on into the cave, still puzzled over the strange experience, but on their way out, they traced the phone line out of the cave and all of the way to the old ticket office. They discovered that the phones were disconnected! There was no way that it could have rung in the cave and no way that anyone could have been on the other end of the line.. and yet it happened! Perhaps it was a telephone call from the other side!

So, are they really ghosts in famous Mammoth Cave? If the stories of witnesses and guides from almost the past two centuries can be believed, there are. Combine these accounts with hesitant reports from scientists and trained skeptics, who can't explain what they have encountered in the cave, and you certainly have an unusual situation on your hands!

But if nothing else, the cave is certainly ripe for a haunting and the legends alone draw thousands of eager visitors each year. The mystery, the history, the cave explorers who have never returned, the tragedy, the terror and the death have created just what may be one of the most haunted places in the world!

THE GRAND OLD LADY OF THE OZARKS

Hauntings at the Crescent Hotel

Located in remote resort town of Eureka Springs, Arkansas, stands the gothic Crescent Hotel. Called by some the Grand Old Lady of the Ozarks,' the hotel has served as many things over the years and yet strangely, each incarnation was reported to be haunted and each one also contributed to the legion of phantoms believed to walk the corridors of the building. If there is a single place in the Ozark Mountain region that can be called most haunted, it is this one!

The hotel was built on the crest of West Mountain between 1884 and 1886 and may have gained its first ghost when a workman fell from the roof during the construction. His body landed in the second floor area where Room 218 is now located. I doubt that it's a coincidence that this room is considered to be one of the most haunted in the hotel!

The Crescent was designed by Isaac L. Taylor, a well-known Missouri architect who was famous for a number of buildings in St. Louis and who would go on to greater fame for his designs during the 1904 World's Fair. The financing for the hotel came from a number of wealthy individuals and businessmen, including Powell Clayton, the governor of Arkansas from 1868 to 1870, and later the U.S. Ambassador to Mexico. Clayton formed the Eureka

Improvement Company to seek investors and to acquire land, hoping to take advantage of the boom time of the period. Many of the other investors included officials with the Frisco Railroad.

The construction of the hotel, and development in the area, was so important at that time thanks to the national attention that had come to Eureka Springs (and other locations in Arkansas) for the healing waters that were bubbling from the earth nearby. During the late 1800s, people traveled from all over the country to take in the waters and to hopefully ease and cure their particular ailments. In addition, spring water could also be bottled and shipped out, further enhancing the small town's reputation.

The officials from the railroad were involved in the development plans because of the excursion train trips that had become so popular in the 1880s. The Frisco Railroad had built a spur from Seligman, Missouri to Eureka Springs to accommodate the tourists who wanted to visit the area. It was in their best interest to also develop a fine hotel for them to stay in. As the Crescent neared completion, liveried footmen would meet guests at the railroad depot and transport them by coach to the portico the new hotel.

The hotel itself combined a number of architectural styles to create a unique (and sometimes foreboding) setting. It is equipped with numerous towers, overhanging balconies and granite walls that are more than 18 inches thick. Numerous renovations have altered the five-story interior, but the lobby is still fitted with a massive stone fireplace that dominates the room. At one time, more than 500 people could be seated in the dining room. Electric lights were included in the original construction, as were bathrooms and modern plumbing fixtures. The lawn outside was decorated with gazebos, winding boardwalks and flower gardens and guests were offered tennis courts, croquet and other outdoor recreations.

The Crescent became almost immediately popular and attracted people from all over the south. It flourished for several years and from 1902 to 1907, it was taken over by the Frisco Railroad, which leased the property as a summer hotel. Not long after, people began to realize that while the local hot springs were certainly wonderful, they held no curative powers. The springs soon lost the interest of the wealthier class, who had many other pursuits in that gilded age, and business for the town dropped off. The loss of revenue convinced the railroad to quickly abandon their attempt at running a hotel.

The next 60 years were not good ones for the Crescent. It was open year-round, but it was starting to slip into a more run-down and decrepit condition. Various attempts were made to keep the place up and running, but as time passed, Eureka Springs lost its past prominence and the hotel became a forgotten curiosity. But it did not stand empty, as history goes on to testify.

In 1908, the hotel was opened as the Crescent College and Conservatory for Young Women and served as an exclusive academy for wealthy ladies. During the summer it still catered to the tourist crowd, but the money it made was not enough to keep the aging monolith in business. The costs of running, heating and repairing the place were so overwhelming that they were not ever offset by the staggering tuition charged to the students. The school closed in 1924 and then reopened briefly from 1930 to 1934 as a junior college.

By the 1920s, the automobile was transforming Arkansas into a vacation state. One estimate even claimed that nearly a half million people drove to the Ozarks for vacations in 1929, a staggering number for the time. Because of this, there were a number of businesses that leased the Crescent as a summer resort after the school closed down.

However, in 1937, Norman Baker leased the hotel for another purpose altogether. These were the darkest days of the hotel and according to most, the time when the haunting really began at the Crescent Hotel. The deeds committed during this era have unquestionably had a lasting impact on the building—and perhaps on the spirits who still linger here.

When Baker took over the hotel, he had plans to turn the place into a hospital and health resort. Baker was an Iowa-born charlatan who had made his fortune by inventing the Calliaphone, an organ played with air pressure and not steam. He had made millions of dollars by 1934 but he was never content with this. He considered himself something of a medical expert, although he had no training. He claimed to have discovered a number of cures for various ailments but he was sure that organized medicine was conspiring to keep these "miracle medicines" from the market. He was also sure that these same enemies were trying to kill him.

Baker started a hospital in Muscatine, Iowa but ran afoul of the law over his "cure" for cancer. He was convicted of practicing medicine without a license in 1936 and all of his medicines were condemned by the American Medical Association. Nevertheless, he purchased the Crescent Hotel and remodeled it, tragically tearing out the distinctive wooden handrails and balconies and painting the wonderful woodwork in garish shades of red, orange, black and yellow. He decorated his own penthouse in shades of purple. He also added a few other touches to his private rooms, hanging machine guns on the walls and installing secret escape passages that would save him should his AMA "enemies" attack.

Baker moved his cancer patients from Iowa to Arkansas and he advertised the health resort by saying that no X-rays or operations were performed to save his patients lives. The cures mostly consisted of drinking the natural spring water of the area and various home remedies, or so the official stories say. According to most reports, no one was actually killed by Baker's medical claims, but local legend tells a different story.

The legends say that when remodeling has been done at the hotel over the years, dozens of human skeletons have been discovered secreted within the walls. It has also been said that somewhere within the place are jars of preserved body parts that were hidden so as to not scare off prospective buyers. They still have not been found to this day.

These same stories also claim that Baker was no harmless

quack, but a dangerous and terrible man who experimented on both the dead and the living. One of his miracle cures for brain tumors was to allegedly peel open the patient's scalp and then pour a mixture of spring water and ground watermelon seeds directly onto the brain. Dozens of the patients died and Baker was said to have hidden the bodies for weeks until they could be burned in the incinerator in the middle of night. As his publicity claimed that he could cure cancer in a matter of weeks, he had to keep the press from finding out that many of his patients died every month. It has been said that he would put the extreme and advanced cases into an asylum, where they would die in extreme pain. That way, no one would know that they actually died of cancer.

These are the legends that have been told, although most sources will say that these events never actually took place. They will say that they are nothing more than tall tales that have been attached to the Crescent over the years. And perhaps they are right.

Regardless, federal authorities caught up with Baker and he was charged with using the mail to defraud the public about his false medical claims. He was convicted in 1940 and sentenced to four years in Leavenworth. The hospital closed and Baker vanished into history. But would those who died at his health resort disappear so easily?

The brooding old hotel stayed closed until 1946, when new investors took it over and began trying to restore the place. The hard years still showed and the hotel was described as being "seedily elegant." Since then however, it has started to regain it's lost glory and it remains an odd and historical piece of Ozark history. It also remains haunted.

Staff members receive frequent reports from overnight guests of strange goings-on in their rooms and in the hallways. Room 424 has had several visitations but the most famous haunted spot is the previously mentioned Room 218. Several guests and employees have encountered strange sounds and sensations in that room. Doors have slammed shut and some people claim to have been shaken awake at night. One man, a salesman, was asleep in Room 218 one night when his shoulder was violently shaken back and forth. He awakened just long enough to hear footsteps hurry across the floor. He saw no one in the room.

Who this particular ghost may be is unknown, although some believe it is the spirit of the man who was killed during the hotel's construction. His body was said to have fallen just about where the room is currently located. Other than that, there doesn't seem to be any particular macabre history about this room. A story of the hotel has it that the wife of one of the hotel's past owners stayed in the room. At one point in the middle of the night, she ran screaming from the room, claiming that she had seen blood spattered all over the walls. Several staff members ran up to take a look but found no blood and nothing else out of the ordinary. Could the spectral blood have been connected to the fallen construction worker? Or perhaps an operating room from Dr. Baker's days of depravity?

Another ghost of the hotel is that of a distinguished-looking man with a mustache and beard and who dresses in old-fashioned, formal clothing. He seems to favor the lobby of the hotel and a bar that is decorated in the style of the Victorian era. People who claim they have talked to the man say that he never responds, he only sits quietly and then vanishes. In an interview, a staff member recounted one odd experience with the silent ghost: "During the summer, we had two auditors work for us because we're so busy. One of these men left the front desk to get a drink of water in the bar, after it was closed. He told me that he saw some guy sitting on a barstool, staring straight ahead. He didn't say anything and he didn't move. Our guy left to get his partner, who was still at the front desk. They came back and spoke to the man. They thought he was drunk."

When the man again did not respond, the two auditors decided to leave him alone and go back to work. As they looked back over their shoulders on the way out of the bar though, they saw that the barstool was now empty. The man was nowhere in the room.

"One of them started searching for the man," the staff member added. "He looked around the lobby, which is about 25 to 30 yards across, everywhere in that area. The auditor who was looking around went over to the steps (a staircase ascends from the lobby). The fellow from the bar was on the second-floor landing, looking down at him. He went up but as he got to the second floor, he felt something push him back down again. That's when he got the manager and told him what had happened."

It's possible that the era of Baker's hospital may have left the greatest ghostly impression on the place. In July 1987, a guest claimed that she saw a nurse pushing a gurney down the hallway in the middle of the night. The nurse reached the wall and then vanished. It was later learned that a number of other people had witnessed the same vision and had seen it reenacted in just the same way.

An apparition that is believed to be Baker himself has been spotted around the old recreation room, near the foot of the stairs going to the first floor. Those who have seen him say that he looks lost, first going one way and then another. Could Baker be trapped in the hotel, perhaps paying for misdeeds that were committed many years ago?

Some time back, an antique switchboard from the days of the hospital was finally removed because of all of the problems it caused. A staff member explained: "In the summer we would get phone calls on the switchboard from the basement recreation room. There was no one on the other end because the room was unused and locked. We could check it out and find that the phone had been taken off the hook. There was only one way in or out of the place and the key was kept at the front desk."

This same staff member checked out the recreation room one night after receiving another of the strange calls. He found the phone on the hook, but he still maintains that he felt another presence in the room with him. "I just wanted to get out," he added.

He locked the door and went back upstairs, but within five

minutes the switchboard buzzer went off again, indicating that a call was coming from the same room that he had just left. This time, he decided not to go and check it out!

To go along with all of the stories, accounts and experiences, the hotel even has a legendary ghost photo from Room 202. No one knows who took it or why, but the photo contains a misty figure slouching in the closet of the room. The room was empty except for the photographer at the time.

So what makes the Crescent Hotel such a haunted place? Are memories from the past somehow stored here, replaying themselves over and over again on a regular basis to the fear and delight of the living? Or are the deeds of the past simply revisiting the present, reminding us that history is never really forgotten? Whatever the reason for the strange happenings though, the Crescent Hotel remains one of the South's most haunted spots and the perfect vacation place for those with ghosts in mind.

THE MOST HAUNTED
PLANTATION IN THE SOUTH

The Mysterious History of the Myrtles Plantation

Handprints in the mirrors, footsteps on the stairs, mysterious smells, vanishing objects, death by poison, hangings, murder and gunfire—the Myrtles Plantation in the West Feliciana town of St. Francisville, Louisiana holds the rather dubious record of hosting more ghostly phenomena than just about any other house in the country. But what could be more dubious than the honor itself—perhaps some of the questionable history that has been presented to explain why the house is so haunted in the first place!

Long perceived as one of the most haunted houses in America, the Myrtles attracts an almost endless stream of visitors each year and many of them come in search of ghosts. It is not my purpose to do anything to discourage these visitors from coming—or even to discourage them from looking for the ghosts that they can almost certainly find here. The purpose behind sharing the truth of the Myrtles is to question the "facts" as they have been presented by several generations of the plantation's owners and guides—facts and history that many of them know is blatantly false. I have no wish to try and debunk the ghosts, merely the identities that they have been given over the years. The Myrtles, according to hundreds of people who have encountered the unexplained here, is haunted—but not for the reasons that we have all been told.

But why go to the trouble to debunk the myths that have been created over the last fifty-some-odd years? Surely, they aren't hurting anyone, so why bother to expose them as the creation of rich imaginations? To that, I can only say that no dedicated ghost hunter should be afraid to seek the truth. As the history of a house is the most important key to discovering just why it might be haunted in the first place, it seems to be imperative to discover the real history of the site. It has often been recommended to sift through the legends and folklore of the place in a search for a kernel of truth. This is exactly what I did when I began researching the history of the Myrtles—examining the lore in a search for the truth. After a lot of hard work, I believe that I have found it. It might not be as glamorous as the legends of the Myrtles Plantation that we have all heard about but it is certainly strange. The real history of the plantation is filled with death, tragedy and despair, leading us to wonder why a fanciful history was created in its place. That question will likely never be answered but many others will.

The History of the Myrtles Plantation: Truth & Legends

The Myrtles Plantation was constructed by David Bradford in 1794 and since that time, has allegedly been the scene of at least 10 murders. In truth, only one person was ever murdered here but, as has been stated already, some of the people who have owned the house have never let the truth stand in the way of a good story. But as the reader will soon discover, the plantation has an unusual history that genuinely did occur, and one that may, and likely has, left its own real ghosts behind.

David Bradford was born in America to Irish immigrants and was one of five children. In 1777, he purchased a tract of land and a small stone house near Washington County, Pennsylvania. He became a successful attorney, businessman and Deputy Attorney General for the county. His first attempt to marry ended only days before his wedding (nothing is known about this) but he later met and married Elizabeth Porter in 1785 and started a family.

As his family and business grew, Bradford needed a larger home and built a new one in the town of Washington. The house became well known in the region for its size and remarkable craftsmanship, with a mahogany staircase and woodwork imported from England. Many of the items had to be transported from the east coast and over the Pennsylvania mountains at great expense. Bradford would use the parlor of the house as an office, where he would meet with his clients.

Unfortunately, he was not able to enjoy the house for long. In October 1794, he was forced to flee, leaving his family behind. Bradford became involved in the infamous Whiskey Rebellion and legend has it that President George Washington placed a price on the man's head for his role in the affair. The Whiskey Rebellion took place in western Pennsylvania and began as a series of grievances over high prices and taxes forced on those living along the frontier at that time. The complaints eventually erupted into violence when a mob attacked and burned down the home of a local tax collector. In the months that followed, residents resisted a tax that had been placed on whiskey and while most of the protests were nonviolent, Washington mobilized a militia and sent it in to suppress the rebellion. Once the protests were brought under control, Bradford left the region on the advice of some of the other principals in the affair.

After leaving Washington, Bradford first went to Pittsburgh.

Leaving his family in safety, he traveled down the Ohio River to the Mississippi. He eventually settled at Bayou Sarah, near what is now St. Francisville, Louisiana. Bradford was no stranger to this area. He had originally traveled here in 1792 to try and obtain a land grant from Spain. When he returned in 1796, he purchased 600 acres of land and a year later, built a modest, eight-room home that he named Laurel Grove. He lived here alone until 1799, when he received a pardon for his role in the Whiskey Rebellion from newly elected President John Adams.

After receiving the pardon, Bradford returned to Pennsylvania to bring his wife and five children back to Louisiana. He brought them to live at Bayou Sarah and they settled into a comfortable life here. Bradford occasionally took in students who wanted to study the law.

Clark Woodrooff was born in Litchfield County, Connecticut in August 1791. Having no desire to follow in his father's footsteps as a farmer, he left Connecticut at the age of 19 and sought his fortune on the Mississippi River, ending up in Bayou Sarah. He arrived in 1810, the same year that citizens of the Feliciana parish rose up in revolt against the Spanish garrison at Baton Rouge. They overthrew the Spanish and then set up a new territory with its capital being St. Francisville.

Still seeking to make his fortune, Woodrooff placed an advertisement in the new St. Francisville newspaper, the *Time Piece*, in the summer of 1811. He informed the public that "an academy would be opening on the first Monday in September for the reception of students." He planned to offer English, grammar, astronomy, geography, elocution, composition, penmanship and Greek and Latin languages. The academy was apparently short-lived for in 1814, he joined Colonel Hide's cavalry regiment from the Feliciana parish to fight alongside Andrew Jackson at the Battle of New Orleans. When the smoke cleared and the War of 1812 had ended, Woodrooff returned to St. Francisville with the intention of studying law.

He began his studies with Judge David Bradford and soon earned his degree. He also succumbed to the charms of the Bradford daughter, the lovely Sarah Mathilda. Their romance blossomed under the shade of the crape myrtle trees that reportedly gave the home its lasting name. The young couple was married on November 19, 1817 and for their honeymoon, Woodrooff took his new bride to the Hermitage, the Tennessee home of his friend, Andrew Jackson.

After the death of David Bradford, Woodrooff managed Laurel Grove for his mother-in-law, Elizabeth. He expanded the holdings of the plantation and planted about 650 acres of indigo and cotton. Together, he and Sarah Mathilda had three children, Cornelia Gale, James, and Mary Octavia. Tragically though, their happiness would not last.

On July 21, 1823, Sarah Mathilda died after contracting yellow fever. The disease was spread through a number of epidemics that swept through Louisiana in those days. Hardly a family in the region went untouched by tragedy and despair. Although heartbroken, Woodrooff continued to manage the plantation and to care for his children with help from Elizabeth. But the dark days were not yet over. On July 15, 1824, his only son James, also died from yellow fever, and two months later, in September, Cornelia Gale was also felled by the dreaded disease.

Woodrooff's life would never be the same but he managed to purchase the farm outright from his mother-in-law. She continued to live at Laurel Grove with her son-in-law and granddaughter Octavia until her death in 1830.

After Elizabeth died, Woodrooff turned his attentions away from farming to the practice of law. He and Octavia moved away from Laurel Grove, and he left the plantation under the management of a caretaker. On January 1, 1834, he sold Laurel Grove to Ruffin Grey Stirling.

By this time, Woodrooff was living on Rampart Street in New Orleans and had changed the spelling of his last name to Woodruff.

He had also been elected as the president of public works for the city. During this period, Octavia was sent to a finishing school in New Haven, Connecticut but she returned home to live with her father in 1836. Two years later, she married Colonel Lorenzo Augustus Besancon and moved to his plantation, Oaklawn, five miles north of New Orleans.

In 1840, the Louisiana governor, Isaac Johnson, appointed Woodruff to the newly created office of Auditor of Public Works where he served for one term. Then, at 60 years of age, he retired and moved to Oaklawn to live with Octavia and her husband. He devoted the remainder of his life to the study of chemistry and physics and died on November 25, 1851.

In 1834, Laurel Grove was purchased by Ruffin Grey Stirling. The Stirlings were a very wealthy family who owned several plantations on both sides of the Mississippi River. On January 1, Ruffin Grey Stirling and his wife, Mary Cobb, took over the house, land, buildings and all of the slaves that had been bought from Elizabeth Bradford by her son-in-law.

Since the Stirlings were so well thought of in the community, they needed a house that was befitting their social status. They decided to remodel Laurel Grove. Stirling added the broad central hallway of the house and the entire southern section. The walls of the original house were removed and repositioned to create four large rooms that were used as identical ladies' and gentlemen's parlors, a formal dining room and a game room. Year-long trips to Europe to purchase fine furnishings resulted in the importation of skilled craftsmen as well. Elaborate plaster cornices were created for many of the rooms, made from a mixture of clay, Spanish moss and cattle hair. On the outside of the house, Stirling added a 107-foot long front gallery that was supported by cast-iron support posts and railings. The original roof of the house was extended to encompass the new addition, copying the existing dormers to maintain a smooth line. The addition had higher ceilings than the original house so the second story floor was raised one foot. The completed project nearby doubled the size of David Bradford's house and in keeping with the renovations, the name of the plantation was officially changed to the Myrtles.

Four years after the completion of the project, Stirling died on July 17, 1854 of consumption. He left his vast holdings in the care of his wife, Mary Cobb, who most referred to as a remarkable woman. Many other plantation owners stated that she "had the business acumen of a man," which was high praise for a woman in those days, and she managed to run all of her and her husband's farms almost single-handedly, for many years.

In spite of this, the family was often visited by tragedy. Of nine children, only four of them lived to be old enough to marry. The oldest son, Lewis, died in the same year as his father, and daughter Sarah Mulford's husband was actually murdered on the front porch of the house after the Civil War. The war itself wreaked havoc on the Myrtles and the Stirling family. Many of the family's personal belongings were looted and destroyed by Federal soldiers and the wealth that they had accumulated was ultimately in worthless Confederate currency. To make matters worse, Mary Cobb had invested heavily in sugar plantations that had been ravaged by the war. She eventually lost all of her property. She never let the tragedies of the war, and others that followed after, overcome her however, and she held onto the Myrtles until her death in August 1880. She is buried next to her husband in a family plot at Grace Church in St. Francisville.

William Winter had been born to Captain Samuel Winter and Sarah Bowman on October 28, 1820 in Bath, Maine. Little is known about his life or how he managed to meet Sarah Mulford Stirling. However, they were married on June 3, 1852 at the Myrtles and together, they had six children, Mary, Sarah, Kate, Ruffin, William and Francis. Kate died from typhoid at the age of three. The Winters first lived at Gantmore plantation, near Clinton, Louisiana and then bought a plantation on the west side of the Mississippi known as Arbroath.

After the Civil War, William was named as agent and attorney by Mary Cobb Stirling to help her with the remaining lands, including Ingleside, Crescent Park, Botany Bay and the Myrtles. In return, Mary gave William the use of the Myrtles as his home. Times were terrible though, and Winter was unable to hold onto it. By December 1867, he was completely bankrupt, and the Myrtles was sold by the U.S. Marshal to the New York Warehouse & Security Company on April 15, 1868. Two years later however, the property was sold back to Mrs. Sarah M. Winter. It is unknown just what occurred to cause this reversal of fortune but it seemed as though things were improving for the family once again.

But soon after, tragedy struck the Myrtles once more. According to the January 1871 issue of the *Point Coupee Democrat* newspaper, Winter was teaching a Sunday School lesson in the gentlemen's parlor of the house when he heard someone approach the house on horseback. After the stranger called out to him and told him that he had some business with him, Winter went out onto the side gallery of the house and was shot. He collapsed onto the porch and died. Those inside of the house, stunned by the sound of gunfire and the retreating horse, hurried outside to find the fallen man. Winter died on January 26, 1871 and was buried the following day at Grace Church. The newspaper reported that a man named E.S. Webber was to stand trial for Winter's murder but no outcome of the case was ever recorded. As far as is known, Winter's killer remains unidentified and unpunished.

Sarah was devastated by the incident and never remarried. She remained at the Myrtles with her mother and brothers until her death in April 1878 at the age of only 44.

After the death of Mary Cobb Stirling in 1880, the Myrtles was purchased by Stephen Stirling, one of her sons. He bought out his brothers but only maintained ownership of the house until March 1886. There are some who say that he squandered what was left of his fortune and lost the plantation in a game of chance, but most likely, the place was just too deep in debt. He sold the

Myrtles to Oran D. Brooks, ending his family's ownership. Brooks kept it until January 1889 when, after a series of transfers, it was purchased by Harrison Milton Williams, a Mississippi widower who brought his young son and second wife, Fannie Lintot Haralson, to the house in 1891.

Injured during the Civil War, Williams planted cotton and gained a reputation as a hard-working and industrious man. He and his family, which grew to include his wife and seven children, kept the Myrtles going during the hard times of the post-war South. But tragedy was soon to strike the Myrtles again.

During a storm, the Williams' oldest son, Harry, was trying to gather up some stray cattle and fell into the Mississippi and drowned. Shattered with grief, Harrison and Fannie turned over management of the property to another son, Surget Minor Williams. He later married a local girl named Jessie Folkes and provided a home at the Myrtles for his spinster sister and maiden aunt, Katie. Secretly called "the Colonel" behind her back, Katie was a true Southern character. Eccentric and kind, but with a gruff exterior, she kept life interesting at the house for years.

By the 1950s, the property surrounding the house had been divided among the Williams heirs and the house itself was sold to Marjorie Munson, an Oklahoma widow who had been made wealthy by chicken farms. It was at this point, they say, that the ghost stories of the house began. They started innocently enough but soon, what may have been real-life ghostly occurrences took on a life of their own.

Ghost Stories of the Myrtles:
Separating Fact From Fiction

There is no question that the most famous ghostly tale of the Myrtles is that of Chloe, the vengeful slave who murdered the wife and two daughters of Clark Woodruff in a fit of jealously and anger.

Those who have been reading the article so far have already guessed that there are some serious flaws in this story but for the sake of being complete, we have include the story here as it has long been told by owners and guides at the house.

According to the story, the troubles that led to the haunting at the Myrtles began in 1817 when Sarah Mathilda married Clark Woodruff. Sara Matilda had given birth to two daughters and was carrying a third child, when an event took place that still haunts the Myrtles today.

Woodruff, had a reputation in the region for integrity with men and with the law, but was also known for being promiscuous. While his wife was pregnant with their third child, he started an intimate relationship with one of his slaves. This particular woman, Chloe, was a household servant who, while she hated being forced to give in to Woodruff's sexual demands, realized that if she didn't, could be sent to work in the fields, which was the most brutal of the slave's work.

Eventually, Woodruff tired of Chloe and chose another woman with whom to carry on. Chloe feared the worst, sure that she was going to be sent to the fields, and she began eavesdropping on the Woodruff family's private conversations, dreading the mention of her name. One day, the Judge caught her at this and ordered that one of her ears be cut off to teach her a lesson and to put her in her place. After that time, she always wore a green turban around her head to hide the ugly scar that the knife had left behind.

What actually happened next is still unclear. Some claim that what occurred was done so that the family would just get sick and then Chloe could nurse them back to health and earn the Judge's gratitude. In this way, she would be safe from ever being returned to the fields. Others say that her motives were not so pure and that what she did was for one reason only—revenge!

For whatever reason, Chloe put a small amount of poison into a birthday cake that was made in honor of the Woodruff's oldest daughter. Mixed in with the flour and sugar was a handful of crushed oleander flowers. The two children, and Sarah Mathilda, each had slices of the poisoned cake but Woodruff didn't eat any of it. Before the end of the day, all of them were very sick. Chloe patiently attended to their needs, never realizing (if it was an accident) that she had given them too much poison. In a matter of hours, all three of them were dead.

The other slaves, perhaps afraid that their owner would punish them also, dragged Chloe from her room and hanged her from a nearby tree. Her body was later cut down, weighted with rocks and thrown into the river. Woodruff closed off the children's dining room, where the party was held, and never allowed it to be used again as long as he lived.

Since her death, the ghost of Chloe has been reported at the Myrtles and was even accidentally photographed by a past owner. The plantation still sells picture postcards today with the cloudy image of what is purported to be Chloe standing between two of the buildings. The former slave is thought to be the most frequently encountered ghost at the Myrtles. She has often been seen in her green turban, wandering the place at night. Sometimes the cries of little children accompany her appearances and at other times, those who are sleeping are startled awake by her face, peering at them from the side of the bed.

I am sure that after reading this story, even the most non-discerning readers have discovered a number of errors and problems with the tale. In fact, there are so many errors that it's difficult to know where to begin. However, to start, it's a shame that the character of Clark Woodruff has been so thoroughly damaged over the years with stories about his adulterous affairs with his slaves and claims that he had the ear cut off of one of his lovers. Sadly, these stories have been accepted as fact, even though no evidence whatsoever exists to say that they are true. In fact, history seems to show that Woodruff was very devoted to his wife and in fact, was so distraught over her death that he never remarried.

Before we get to the problem of Chloe's existence, we should also examine the alleged murders of Sarah Mathilda and her two daughters. In this case, the legend has twisted the truth so far that it is unrecognizable. Sarah Mathilda was not murdered. She died tragically from yellow fever (according to historical record) in 1823. Her children, a son and a daughter—not both daughters— died more than a year after she did. They certainly did not die from the result of a poisoned birthday cake. Also, with this legend, Octavia would not have existed at all (her mother was supposed to have been pregnant when murdered) but we know that she lived with her father, got married and lived to a ripe old age. In addition, Woodruff was not killed either. He died peacefully at his daughter and son-in-law's plantation in 1851.

The key to the legend of course, is Chloe, the murderous slave. The problem with this is that as far as we can tell, Chloe never existed at all. Not only did she not murder members of the Woodruff family but it's unlikely that the family ever even had a slave by this name. Countless hours have been spent looking through the property records of the Woodruff family, which are still available and on file as public record in St. Francisville, searching for any evidence that Chloe existed. It was a great disappointment to learn that the Woodruffs had never owned a slave, or had any record of, a slave named Chloe, or Cleo, as she appears in some versions of the story. The records list all of the other slaves owned by the Woodruff family but Chloe simply did not exist.

So how did such a story get started?

In the 1950s, the Myrtles was owned by wealthy widow Marjorie Munson, who began to notice that odd things were occurring in the house. Wondering if perhaps the old mansion might be haunted, she asked around and that's when the legend of Chloe got its start. According to the granddaughter of Harrison and Fannie Williams, Lucile Lawrason, her aunts used to talk about the ghost of an old woman who haunted the Myrtles and who wore a green bonnet. They often laughed about it and it became a family story. She was never given a name and in fact, the ghost with the green bonnet from the story was described as an older woman, never as a young slave who might have been involved in an affair with the owner of the house. Regardless, someone repeated this story of the Williams' family ghost to Marjorie Munson and she soon penned a song about the ghost of the Myrtles, a woman in a green beret.

As time wore on, the story grew and changed. The Myrtles changed hands several more times and in the 1970s, it was restored again under the ownership of Arlin Dease and Mr. and Mrs. Robert F. Ward. During this period, the story grew even larger and was greatly embellished to include the poison murders and the severed ear. Up until this point though, it was largely just a story that was passed on by word of mouth and it received little attention outside of the area. All of that changed though when James and Frances Kermeen Myers passed through on a riverboat and decided to purchase the Myrtles. The house came furnished with period antiques and enough ghost stories to attract people from all over the country.

Soon, the story of the Myrtles was appearing in magazines and books and receiving a warm reception from ghost enthusiasts, who had no idea that what they were hearing was a badly skewed version of the truth. The house appeared in a November 1980 issue of LIFE magazine but the first book mention that I have been able to find about the house was in a book by author Richard Winer. Both the magazine article and the Winer book mentioned the poison deaths of Sarah Mathilda and her daughters.

As time went on and more books and television shows came calling at the Myrtles, the story changed again and this time, took on even more murders. In addition to the deaths of Sarah Mathilda, her daughters and Chloe, it was alleged that as many as six other people had also been killed in the house. One of them, Lewis Stirling, the oldest son of Ruffin Grey Stirling, was claimed to have been stabbed to death in the house over a gambling debt. However, burial records in St. Francisville state that he died in October 1854 from yellow fever.

According to legend, three Union soldiers were killed in the house after they broke in and attempted to loot the place. They were allegedly shot to death in the gentlemen's parlor, leaving bloodstains on the floor that refused to be wiped away. Once fanciful account has it that years later, after the Myrtles was opened as an inn, a maid was mopping the floor and came to a spot that, no matter how hard she pushed, she was unable to reach. Supposedly, the spot was the same size as a human body and this was said to have been where one of the Union soldiers fell. The strange phenomenon was said to have lasted for a month and has not occurred since. The only problem with this story is that no soldiers were ever killed in the house. There are no records or evidence to say that there were and in fact, surviving family members denied the story was true.

Another murder allegedly occurred in 1927, when a caretaker at the house was killed during a robbery. Once again, no record exists of this crime and something as recent as this would have been widely reported. The only event even close to this, which may have spawned this part of the story, occurred when the brother of Fannie Williams, Eddie Haralson, was living in a small house on the property. He was killed while being robbed but this did not occur in the main house, as the story states.

The only verifiable murder to occur at the Myrtles was that of William Drew Winter and it differs wildly from the legends that have been told. As described previously, Winter was lured out of the house by a rider, who shot him to death on the side porch. It is here where the stories take a turn for the worse. In the legend, Winter was shot and then mortally wounded, staggered back into the house, passed through the gentlemen's parlor and the ladies parlor and onto the staircase that rises from the central hallway. He then managed to climb just high enough to die in his beloved's arms on exactly the 17th step. It has since been claimed that ghostly footsteps have been heard coming into the house, walking to the stairs and then climbing to the 17th step where they, of course, come to an end.

While dramatic, this event never happened either. Winter was indeed murdered on the front porch by an unknown assailant but after being shot, he immediately fell down and died. His bloody trip through the house never took place—information that was easily found in historical records.

So, is the Myrtles really haunted? The purpose of exposing the truth behind the legends of the Myrtles has never been to say that the Myrtles Plantation is not haunted. In fact, there is no denying that the sheer number of accounts that have been reported and collected here would cause the house to qualify as one of the most haunted sites in the country. However, as you can see from the preceding pages, the house may be haunted—but not for the reasons that have been claimed for so many years.

In all likelihood, the infamous Chloe never existed and even if she did, historical records prove that Sarah Mathilda and her children were never murdered but died from a terrible disease instead. Instead of 10 murders in the house, only one occurred and when William Winter died, he certainly did not stagger up the staircase to die on the 17th step, as the stories of his phantom footsteps allegedly bear out. Such tales belong in the realm of fiction and ghostlore—stories that were created to explain the weird goings-on that were really taking place at the Myrtles.

The house may really be haunted by the ghost of a woman in a green turban or bonnet. The Williams family had an ongoing tale of her and while it may have been a story that was never meant to be told outside the family, the story was told regardless. They admit that while she did exist, no identity was ever given to her. It's also very likely that something unusual was going on at the Myrtles when Marjorie Munson lived there, which led to her seeking answers and to her first introduction to the ghost in the green headdress. Did she see the ghost? Who knows— but many others have claimed that they have.

Frances Myers claimed that she encountered the ghost in the green turban in 1987. She was asleep in one of the downstairs bedrooms when she was awakened suddenly by a black woman wearing a green turban and a long dress. She was standing silently beside the bed, holding a metal candlestick in her hand. She was so real that the candle even gave off a soft glow. Knowing nothing about ghosts, she was terrified and pulled the covers over her head and started screaming! Then she slowly looked out and reached out a hand to touch the woman, who had never moved, and to her amazement, the apparition vanished.

Others claim that they have also seen the ghost and in fact, she was purportedly photographed a number of years ago. The resulting image seems to show a woman that does not fit the description of a young woman like Chloe would have been. In fact, it looks more like the older woman that was described by the Williams family. Could this be the real ghost of the Myrtles?

Even after leaving out the ridiculous stories of the poisonings and Winter's dramatic death on the staircase, the history of the Myrtles is still filled with more than enough trauma and tragedy to cause the place to become haunted. There were a number of deaths in the house, from yellow fever alone, and it's certainly possible that any of the deceased might have stayed behind after death. If ghosts stay behind in this world because of unfinished business, there are a number of candidates to be the restless ghosts of the plantation's stories.

And, if we believe the stories, the place truly is infested by spirits from different periods in the history of the house. There have been many reports of children who are seen playing on the wide verandah of the house, in the hallways and in the rooms. The small boy and girl may be the Woodruff children who, while not poisoned, died within months of each other during one of the many yellow fever epidemics that brought tragedy to the Myrtles. A young girl, with long curly hair and wearing an ankle-length dress, has been seen floating outside the window of the game room, cupping her hands and trying to peer inside through the glass. Is she Cornelia Gale Woodruff, or perhaps one of the Stirling children who did not survive until adulthood?

The grand piano on the first floor plays by itself, usually repeating the same chord over and over again. Sometimes it continues on through the night. When someone comes into the room to check on the sound, the music stops and will only start again when they leave.

Scores of people have filed strange reports about the house. In recent times, various owners have taken advantage of the Myrtles' infamous reputation and the place is now open to guests for tours and as a haunted bed and breakfast. Rooms are rented in the house and in cottages on the grounds. The plantation has played host to a wide variety of guests from curiosity-seekers to historians to ghost hunters. Over the years, a number of films and documentaries have also been shot on the ground and many of them have been paranormal in nature.

One film, which was decidedly not paranormal, was a television mini-series remake of *The Long Hot Summer*, starring Don Johnson, Cybill Shepherd, Ava Gardner and Jason Robards. A portion of the show was shot at the Myrtles and it was not an experience that the cast and crew would soon forget. One day, the crew moved the furniture in the game room and the dining room for filming and then left the room. When they returned, they reported that the furniture had been moved back to its original position. No one was inside of either room while the crew was absent! This happened several times, to the dismay of the crew, although they did manage to get the shots they needed. They added that the cast was happy to move on to another set once the filming at the Myrtles was completed.

The employees at the house often get the worst of the events that happen here. They are often exposed, first-hand, to happenings that would have weaker folks running from the place in terror. And some of them do! One employee, a gateman, was hired to greet guests at the front gate each day. One day while he was at work, a woman in a white, old-fashioned dress walked through the gate without speaking to him. She walked up to the house and vanished through the front door without ever opening it. The gateman quit his job and never returned to the house.

As you can see, the Myrtles can be a perplexing place. History has shown that many of the stories that have been told about the place, mostly to explain the hauntings, never actually occurred. In spite of this, the house seems to be haunted anyway. The truth seems to be an elusive thing at this grand old plantation house but there seems to be no question for those who have stayed or visited here that it is a spirited place. At the Myrtles, the ghosts of the past are never very far away from the present—whether we know their identities or not.

THE THING THAT WENT BUMP IN THE NIGHT

The Infamous Bell Witch of Tennessee

There is perhaps no haunting in the South that resonates as strongly today as the events that took place on the farm of John Bell in rural Tennessee. The story stands unique in the annals of folklore as one of the rare cases in which a ghost not only injured the residents of the haunted house, but also caused the death of one of them!

Although the events in the case took place in the early 1800s, they have not yet been forgotten. This may not be just because of the sensational aspects of the story but also may be because the land where the Bell farm once stood remains haunted today! And in fact, it may just be one of the most haunted places in America!

Just across the Tennessee border from the state of Kentucky is the sleepy little town of Adams, Tennessee. This small village has been here for many years and once served as a busy station for travelers. Today, the town is mostly forgotten. It lies off the path of the nearby interstate and only a narrow, two-lane highway connects it to the outside world.

Adams has made its mark in history though, and in a way that few small towns can boast, nor most likely would they care to. This Tennessee town was the home of the one of the most famous ghosts in the history of supernatural lore. It was here in the early 1800s, that the infamous Bell Witch took up residence, and many believe, she has never left.

John Bell, on whose farm the strange events came to pass, was born in Halifax County, North Carolina in 1750. He was the son of a Scottish farmer and was considered by most to be a hard-working young man. He was apprenticed in the cooper (barrel-making) business as a boy, but chose to become a farmer instead. In 1782, Bell married Lucy Williams, the daughter of a prosperous businessman. Shortly after the wedding, using money that he had saved, Bell purchased a small farm and he and his wife settled down to raise a family. Here, where the Bell family lived for the next 22 years, Lucy Bell bore her husband six children.

Then, in 1804, Bell decided to pull up stakes and move west to the new frontier of Tennessee. He was 54 years old when the family came to Robertson County. He purchased 1000 acres of land on the Red River, about 40 miles north of Nashville and near the settlement that would later be called Adams Station. Bell constructed a double, one and a half story log cabin on the property, along with housing for the slaves and several outbuildings. It wasn't long before the wealthy farmer became one of the leading pillars of the nearby and prosperous settlement.

The Bell family settled quite comfortably into life in the community. By 1817, they had nine children, seven sons and two daughters, named Jesse, John Jr., Drew, Benjamin, Esther, Zadok, Elizabeth, Richard Williams and Joel Egbert. Sadly, Benjamin died very young and while Zadok became a brilliant lawyer in Alabama, he passed away at a very early age.

As the years passed, John Bell became a well-liked and much respected man of the community. His neighbors and friends admired him and the men of the area often sought out his opinions. In addition, nothing but kind words were ever expressed about Lucy Bell, who was loved by everyone. Her home was always open to travelers and the house was a frequent location for social gatherings.

One of those who attended nearly every event at the Bell home was Richard Powell, a handsome schoolteacher who was also well liked in the community. He was the master of the local school and had tutored several of the Bell children, including Elizabeth (who was known to the family as Betsy). She was now starting to grow into womanhood and it was no secret that Powell was enamored of the girl. However, as she was still too young for courtship, Powell would often invent excuses to visit the Bell farm in order to see her.

Nor was Powell alone in his admiration for Betsy. A local young man named Joshua Gardner, who was much closer to Betsy's age, was also in love with her. It was well known that Betsy returned his affections, although it was an affair that would end tragically in the years to come.

It was in 1817 when the strange events began. It was time that became forever known to future generations of the Bell family as the beginning of "our family troubles."

The first mysterious occurrence took place when John Bell saw a strange-looking animal on his property. He was walking across one of his cornfields when he saw the creature squatting between the rows. Bell described it as "a strange animal, unlike any he had ever seen." He concluded that it was "probably a dog," and having his gun with him, he fired at the animal. The creature quickly turned and ran away. Bell would state that he had no idea if his bullet hit the animal or not.

The second odd sighting took place a few days later. It was late afternoon and Drew Bell spotted a very large bird, which he assumed was a wild turkey, sitting on a fence row. He hurried into the house to fetch his gun but when he got within shooting distance of the bird, it spread its wings and flew off. At that point, Drew realized that it had not been a turkey at all, but what has been

A drawing of the Bell Witch ghost

The Old John Bell House

called "an unknown bird of extraordinary size." He shot at the bird anyway and it appeared to fall to the ground. When he ran over to look at the carcass, the creature had vanished.

Then, one evening, a short time after this, Betsy Bell walked out with the children toward the edge of the forest. There, among the trees, she saw something that she described as "a pretty little girl in a green dress," dangling from the limbs of a tall oak tree. When she approached the girl, the apparition abruptly vanished.

The haunting began at the house in early 1818 with a series of sounds around the exterior of the house. They began as booming, vibrating shakes that first made the family think they might be caused by an earthquake. The terrible earthquake along the New Madrid fault in 1811 had rocked Tennessee and the Bell family feared that another massive quake might be coming.

Those fears were soon replaced by new ones as knockings began to sound on the front door of the house. When a family member would go to let the caller in, they would find that no one was present. The knockings and rappings were soon followed by hideous scratching sounds. It sounded as though the wood was being peeled from the outside walls, although no cause could be discovered for the noises.

Before long, the frightening sounds moved inside. They began as gnawing, scratching and scraping sounds that seemed to emanate from the bedroom belonging to the Bell sons. They would jump out of bed and light a candle, trying to find the source of the noise, but it would then stop. As soon as the candle was put out, they would start again.

This continued for weeks and then, a new wrinkle was added. Each time the boys would rise from their beds, the sound would cease in their room and would begin to be heard in Betsy's room instead. From there, it would travel to John and Lucy's bed chamber, finally rousing the whole household. The irritating sound would continue from room to room, stopping when everyone was awake and starting again when they all went back to bed.

The sounds continued and began to change. The sound of the scratching rat was joined by that which sounded like a large dog, pawing at the wooden floor. Other noises were described as sounding like two large animals dragging trace chains through the house. Richard Bell also recalled the sound being like "heavy stones falling" and like "chairs falling over."

The crashing and scratching sounds were frightening, but not as terrifying as the noises that followed. It was not uncommon for the Bells to be awakened in the darkness by a noise like the smacking of lips, gulping sounds and eerie gurgling and choking; sounds seemingly made by a human throat, although no living person was present. The nerves of the Bell family were beginning to unravel, as the sounds became a nightly occurrence.

The inhuman sounds were followed by the unseen hands that began to plague the household and they troubled Betsy more than anyone else. Items were broken around the house and blankets were pulled from the beds. "The phenomena was pulling the cover off the beds as fast as we could replace it," Bell stated.

The hands also did more than trouble inanimate objects. Hair was pulled and the children were slapped and poked, causing them to cry in pain. Betsy was once slapped so hard that her cheeks stayed a bright red color for hours.

Whatever the cause of this unseen force, the violence of it seemed to be especially directed at Betsy Bell. She would often run screaming from her room in terror as the unseen hands prodded, pinched and poked her. Strangely, it would be noticed later that the force became even more cruel to Betsy after she entertained her young suitor, Joshua Gardner, at the house. For some reason, the spirit seemed to want to punish her whenever Joshua would call.

By this time, John Bell was out of ideas and explanations for the mysterious occurrences. To make matters worse, he had also begun to develop a nervous condition that affected his tongue and jaw muscles. This affliction caused him great difficulty when trying to eat and chew. When his doctor's cures failed to help him, he started to believe that the illness was caused by the force which had invaded his home. Desperately seeking answers, he realized that he needed to appeal to someone outside of the household for assistance. At this point, Bell decided to enlist help from his friend and neighbor, James Johnson.

At Bell's request, Johnson and his wife came to spend the night at the Bell farm. He was determined to conduct an investigation that would lead him to the bottom of the events. That night, as everyone prepared to go to bed, Johnson, who was a devout Christian, read a chapter from the Bible and prayed fervently for the family to be delivered from the frightful disturbances, or at least for their origins to be revealed.

Almost as soon as the candles in the house were extinguished, the strange sounds began as usual, although this time they were even more violent, as though to show Johnson just what the force was capable of. The gnawing, knocking and scratching sounds began immediately and the disturbances continued to escalate as chairs overturned, blankets flew from the beds, and objects flew from one side of the room to the other.

James Johnson listened attentively to all of the sounds that he heard and closely observed the other incidents that were taking place. He realized, from the sounds of teeth grinding and the smacking of lips that an intelligent force seemed to be at work. He was determined to try and communicate with it and finally called out. "In the name of the Lord, what or who are you?" he cried, "What do you want and why are you here?"

As though shocked, the disturbances suddenly halted and the house remained quiet for some time. Unfortunately, it didn't last, and the violence began again with the ripping of the covers from one of the beds. The disturbances moved from room to room, settling in for an attack against Betsy Bell. The young girl was slapped and pummeled mercilessly.

When the events of the evening finally came to a halt, Bell's wife and children, along with Johnson's wife, retired to bed, hoping to find at least some restless sleep. John Bell and James Johnson sat up late into the early morning hours, huddled around a candle in the front room. They whispered back and forth as Johnson tried to make some sense of what he had witnessed that night. He had arrived at the conclusion that the phenomenon was definitely "beyond his comprehension." He did believe, however, that it possessed an uncanny intelligence, based on the fact that it had ceased action when spoken to. By this, Johnson deduced that it could understand language.

He advised Bell to invite their other friends into the investigation and Bell took his advice. They formed a committee to investigate whatever was going on in the house. John Bell had chosen these men with care and had apparently chosen well, as each one of them stayed at his side until the very end.

Regardless of the diligence of the committee, the household was soon in chaos. Word began to spread of the strange events and friends, and even strangers, came to the farm to see what was happening. Dozens of people heard the clear banging and rapping sounds, inexplicable lights were reported in the yard and chunks of rock and wood were thrown at the curious guests. From all over Kentucky and Tennessee came exorcists and witch-finders, all of them claiming they could expel the evil force from the Bell house. Their efforts were all in vain as the disturbances soon had them fleeing from the premises!

The committee formed by Bell, Johnson and their friends continued to search for answers. They set up experiments, trying to communicate with the force, and they kept a close eye on all of the events that took place. They set up watches that lasted throughout the night, but it did no good and, if anything, the attacks increased in their violence. Betsy was treated brutally and she began to have fainting spells and sensations of the breath being sucked out of her body. She was being scratched and her flesh would bleed as though she was being pierced with invisible pins and needles.

Meanwhile, James Johnson continued with his investigations

and theories of the force being controlled by an intelligent being of some sort. He, along with other members of the committee began speaking to the witch (as they had begun calling the force), asking it to speak and tell them what it wanted.

Questions were asked which required either yes or no answers, or which could be answered with numbers, and the replies would come in knocks or raps, as if an invisible fist were tapping on the wall. This went on for some time but the committee members continued to harass the witch with questions, daring the presence to speak.

Soon, it began to whistle in reply to the questions. It was not the whistling which one associates with trying to produce a musical melody, but a whistling, rasping sound, as if someone is trying very hard to speak! The whistling progressed and developed until it became a weak, indistinct whisper. Words were being formed but they could not be understood, at least at first.

"I do not remember the first intelligent utterance, which, however, was of no significance," wrote Richard Bell, "but the voice soon developed sufficient strength to be distinctly heard by every one in the room."

The scratching, rappings and whispers had become a voice. The spirit that had wreaked havoc in the Bell house was now beginning to talk. The problem was, once the witch began to speak, she would never be silent again!

The close-throated whistling noises soon turned into faint, indistinct words and the voice of the witch began to gain strength. Not surprisingly, the word spread quickly about this new wrinkle to the mystery. Soon, members of John Bell's investigative committee, and other interested parties, descended on the harassed household, increasing their efforts to get the witch to talk. Their goal was to try and get the witch to disclose her reasons for being at the Bell house; although little did they know that their efforts would be rewarded with literally months of lies, trickery and verbal abuse!

One of the first real statements the witch made after gaining the ability to speak was the answer to who she really was and why she was there. It would be a very ambiguous answer, but it would be one of the only completely honest answers she would ever give as to why the haunting was taking place.

"Who are you and what do you want?" one of the committee members demanded of the witch.

"I am a spirit," came the reply, "I was once very happy but have been disturbed."

The next occasion when the voice of the spirit was heard was on a Sunday night, not long after its initial contact with the investigators. By this time, the voice of the witch was much stronger and on this night occurred the spirit's first intrusion into the matters of the Bell family.

The family was seated in the front room of the house, discussing an impending trip that was to be made by the younger John Bell. He was going to North Carolina to tie up some business dealings that his father still maintained there. He was planning to leave by horseback at dawn the following morning. The trip was of great interest to the rest of the family, especially the younger children, and there was much talk about the long journey ahead of him, how long he would be away, the best route to take and of course, talk of the business matters themselves.

As was usual during this time period, a number of friends were also at the house. They too were giving John some good-natured advice about his trip, but then came some advice from an unexpected source!

From nowhere came the voice of the witch. "Do not leave on your journey," the witch said to him. She informed John that he would have a hard and tiresome trip, which would be plagued with bad luck. The estate that he was to close for his father would instead not be completed for some time and John would return from the arduous journey empty-handed. In addition, the spirit also told him of a young woman from Virginia who was coming to Robertson County to visit some friends and would arrive the following afternoon. Not only was this woman beautiful, but she was wealthy as well, and if John stayed in Tennessee, he would be able to win this young lady's heart.

John laughed at the revelations of the witch and left the following morning for North Carolina, just as he had planned. The trip turned out to be a particularly miserable one, and he was not able to return home for more than six months. When he did come back to Tennessee, he brought no money with him.

To make matters worse, just a few hours after John's departure, a very attractive young lady from Virginia arrived in the community. She visited her friends for several months and then departed just before John's return. Just as the witch predicted, the two of them never met.

Over the course of the next few weeks, the voice of the witch began to be heard more and more often. The committee members continued to visit the house and pressed the spirit with questions. They had succeeded in getting the witch to admit that she was a disturbed spirit, but now the most urgent questions were how the spirit had been disturbed; and what could be done to remedy the situation.

"I am the spirit of a person who was buried in the woods nearby," the witch told the investigators, "and my grave has been disturbed...my bones disinterred and scattered."

While this statement seems rather strange, it actually stirred a memory for the Bell family. It recalled an incident that had taken place years before and by now had been entirely forgotten. Several seasons earlier, the farm hands had been clearing some land and had stumbled upon a large mound, which John Bell had guessed to be an Indian grave. The slaves had worked around the mound, careful not to disturb it.

A few days later, a local boy named Corban Hall had visited the farm and Drew had told him about the discovery of the Indian grave. The two boys decided to open up the grave and see if they could find any relics with which the Indians buried their dead.

They set to digging and although they found no relics, they did find a collection on ancient bones, which were promptly scattered. Although the bones were returned to the grave, could they have been disturbed in such a way that the farm became haunted?

The excitement in the community grew as word spread of the witch's increasing number of communications. People came from around the area and from the far-flung regions to hear the unexplained voice. The stories attracted the believers in the unknown who credited the spirit as being the ghost of an Indian; an evil spirit; and even the result of genuine witchcraft.

The accounts also brought the skeptics, who came to the Bell farm intent on exposing the haunting as a hoax. Most of them ended up leaving in a state of puzzlement, while others expressed their opinions about the witch. Some charged that the voice was a sort of trickery being worked by the Bell family in order to draw crowds to the farm and make money off of them.

Unfortunately (at least for John Bell's pocketbook), this was not the case. The crowds who came to the farm paid no admission and the Bells allowed them to stay as long as they wished. Most were fed, along with their horses, and many stayed the night in a warm bed. No one ever left the farm hungry and while many offered to pay for their meals, Bell refused to accept their money. Even his friends tried to convince him to accept the donations, insisting that he could not afford to keep entertaining the large crowds.

Through all of it though, Bell refused to take the money. He never considered the witch a wonder or an object of delight. He thought of the creature as "an affliction" and her presence in the house as "a calamity" of a most dire nature. His sense of honor did not allow him to accept money so that visitors could witness something so terrible.

The witch had now gained an audience for her new voice and as the crowds came to the farm, the spirit seemed to bask in the attention. Despite the new attention heaped on the witch though, none of the incidents previously described as taking place in the Bell house had come to an end. Objects still moved about the house at will and most disturbing, of course, were the continued attacks on Betsy Bell and the physical ailments that plagued John Bell.

Strangely, the witch would sometimes regard Betsy with tenderness, only to attack her with terrible force later that same day. As mentioned previously, these attacks were especially severe after a visit by young Joshua Gardner. She was also subject to fainting spells and moments when her breath seemed to be sucked from her body. These incidents would leave her utterly exhausted and lifeless and she would black out for up to 30 or 40 minutes at time. Once she awoke however, she would be completely restored and would have no memory of what had occurred. While serious though, these spells were of less concern than the ailments being suffered by John Bell.

During the first year of the haunting, Bell began to complain of a curious numbness in his mouth that caused his tongue to become stiff and to swell. In fact, his tongue and throat became so swollen that he would be unable to eat for days at time. He even had difficulty swallowing and drinking water, which added to his discomfort. As the haunting progressed, he began to come down with other unexplainable symptoms as well. Most notable were the bizarre facial tics and twitches that he suffered. Once these fits would seize his face, he would be unable to talk or eat and they would sometimes cause him to lose consciousness as well. These odd seizures would last anywhere from a few hours to as long as a week. However, once they passed, he would be in good health until the next attack came along.

The spells gradually increased, both in length and in severity, and undoubtedly carried the man to his grave. The opposite was the case for Betsy Bell. It seemed that as her father's troubles increased, her symptoms began to go away. Eventually, her afflictions stopped completely and she never suffered another symptom of any kind. But why John Bell?

We'll probably never really know but from the very beginning the witch had made it clear that she was going to get Old Jack Bell and would torment him until the end of his life. In addition to his illness, Bell was also physically abused by the witch and many witnesses would recall him being slapped by unseen hands or crying out in pain as he was prodded and stabbed with invisible pins. Whenever Bell's name was mentioned in the presence of the spirit, she would begin screaming and would call Bell every vile and offensive name she could muster up. It was obvious that she violently hated him and his torment would only end with his death. Bell's doctor was helpless when it came to finding a cure for the seizures and ailments. The witch laughed at his efforts and declared that she was the cause of John Bell's problems and no medicine existed which could cure him.

Apparently, the witch was determined to get John Bell any way she could and yet after all of this time, she had never explained why she hated him so much. What had Bell done to cause her to despise him so greatly? And why had the Bell house been singled out for the haunting?

Then, one night, the witch revealed the answer. Her reply came to a question posed to her by the Reverend James Gunn. He asked her once again just who she was and why she was tormenting the Bell family.

The spirit spoke up and announced to Reverend Gunn that she was the witch of a local woman named Kate Batts. To his credit, Gunn did not believe this story but many of the people in the community certainly did and the word spread quickly. This was something that the local people could understand and they clung to the belief that the spirit had somehow been directed against Bell and his family. The belief that the witch could spring from the evil influences of Kate Batts created an answer to the riddle. The idea of some unknown spirit haunting the house for an unknown reason was utterly foreign to them, but now the spirit seemed to have a purpose. Kate Batts' connection to the spirit became so complete in many people's minds that they began referring to the spirit as

Kate, a nickname that has endured after all this time.

Kate Batts was a local, eccentric woman who had no love for John Bell. Curiously, the strange events at the Bell house had begun a short time after a business deal between her and John Bell. Apparently, Bell had sold Batts a slave and had charged her excessive interest in the matter, which led to harsh words between them. It should be noted also that Batts was not the only person to think the deal was disreputable. Bell had been accused by leaders of his own church of dishonesty in the deal and although acquitted by the church, was convicted in August 1817 by the state of Tennessee. This caused the church to reconsider their decision and in January 1818, Bell was expelled from the congregation.

A few local wags were quick to point out Bell's expulsion when the strange events first began to occur at his house, and then once the witch actually claimed to be in league with Kate Batts, they were quick to speak of the connection. As mentioned already, Kate Batts was a rather strange and eccentric woman and counted few friends in the neighborhood. Her husband was an invalid, and so she was forced to handle most of their business interests. She had a reputation for being hard to deal with and after her business deal with John Bell soured, she spent a lot of time maligning his character in Robertson County. Many people were afraid of her and feared incurring her wrath, so she was largely avoided.

Over the years, there have been many stories that have sprung up about John Bell and his relationship with Kate Batts, including that he had murdered her in North Carolina and that he had starved her to death in a smokehouse. Obviously, such stories were untrue as Kate Batts was alive and well during the haunting, and for some years after. In fact, when she learned that the spirit was now calling itself Kate and claimed to be her witch, she demanded that charges be pressed against John Bell as she was sure that this was his way of trying to discredit her in the community.

While it was obvious that she hated the man nearly as much as the spirit did, it is unlikely that she had anything at all to do with the haunting. However, the folklore of the case still makes Kate Batts to blame, but perhaps because it has been so hard to separate the living woman from the spirit who took on her name. Shortly after the announcement to Reverend Gunn, the goblin began to be called Kate by the local folks and she was quick to answer to that name.

So, as Richard Williams Bell said, "for convenience sake, I shall hereafter call the witch Kate, though not out of any disregard for the memory of Mrs. Batts."

The witch would often spar and battle with friends of the Bell family and often even visited them in their own homes when it suited her. In addition, she also made plenty of appearances for total strangers as well and over time, literally hundreds of people witnessed the activity caused by the witch.

The witch made it clear that she was not going to suffer fools lightly though. Throughout the haunting, there were a number of witch-slayers and debunkers who came to the Bell farm, intent on either driving out the witch or proving that the entire affair was a hoax. These detectives, wise men, witch doctors and conjurors were all allowed to practice their schemes and magic arts in any way they wished and without fail, each of them left the farm confessing that the strange events were beyond their understanding.

While many men visited the farm with intentions to get to the bottom of the matter, perhaps the most famous was Andrew Jackson. While most don't know that this famous resident of Tennessee once crossed paths with the Bell Witch, Jackson found the event so memorable that he told anyone who would listen that he "would rather face the whole of the British army than deal with the torment they call the Bell Witch."

Andrew Jackson is remembered by most today as one of the most influential of the pre-Civil War American presidents, but he had a checkered and adventurous career before that. Jackson managed to lead a ragtag army of American militia, soldiers, slaves and pirates and overcame a superior British force in the war of 1812. Jackson became the hero of New Orleans, and today, one of the landmarks of the city is Jackson Square, where a statue of the general on horseback still stands.

One of the men who served Jackson closely during the Battle of New Orleans was John Bell Jr. Jackson had formed a close friendship with the young man, who served him as an aide, and a few years later, when he heard of the strange events on the Bell farm, he decided to investigate.

He brought with him a party of men from Nashville, who brought along their own provisions and supplies. They departed in the late afternoon with a number of mounted men and a large wagon stocked with gear and pulled by four draft horses. The group traveled up the turnpike to Robertson County and at some point, as they neared the Bell farm, one of the men in the party made a joke about the witch.

Suddenly, almost as soon as the words left the man's lips, the large wagon ground to a halt. The driver cracked the reigns over the horse's backs, but no matter how much they pulled, the wheels of the wagon refused to turn. Jackson and several of the other men climbed down from their mounts and looked over the wagon. They could find no reason why the vehicle would not move. Puzzled, they urged the horses on and, to the animals' credit, they tried with all of their might to get the wagon moving again. However, it stayed completely still.

Jackson cursed aloud. "It's the witch!" he shouted.

Then from the trees overhead came a disembodied and highly amused voice. "They can go now, General," it said. Jackson spun around and several of his men spread out to look for the speaker. Of course, they found no one. Then, the voice of Kate came again. "I'll see you all later on tonight," she promised.

Jackson was perplexed when his party reached the Bell farm, but matters of the witch were forgotten for a few hours as he renewed his friendship with John Jr. and became acquainted with the rest of the family. The elder Bell was much impressed with their distinguished guest and accommodations were prepared for him, as was a large dinner.

Jackson's party unloaded the contents of the wagon while the General explained to his friends what had occurred on the turnpike. As the men made camp in the yard, Jackson adjourned inside for a drink and to await the coming of the witch. They sat and talked for several hours about the war, Nashville, and about the Indians who once lived in the area.

Soon, the men from Jackson's party also joined them, and among the number was a man who fancied himself a "witch tamer." The man was full of boasts about his power over the supernatural and made a number of claims that boiled down to the fact that no witch would dare to make an appearance while he was present. He always carried with him, in situations like this, a pistol that was loaded with a silver bullet. He stated that if Kate dared to show up, he would send the creature back from whence she came!

And at first it seemed as though Kate was actually frightened of the man. An hour or more passed with no activity and no sound, other than the soft murmur of conversation. After a time, even General Jackson was beginning to grow impatient. Finally, the witch tamer took matters into his own hands. He stood up on a wooden chair and in a loud voice, dared the witch to appear.

These words were followed by a howl of pain! The witch tamer jumped down from his chair and began dancing about as if his backside were on fire. He hollered loudly and grabbed hold of the seat of his pants. "Help me boys!" he called out. "I'm being stuck by a thousand pins!"

Kate laughed loudly. "I'm right in front of you," she cried, "shoot me!"

The witch tamer drew his pistol and tried to take aim at the air in front of him. He pulled the trigger on the pistol and only a puff of gunpowder smoke emerged from the barrel—the pistol refused to fire! With that, Kate began cackling again.

Still dancing about and holding his back side, the witch tamer began to feel other stinging pains as invisible hands slapped and pinched him. Jackson himself saw the man's head rock back with the force of a slap and saw the red mark appear on his cheek. Then, the man's hands began grasping at his face. "She's pulling my nose off!" he screamed.

The man stumbled forward, looking to the others just as if something was yanking on the end of his nose. Suddenly, he was flung toward the front door, which opened on its own, and was sent sprawling into the dusty front yard. All the while, Kate's voice screeched maniacally, offering obscene advice about how to be a good witch tamer.

But Kate was not done with the men from Nashville just yet. "There is another fraud in your party, General," she told Jackson. "I'll get him tomorrow night!"

The men from Nashville began looking at each other very nervously and to a man, refused to spend the night inside of the house. They retired to the camp outside to sleep, but not before urging Jackson to leave the farm at daybreak. At first, the pleas of the men fell on deaf ears. General Jackson was fascinated by the phenomena and besides that, hoped in some way to assist his friend with the family's troubles. Eventually though, the men convinced Jackson that leaving would be in the best interests of all concerned. They left the next morning at dawn and none of them ever returned to the Bell farm.

After nearly four years of the haunting, John Bell continued to suffer from the same afflictions of the body. By late 1820, his physical condition had grown even worse. The jerking and twitching of his face still continued, as did the swelling of his tongue and the seizures that left him nearly paralyzed for hours and days at a time. The spells became even more violent, and toward the end of his days, Richard Williams Bell accompanied him everywhere he went. The family feared that a seizure would come upon him while working, and if no one was with him, he might fall and be injured.

Around the middle of October, Bell once again became ill. This time, the spell lasted for eight days, and he was confined to his bed the entire time. During his convalescence, the witch stayed by his side. She raved and cursed in the sick room like a maniac, bothering him so that he could not rest and wishing loudly that he would simply die and leave the world a better place.

But once again, John Bell managed to prevail and he came out of the sickness. It was another week before he was back on his feet again, but after this, he felt much stronger. He called Richard early one morning to go with him to the hog pen, which lay about 300 yards from the house. He wanted to make sure that the hogs that were destined for slaughter were separated from those to be kept as stock.

The two had not walked very far before one of John Bell's shoes was jerked from his foot. The incident occurred so quickly that neither of them even had time to think about it. Richard scratched his head and retrieved the shoe, then bent down and slipped it back on his father's foot. He tied the strings quite tightly into a double knot. Then, the two of them started back up the path again.

They had not gone much further when the other shoe flew off in the same manner. Richard fetched it also and tied it in the same manner as the other one. They found the incident quite strange (apparently not realizing it was the work of the witch at this point) and after much discussion continued up the path. Richard would later note in his writings that the shoes had been tied firmly and fit his father quite closely.

They continued to the hog barn without incident and Bell directed the hands as to how he wished the animals to be separated. Once this was finished, he and Richard started back to the house, intent on breakfast. They had not gone very far before both of John Bell's shoes once again were torn from his feet. Seconds later, he was slapped so hard across the face that he had to lie down beside the dirt path, needing a moment to recover from the blow.

While his father rested, Richard replaced the shoes on his feet. Within seconds, they had flown back off again and then Bell's face began the spasmodic twitching that was so horribly familiar. He started to shake and contort and Richard shrank back in fear.

From the air around them came the shrieking voice of Kate, who was cursing and singing. As the sudden spell passed, Richard saw tears begin to stream from his father's eyes. Every bit of courage the beleaguered man had left was now gone.

John Bell took to his bed as soon as they reached the house and he never left the house again.

Over that period of time, Bell continued to decline, and nothing done by his family or friends seemed to ease his suffering. Lucy stayed beside him most of the time, only spelled by John Jr. and the other children. John Bell's friends, and members of the original investigative committee, were as saddened by his decline as the family. It is not hard to imagine that their despair may have been accompanied by feelings of having failed their friend. They had been unable to get to the root of the mystery of the witch and now Bell was paying the price for this.

On the morning of the 19th, Bell failed to rise as he had every other morning. Even as sick as he was, he never failed to stir and take some sort of sustenance, even if it was only water and bread. On this morning, however, he did not awaken. Lucy went to check on him after rising and it appeared that he was sleeping very soundly. She decided to let him rest and sent John and Drew to attend to the livestock while she prepared breakfast. She decided that she would awaken him once the food was prepared.

A little less than an hour passed before Lucy went back into Bell's sick room. She touched her husband gently on the shoulder, but he did not wake up. She then shook him a little harder, but again, there was no sign that he knew she was there. She realized then that while he was alive, he was in some sort of a stupor.

Lucy called out to the rest of the family, and John ran back inside. He had always attended to his father's medicine and he went immediately to the cupboard where it was kept. His father had gone through similar periods before and usually a dose of his medicine would revive him. When John opened the cabinet, he discovered that all of the medicines that had been prescribed to his father had vanished. In place of them was a small, "smoky-looking vial" that was about one-third full of a dark colored liquid. He asked at once if anyone in the house had moved the medicine but all denying touching it, or even knowing what medicine had been there. No one had any idea what may have been in the vial.

Immediately, John sent one of the slaves to Port Royal to fetch the family doctor, George Hopson. A short time before the discovery of the strange vial, several of Bell's friends had arrived at the house. They were as puzzled by the appearance of the bottle as the family was.

The group gathered around the sick bed and continued to try and raise John Bell. Just then, Kate's voice split the air of the room. She laughed loudly. "It's useless to try and relieve Old Jack," she said. "He'll never get up from that bed again."

Angrily, one of the men present questioned her about the smoky vial that had been found in the cupboard. She admitted that she had put it there and claimed that she had given Bell a large dose of it while he had been sleeping, "which fixed him," she added.

This was all of the information that Kate would give in regards to the liquid and no one had any idea where it may have come from, or how John Bell had managed to ingest it. Even if Kate had not brought it into the house, it was possible that Bell, roused in the middle of the night and looking for his medicine, may have swallowed it by mistake. Even so, where the bottle had come from was still unexplained.

It was then suggested that the mysterious liquid be tested on something. One of the men disappeared outside and quickly returned with one of the barn cats that could be found on the property. John Jr. dipped a straw into the vial and then drew it through the cat's mouth, wiping the dark liquid on its tongue. The cat jumped out of his arms as if it had been prodded with a hot poker! It whirled about a few times and then fell to the floor with its legs kicking in the air. The animal was dead in less than a minute. Whatever was in the bottle—it appeared to be deadly.

Bell lay all day and through the night in a coma and could not be roused to swallow any medicine that might counteract the effects of the drug. Dr. Hopson was sure that he had taken, or had been given, the contents of the bottle, as Bell's breath smelled the same as the liquid in the vial. In the throes of despair, the vial and its contents were cast into the fire. A blue blaze shot up into the chimney "like a flash of powder."

John Bell never regained consciousness, and early on the morning of December 20, he took one last shuddering breath and died. His final moments were met by great joy from the witch. She laughed heartily and expressed the hope that Bell would burn in hell. With those chilling words, she departed and was not heard from again until after the funeral.

The burial was held a few days later, and it has been said that the funeral was the largest ever held in Robertson County, before or since. Bell was laid to rest in a small cemetery, a short distance from the Bell house. After the grave was filled, the mourners began to walk away. As they left the scene, the voice of Kate returned, echoing loudly in the cold morning air. She was singing at the top of her spectral lungs. "Row me up some brandy, O!" she squalled in a loud voice and could still be heard celebrating the death of John Bell as the last of the family and friends entered the house.

This ended the most terrifying chapter of the haunting and marked the case of the Bell Witch in the annals of supernatural history forever. It became one of the only cases ever recorded in which a spirit was responsible for the death of one of the principles in the case.

But the Bell Witch was not finished—at least not quite yet.

After the funeral, the activities of the witch seemed to decrease, but she was not quite gone. Kate remained with the family throughout the winter and spring of 1821, but she had changed. She was not quite as vicious as she had once been, not even to Betsy

Bell, around whom her activities continued to be centered.

During the entire haunting, it was made clear that Betsy would be punished as long as she continued to allow herself to be courted by Joshua Gardner. After the death of John Bell however, Kate's activities were not so violent and Betsy and Gardner began to believe that perhaps the witch might allow them to be together in peace.

As it had been with John Bell himself, the witch had never made it clear just why she disliked Joshua Gardner so much. She simply hated him and never explained why. Kate spent a great amount of time pleading with Betsy to end her relationship with him and also made it clear that she would beat the girl until she did so. The odd thing about it was that Kate acted as if she were punishing the girl for her own good!

There was no doubt that Joshua was in love with Betsy, and that the feeling was mutual. Everyone agreed that Joshua and Betsy were very well suited for each other. Everyone but Kate, that is.

Once the violence of the haunting had subsided somewhat, Betsy and Joshua began to renew their relationship, which had previously cooled, thanks to the witch. On Easter Sunday of 1821, the two of them celebrated the holiday by becoming engaged, much to the delight of their families and friends. The following day, the young couple decided to go fishing and to have a picnic along the Red River.

After lunch, Joshua and Betsy sat down on a large rock and cast a line into the water. A few minutes later, the line was seized with great force and the line and pole were both pulled into the water and vanished downstream. At that same moment, the eerily familiar voice of the witch rang out. "Please, Betsy Bell, do not marry Joshua Gardner," Kate intoned. The plea was repeated two more times and then the voice faded away.

This must have been the breaking point for Betsy. She must have finally realized that the witch was never going to leave her alone as long as she continued to stay with Joshua Gardner. So, thus ended the engagement of Elizabeth Bell and Joshua Gardner. The two of them parted that afternoon and as far as I know, never saw one another again.

After arranging his affairs, Joshua Gardner departed from Robertson County and went to live in western Tennessee at a place called Gardner's Station. He lived a long and successful life, married twice and died in 1887 at the age of 84. Whether or not he ever thought of Betsy Bell again is unknown.

In the early summer of 1821, the remaining members of the Bell family were seated around the fireplace after supper. They were talking quietly when something that looked like a cannonball thundered down the chimney and rolled out into the center of the room. It exploded in a cloud of smoke and heavy mist, accompanied by the familiar voice of the witch.

"I am going," Kate cried out. The witch bid them farewell promised that she would return again in seven years to visit the Bell house and every house in the neighborhood.

"This promise was fulfilled as regards to the old homestead," Richard Williams Bell later wrote, "but I do not know that it visited homes in the vicinity. It returned in February 1828."

The return of the witch was marked by the same sort of activity as when the original haunting first began. It started with scratching sounds on the exterior weatherboards of the house, then moved to strange sounds inside of the house. Soon, the blankets were being pulled from the beds and objects were vanishing and then appearing again in other locations.

The Bells, who still lived in the house, made a pact amongst themselves. They were determined to ignore the activity and if spoken to by the spirit, they would ignore it. In this way, they hoped the visitation might end quickly. And so it did; the witch departed from the house after a few weeks, never speaking and apparently unconcerned with the remaining members of the family.

The most active elements of the witch's 1828 visit took place at the home of John Bell Jr., who had built a house on land that he had inherited from his father. It was a short distance away from the original homestead and in early March, the witch came to visit him there. During her brief re-appearance, the witch was said to make several accurate predictions about the future, including the end of slavery, the Civil War, the rise of the United States as a world power; the coming of World War I and World War II; and the end of the world. To this last prediction, the witch did not give a date but only the information that the world would end with the temperature of the planet rising so high that it would become uninhabitable.

Kate stayed with John Bell for several months. On the final night of her visit, promised to return once again in 107 years (1935), and while there is no record that she ever did so, there are some that maintain that the spirit of the Bell Witch has never left Adams, Tennessee at all.

The old Bell farm was located about one mile from Adams Station (now Adams), Tennessee, a small village that officially came into existence in 1859 during the building of the Edgefield and Kentucky Railroad. The farm was located along the Red River and the section on which the house was located is still in the Bell family today. It is private property owned by Mr. Carney Bell.

The Bell house was a double log home, which was one-and-a-half stories high. It was weather-boarded on the outside and had six large rooms and two halls, making it one of the finest houses in the county during its time. It was located about a half-mile from the river and there was a large orchard in the back. The lawn was covered with pear trees, and several outbuildings were also located on the property. During its heyday, it was a comfortable and very functional working farm.

The thriving spot also got its share of visitors, even before the haunting, as it was located on a main, public road. This dirt highway, known as the Brown's Ford and Springfield road, ran about 100 yards from the house. It was said that during the excitement over the witch, it was not uncommon to find a horse hitched to every fence corner of the farm, as the house and yard were often filled with people coming to investigate the sensation. Travelers still continued to pass this way, even after the Bell house was abandoned.

After the death of Lucy Bell, who continued to stay on in the house after her children were gone, no one cared to occupy the place. For some time, the house was used for storing grain and then was torn down. Today, there is little sign that a house once stood there. Only a few stones of the foundation can be seen and the remains of an old well. The land around the house site has since been turned into farming ground, although strangely, the actual location of the house remains untouched.

After the house was abandoned, a number of those who traveled along the old public road began to make reports of strange incidents taking place there. Some claimed to see apparitions wandering about the weed-choked yard and others said that unexplained lights and glowing objects flitted about the fields. Of course, it is possible that these stories can be accounted for as the overactive imaginations of those who knew of the odd stories of this property and who claimed the activities as being the leftover effects of the Bell Witch. But what of the tales that were not so easy to explain?

Some of the weird reports came from travelers with no connections to the immediate area and who knew nothing of the property. A few of the stories also came from reputable residents of the region, who claimed to see a glowing light emanating from the windows of the Bell house, even though the structure had long been empty and abandoned.

Was it possible that the Bell Witch could have left some sort of lingering atmosphere on the area?

Near the Red River, on the former Bell farm, is a cavern that has been called the Bell Witch Cave. Many people believe that when the spirit of the witch departed from the torment of the Bell family, she went into this cave.

While the cave had become quite famous in recent years, there is little mention of it in contemporary accounts of the haunting. It is believed that the cave might have been used for the cool storage of food in those days, thanks to the fact that it remains a constant 56 degrees. It was also mentioned in some accounts that Kate's voice was often heard nearby and one day, Betsy Bell and several of her friends had a close encounter with the witch inside of the cave.

The cave itself is located in the center of a large bluff that overlooks the river. The mouth of the cave opens widely but entrance to the cavern itself must be gained through a fairly long tunnel. The cave is not large compared to most commercial caves, however its true length is unknown because of narrow passages which go beyond the 500 or so feet accessible to visitors. Although geologically, this is a dry cave that has been carved from limestone, in wet weather, a stream gushes from the mouth of the cavern and tumbles over a cliff into the river below. This makes the cave nearly impossible to navigate and even shouted conversations become inaudible over the roar of the water.

In dry times, the cave has proven to be quite an attraction to curiosity-seekers and ghost hunters. Once you pass through the entrance passage, the visitor enters a large room that opens into yet another tunnel and an overhead passageway. Another large room can be found at the rear of the explored portion of the cave, but from that point on the tunnels become smaller, narrower and much more dangerous.

One day, Betsy Bell and some of her friends were exploring the cave, using candles as a source of light. One of the boys came to a place where he had to get down on his belly and wriggle through. He inched along the passage before becoming stuck! He twisted around trying to get free and in his panic, dropped his candle and it was snuffed out. He called for help and while his friends could hear him, could not find him in the total blackness of the cave.

Suddenly, the boy heard the voice of the witch coming out of the darkness behind him. "I'll get you out," Kate assured him and the boy began to feel his legs being pulled as if twin vices had been cinched around his ankles. He was dragged through the muddy cave all of the way back to the entrance and was deposited there in small pool of water. He was a bit worse for wear, but at least he was alive!

The Bell Witch Cave became an attraction thanks to a man named Bill Eden, who owned the property for a number of years. He was a wealth of information about the cave and about the fact that strange occurrences were continuing to take place on the land that once belonged to John Bell. Although he was mainly a farmer, Eden did make some early improvements to the cave by adding electrical lights, but that was about all.

Despite being undeveloped, the cave managed to attract hundreds of visitors every year who wanted to be shown through it. Bill always obliged although he was always puzzled about how they found the place. There were no signs to point the way at that time but somehow people found it and they always asked to hear the stories of the witch, and the stories that Eden spun from his own weird experiences at the place.

Eden bought the farm where the cave is located in 1964, and owned the place for 17 years. However, he had lived on various parts of the Bell farm for more than 40 years. He and his wife, Frances, had resided in various farmhouses around the property and both could recall a number of strange incidents that had occurred in them. It seemed that every house had come with knocking noises, apparitions or other unexplained oddities.

Eventually, Bill grew tired of living in old, haunted farmhouses so he tore down an old Bell family house and built a modern, one-story brick home (which still stands today) in its place. This however, did not bring an end to the strange events there, as the current owners can tell you!

But perhaps it is the property, and not the house, which is haunted! Years before Eden had lived there, while the other house was still standing, a section of woods had run from the house all of the way to Adams, which is about a mile to the south. Those who traveled from the immediate vicinity into Adams at that time would take a well-worn path that provided a short cut into town.

The stories said that sometimes, just as darkness was falling, a figure would walk down the path and out of the woods and into a low place in the yard. This figure would never stop walking and would go down toward a big oak tree and then vanish from sight. This would happen only periodically and there seemed to be no set pattern as to when this figure might appear.

Another tale about the land where Eden built the new brick house stated that for many years, a bright light was seen there almost every night. This mysterious orb looked much like a lantern, although no earthly hand could be seen carrying it. The light would rise from just below the top of the bluff and float high into the air before coming to rest in a large oak tree in front of the original house. One night, the man of the house decided that he was going to shoot that light out of the tree. He went into the house and got his rifle. Then, taking careful aim, he fired. As the rifle cracked, the light tumbled down through the branches of the tree and vanished into the grass and brush beneath it.

Everyone who had gathered to watch this ran over to see where the light had gone and just what the strange object had been. Despite a careful search though, they found nothing. The light returned again three days later but how long it stayed is unknown.

And there were many other stories to tell in regards to the Bell Witch Cave! Many of the strange experiences actually happened to Bill Eden himself, while others involved visitors to the cave. For instance, a woman came to visit one day and asked to go down and see the cave. She had brought a group of friends along and in all, about fifteen people followed Eden down the rather treacherous path to the cave's entrance. All at once, the woman in charge of the group abruptly sat down in the middle of the path. One of the people who was with her asked why she was sitting there, and she answered that she wasn't! She claimed that a heavy weight, which felt like a ton of lead, was pressing her down to the ground and she couldn't get up. Several members of the group managed to get the lady to her feet and got her back up the hill to her car.

Bill Eden could also recount a number of encounters he had on his own in the cave. "You can hear footsteps in there all the time and I saw one thing," he said in the interview. "Lots of people come out here expecting to see a ghost or a witch of whatever you want to call it. I just call it a spirit…and it looked like a person with its back turned to you. Looked like it was built out of real white-looking heavy fog or snow, or something real solid white. But you couldn't see through it. It had the complete figure of a person till it got down to about its ankles. It wasn't touching the floor at all. It was just drifting…bouncing along."

On another occasion, Eden was leading a man, his wife and grown son on a tour of the cave. They were all walking along through the cave, and Eden was pointing out some of the rock formations in the cavern, along with telling tales of the witch. The group was standing in the back room of the cave (as far back as the tour goes) when the woman happened to look up over some rock formations. Suddenly, she began to scream! "Look at that woman!" she screamed at Eden and her family. "She's not walking! She's floating through the air!"

The men looked to where she pointed and then looked at each other. None of them saw anything! Eden looked over at the woman again and by this time, her knees had buckled and she had fallen to the floor of the cave. They quickly helped her up and started walking her toward the front of the cave.

When they made it to the front room, another strange occurrence took place. Close by the entrance to the passage which connects the two large rooms, there is a limestone outcropping which comes out from the wall. As they got close to this limestone section, they heard what sounded like loud, raspy breathing coming (it seemed) from the rock itself! Eden would later say that it was like the hard and labored breathing of a person, which became more labored until it was finally the struggling breath of someone dying. Of course, no matter what it sounded like, it was quite frightening in the dark recesses of the cave!

224

The woman almost collapsed again and she began to weep. She turned to Eden, quite angry, and stated that he ought to be arrested for rigging the cave in that way! "You're going to kill somebody if you don't stop!" she declared.

Eden replied that he had no idea what she had seen, and whatever that breathing sound had been, he had done nothing to rig things up. Her husband came to Bill's defense and assured her that he had seen no wires or anything else to indicate that Eden had rigged things to happen in the cave. The lady slowly became convinced, although I imagine this was the last time that she visited the Bell Witch Cave!

In the early summer of 1977, several soldiers from Fort Campbell came over to visit the cave. Eden took the young men on a tour and ended up in the back room, where all of them sat around talking and Eden told his stories of the odd events on the farm.

One of the men politely expressed some doubts about the validity of the story. He had been to many places that were supposedly haunted and nothing out of the ordinary had ever occurred to him. Eden laughed and shrugged his shoulders. The man could believe whatever he wanted to, but as for Bill, well, he had seen enough things on the farm to know that something unexplainable was going on.

"If something happened, you probably wouldn't ever come back here again," Bill added with a grin.

The group sat and talked for a short while longer and then they all got up to leave…all except for the young man who had spoken up about his disbelief in ghosts. "Mr. Eden! Come here and help me," the soldier said. "I can't get up."

Eden and the man's friends all assumed that he was joking, and they all began to laugh. It wasn't until Bill took a good look at the man that he realized that something really was wrong. The young man was now begging for help and his face was drenched so badly with sweat that it looked like someone had poured a bucket of water over him. When Eden took hold of his hand to help him up, he could feel the man's hand was cold and clammy as if he were going into shock.

The man continued to call for help and claimed that he could feel strong arms wrapped around his chest. They were squeezing him tightly, he said, and he was unable to breathe. Eden and the other men helped their friend to his feet and while the soldiers supported him, Bill wiped his face off with some run-off water from the cave. When the soldier got to feeling better, they took him outside of the cave. By the time they were ready to leave, the young man had completely recovered and was suffering no ill effects from his harrowing experience.

As he was heading to his car, he stopped and shook Bill Eden's hand. "Well, you were right about one thing, Mr. Eden," the young soldier said. "I won't ever be back here again."

The winter rains in Tennessee wreak havoc on the Bell Witch Cave, which is why Bill Eden (and the current owners) usually only opened the cave during the summer and early autumn months. Each spring, Bill always had a lot of work to do on the floor of the cave where the rushing water had carved out small holes and ditches.

One Sunday morning, Eden had taken his shovel and rake and was working back some distance in the cave, trying to level out the more damaged portions of the floor. He was chopping at and smoothing over the gravel when he heard a noise that he was not making himself. He spun around because he realized that it was coming from behind him, from the further recesses of the cave.

In the darkness, he could hear the distinct sound of someone walking down the passage, his or her feet crunching in the gravel on the floor. The sounds kept coming, moving toward him, until they stopped a few feet away. Eden strained his eyes to peer into the shadows, but he could see no one there.

"Something I can do for you?" he called out, but he got no answer. He called again, but still no answer came.

Although he most likely would have hated to admit it, I imagine this incident raised the hairs on the back of Bill's neck. He decided that he would probably get more work done near the entrance of the cave, where it was much lighter, so he picked up his tools and headed in that direction. He walked up front and as he passed through the first room, he noticed his dog sleeping on the little ledge over on the left side of the room.

For the next thirty minutes or so, Eden worked on the floor between the iron gate at the mouth of the cave and the first room. He had just stopped for a moment to rest when he heard the familiar footsteps, tracking through the gravel once more. They were once again coming from the back of the cave and quickly approached the first room, where Bill's dog was sleeping.

Suddenly, the animal's ears pricked up and he jumped to his feet. The hackles raised on the back of his neck and Bill saw his lips curl back to reveal the dog's rather intimidating set of teeth. The animal didn't move, though. He just stood there, looking directly at the spot where the footsteps had last been heard.

The gravel began crunching again and moved forward, in the direction of where Bill was standing. As the sounds moved past the dog, he stared ahead, as though watching someone that Eden was unable to see. The footsteps came directly toward Bill, passed by him, and then continued to the outside of the cave.

Immediately after, both Bill and the dog hurried outside into the sunlight. He admitted later that he did not have the nerve to go back inside right away, nor for several days afterward. From that time on, that particular dog never entered the main part of the cave again. He would follow people to the steel gate, which is about 30 feet inside, but then he would either wait there or return outside. Whatever he had seen that day had frightened him away for good!

And those were not the end of the stories told by Bill Eden about the farm and about the Bell Witch Cave. There were many other incidents which took place and Eden never got tired of telling the tales to just about anyone who would listen.

"They call me William, they call me W.M., they call me Bill, they call me Judd, and they call me the Bell Witch Man. This was the way that Bill Eden introduced himself to author Richard Winer in 1978. A few short years later, Bill Eden passed away and sadly, his death closed a fascinating chapter in the history of the Bell Witch saga. There is no doubt about it, Mr. Eden was a true American character and the impression that he left on the place, like the impression left by Kate herself, will always remain.

The present-day owners of the Bell Witch Cave, and the piece of the old Bell farm made so famous by Bill Eden, are Chris and Walter Kirby. Walter is a tobacco farmer and Chris manages to stay busy managing the upkeep and tours of the cave. In the summer months, this task is more than a full-time job.

The Kirbys purchased the land in April of 1993. The place had been empty for several years, after the death of Bill Eden, but by that summer, the cave was open again for business. Over the course of the next year or so, they made a number of improvements to the cave, which included new lights, a new electrical system, an improved path to the cave, wooden walkways to cross the most treacherous areas of the trail, and a number of other things. These improvements continue today.

It wasn't long after the Kirbys moved to the farm, and began conducting tours in the cave, before they realized things were not quite right on the property. They began to notice first that there were strange noises that didn't have an easy explanation. "We've heard them in the cave and we've heard them in the house," Chris told author Charles Edwin Price. "I feel like if there's anyplace that could be haunted, it's this place here. First of all, it's got the legend of being haunted. There's an Indian burial mound right above the mouth of the cave on the bluff. And the previous owner of the cave died in our bedroom."

Shortly after moving onto the farm, Chris was photographing parts of the property and one of the photos on the developed roll of film turned out to be simply amazing! She saw nothing when she took the photo and yet, on the developed print, was a misty shape that hovered above a sinkhole leading down into the cave. The photo continues to defy explanation.

I first met Chris Kirby in the spring of 1997. I had always heard about the Bell Witch case and knew that there was a cave located on the property that was purported to be haunted. My wife and I were on a trip down south at the time and decided to take a side trip over to Adams. After seeing the Bellwood Cemetery and the old Bell School, we headed for the cave. In a town the size of Adams, it's not hard to find but it can easily be reached by turning off Highway 41, right next to the Bell School. You can't miss the sign for the cave alongside the roadway and a right turn takes you onto a curving gravel road and up to a small brick house, which was built by Bill Eden. There is a sign here that reads "Bell Cave Parking."

Over to the right of the parking lot is a large, wooded area that contains the sinkhole near where Chris took the photograph of the strange mist. Behind the house is the trail that leads down to the cave.

The entrance to the cave is closed off by a locked, heavy steel gate. It is supposed to stop unauthorized visitors from entering the cave, which can be very dangerous, especially in the darkness. There are many sections of the cave which remain unexplored and this fact, along with the ghost stories, proves to be a real magnet for teenagers and curiosity seekers. Chris stated that they always worry that someone will be hurt in there because the gate does not always stop the trespassers. They even had two break-ins within a few weeks of buying the property. In fact, the trespassing becomes so bad at certain times of year that the Kirbys have been forced to prosecute anyone caught inside of the cave at night.

After taking us down to the cave, Chris told us about some of the strange incidents that have taken place on the property. The oddities have been weird enough, and frightening enough, to lead her to tell us that she had never been in the cave by herself before…nor did ever intend to go there alone.

One day, Chris and her dog were leading a tour of the cave for a group of visitors. She was just opening the steel gate which leads inside when she heard a strange sound...the same sort of sound described by Bill Eden and one of his tour groups years before. "It sounded like real raspy breathing sounds," she said, "like someone couldn't get their breath. It only lasted for a minute and then it was gone." Chris looked back to her tour group, but they were quietly talking amongst themselves and hadn't heard a thing.

The tour continued through the first room, down the narrow passage and into the second room. Here, as is the tradition in Bell Witch Cave Tours, Chris began telling stories of the witch, the haunting and strange incidents on the farm. As she was talking, the dog suddenly reacted to something that no one else could see. The hair on the animal's back stood up and she began showing her teeth and growling. The tour group asked what was wrong with the dog, but Chris had no idea. She was finally able to calm the dog down, but then the animal began whining and tucked her tail between her legs. She cowered back against Chris and at that same moment, the flashlight in Chris' hand suddenly went out!

"I guessed that it was just the battery at first," Chris remembered, "but then a lady's video camera stopped working too. We were all standing there in the dark and I'll tell you, I was ready to get out of there and everyone else was too!"

Chris also told us about the strange apparitions that she and visitors to the cave have reported. Some of these shapes are misty and fog-like, sometimes appearing in different parts of the cave, only to vanish when approached. She also recalled another type of image they had seen. "It looked like heat waves that come up over the highway in the summer time," she explained. "You can see them out of the corner of your eye and then they're gone."

Since that time, I have visited and have talked with the Kirbys many times and there is no question that the strange incidents on the farm have continued.

But what is it about this farm? Is the old property and the cave really haunted by the Bell Witch? Or does something even stranger walk here? I can't say for sure, although I can say with some certainty that this land is haunted. If the Bell Witch was as real as the reports have led me to believe, then I don't think she has ever left here either. And it didn't take much to convince me of that.

I have walked the old Bell farm and stood next to the grave where John Bell is buried. I have been amazed at the beauty of the hollows and the woods of Robertson County and I have thrilled to the thunder of the Red River after a summer rain.

And I have walked into the gloom of the ominous Bell Witch Cave and that was enough to convince me that something strange is in the place. This land is tainted and there is a darkness that lurks here unlike anything else that I have ever encountered. This is truly one of America's most haunted places!

Chapter Four

GHOSTS OF THE WEST

The Ghosts & Spirits of the Queen Mary

When most of us think about America's western states, we conjure up images of unbroken country, high desert, rolling plains, mountains and perhaps even the long ribbons of highway that cross the land. It's true that many ghosts roam these vast regions, but perhaps one of the most haunted sites in the west has nothing to do with land at all. This haunted site just happens to be a ship!

The passengers who sail aboard this unmoving vessel now are not names that you will find on any manifest, nor do they enjoy the entertainment and the fine food that can still be found aboard the ship today. And yet they have been with her for years....these mysterious passengers are the ghosts of the legendary *Queen Mary*!

The *Queen Mary* was commissioned in 1934 and for many years was the undisputed ruler of the oceans. She set sail on her maiden voyage in May 1936 and quickly became known as the ultimate form of international travel. During the 1930s and in the years following World War II, her decks played host to the rich and famous and included guests like the Marx Brothers, Clark Gable, Charles Lindbergh, Amelia Earhart, Charlie Chaplin, Jean Harlow, Laurel and Hardy and many, many others. The First Class passengers on the ship were treated to every imaginable luxury as the crew and staff were trained to cater to the needs and whims of everyone on board.

A change came in 1939 though, when the British government requisitioned the *Queen Mary* into military service. They gave her a coat of gray paint and started using her to transport troops. The majestic dining salons of the vessel became mess halls that served up to 2,000 soldiers at a time. Her cocktail bars, cabins and state rooms were filled with bunks, as was every available space below decks. Even the swimming pools were boarded over and crowded with cots for the men. The ship was so useful to the Allies that Hitler made her a "marked ship" and offered a $250,000 reward and hero status to the U-Boat commander who could sink her. None of them did! And while the *Queen Mary* was able to avoid the enemy torpedoes during the war, she was unable to avoid tragedy.

The horrific event occurred on October 2, 1942. The *Queen Mary* was sailing on a choppy ocean around the north of Ireland. She carried 10,000 American soldiers, bound for the Clyde River, where the men would disembark. That morning, she was joined by an escort, the cruiser HMS Curacoa and six destroyers.

While danger from German vessels was always present, things were quiet aboard the Curacoa. Lunch had ended and the cooks prepared for the evening meal. Most of the off-watch crew were below decks in their hammocks. Captain John Boutwood was on the ship's bridge and he ordered the destroyers to cruise ahead and shield the *Queen Mary* from mines and U-Boats. Boutwood intended to take position astern of the transport ship as a protection against possible air strikes. All of the ships were ready to take immediate action in case of attack and they had provided similar protection for the *Queen Mary* on three occasions in the past. On Boutwood's orders, the destroyers sailed ahead and Boutwood, also ahead of the liner, readied his ship to fall astern.

On the *Queen Mary*'s bridge, Captain Cyril Illingsworth was in command, along with Senior First Officer Noel Robinson. It was Robinson who first noticed that his ship and the Curacoa were possibly on a converging course. He ordered the helmsman to put the wheel over several degrees to port and at almost the same time, Captain Boutwood realized the situation and took the Curacoa to starboard.

Both of the ships were cruising at almost 30 knots and both bows created a tremendous wake. As the ships nearly converged, the combined wash caused each of the ships to yaw slightly, pushing both of them back toward their original courses. These minor changes caused the *Queen Mary* to nudge the Curacoa's stern and this impact, combined with the ship's own turbulent wash, was enough to throw the cruiser out of control. The Curacoa careened off course and somehow ended up sideways, directly in the path of the *Queen Mary*'s bow!

Before anyone could act, the massive bow sliced into the Curacoa at the middle of the ship. The *Queen Mary* smashed through the smaller vessel without pause. There was no way to slow down, no time for a warning and no distress calls to the men aboard her. They had only seconds to react before the liner tore their ship apart and sent them down below the water. The forward half of the Curacoa was swept along the *Queen Mary*'s port side. Her stern section came to a stop when the seawater flooded her holds and then it pitched downward into the sea. Within minutes, both sections of the ship plunged into icy water, carrying the crew with them. Of the Curacoa's 439 officers and men, 338 of them perished in the sea on that fateful day. The *Queen Mary* suffered only minor damage and there were no injuries aboard the liner. The damage to her hull was so slight that she was able to return to America before being repaired.

After that, she served unscathed for the remainder of the war. Following the surrender of Germany, she was used for carrying American troops home from Europe and in addition, transported as many as 20,000 GI war brides to the United States. The *Queen Mary* operated under military authority for one year after the war and then was returned to the John Brown shipyard in England for conversion back to a luxury liner.

Her post-war service was largely uneventful. For a number of years, she and her sister ship, the Queen Elizabeth, were the preferred method of transatlantic travel for the rich, the famous and the unknown alike. As time passed and the middle 1960s came about, luxury ships began to fall into disfavor. It was faster, and cheaper, by this time to simply catch a plane to wherever you wanted to go. The ocean liners were becoming a thing of the past.

In October 1967, the *Queen Mary* steamed away from England for the last time. Her decks and state rooms were filled with curiosity-seekers and wealthy patrons who wanted to be a part of the ship's final voyage. The crew was made up of the pick of the company's senior staff members, each fulfilling his responsibilities with a nostalgic sadness, for the *Queen Mary* would never sail again.

She ended her 39-day journey in Long Beach, California. The city had purchased the old liner and she would be permanently docked as a floating hotel, convention center, museum and restaurant. She is now listed on the National Register of Historic Places and is open to visitors all year around.

There is no question that the *Queen Mary* has seen a long and strange history over the years and so it comes as no surprise to many that, in addition to her paying guests, the ship plays host to a number of ghosts as well!

Ghost enthusiasts and paranormal researchers have long been of the mind that tragedy and death are the leading causes behind why locations become haunted. Over the years, the *Queen Mary* has seen both. Because of the sheer number of passengers who have walked the decks of ship, accidents and mishaps were bound to happen. One such accident occurred on July 10, 1966 when John Pedder, a worker in the engine room, was crushed to death when the automatic door in Doorway 13 closed on him.

And there have been other deaths on board, some fact and others perhaps, the stuff of legend.

For instance, the ship's first captain, Sir Edgar Britten, died only weeks after the liner's maiden voyage. During the war, when the ship was used as a troop transport, a brawl broke out in one of the ship's galleys and became so serious that the captain radioed a nearby cruiser to send a boarding party to break up the fighting. Before the escort ship's squad could arrive, a ship's cook was allegedly pushed into a hot oven, where he burned to death. There was also a report of a woman drowning in the ship's swimming pool, stories of passengers falling overboard and of course, the terrible accident with the Curacoa off the Irish coast.

Authors Rob and Anne Wlodarski, along with famed ghost hunter Richard Senate, have delved deeply into the ghosts, hauntings and mysteries of the *Queen Mary*. Their own investigations have turned up a myriad of spirits on the vessel and all of them are entwined with the history of the ship.

Another strange death on the ship was that of Senior Second Office W.E. Stark. His ghost has often been spotted in his former quarters and on deck. Stark died in 1949 after joking to some of his friends that he had taken a drink of tetrachloride and lime juice, having mistaken it for gin. He made light of the situation, not realizing how serious it was to become.

Earlier that evening, the Staff Captain had told Stark to take the two Watch Officers to his cabin and help themselves to some gin. The men were all off duty and gladly obliged. From all accounts, it seems that Stark asked Stokes, the Captain's steward, to find the bottle of gin for the Staff Captain's steward was not present at the time. Stokes then went into the Staff Captain's cabin and found a gin bottle in a locked cabinet. The young man had no way of knowing that the bottle was actually cleaning solution and not gin at all. It should be noted that there were no markings on the bottle. He handed the capped bottle to Stark and left the cabin. Stark then poured three gin and limes and instead of waiting for his friends to join him, took a large drink from one of the glasses.

He immediately realized his error and while he joked about it, he did call the ship's doctor, who never expected him to take a turn for the worse. Unfortunately though, Stark began to feel the effects of the poison. By the following day, he was sick in his bunk and by the next, the doctor had advised his transfer to a hospital. The young officer grew even worse and soon lapsed into a coma and died on Thursday, September 22, 1949.

Another ghost believed to haunt the *Queen Mary* is Leonard "Lobster" Horsborough, a former cook. He served aboard the ship for 15 years and then passed away on November 13, 1967, during the vessel's final voyage. He died from complications brought on by a heat stroke and eventual heart failure and was buried at sea. Although no formal notice was given about his service, a large and curious crowd gathered and some have suggested that perhaps the lack of formality given to Horsborough's burial may be the reason his spirit lingers behind. Since his death, tales have often been told of the kitchen area here being haunted and his presence is often seen, heard and felt here. Combined with the cook who was supposedly roasted to death during the war, the galley has the potential to be a very haunted place.

In addition to these ghosts, there are also reported encounters with a man in a white boiler suit who has been seen and heard many times below deck. He has been described as being in his forties and he is dressed in the type of uniform worn by engineers and mechanics in the 1930s. There is also a spectral man in gray overalls who has also been seen below deck. He has dark hair and a long beard and is also believed to be a mechanic or a maintenance worker from the early days who has chosen to remain behind on the *Queen Mary* for some reason.

These spirits are joined by a friendly spirit that has been

dubbed Miss Turner. She is thought to have been a telephone switchboard operator on the ship. Another ghostly woman is said to be Mrs. Kilburn, who has been described as wearing a gray uniform with starched white cuffs. She was in charge of the stewardesses and stewards during the voyages and perhaps her efficient manner keeps her around even today, still watching over the comings and goings on the ship.

And while there is no historical documentation for the existence of the Lady in White who haunts the *Queen Mary*, she is frequently seen aboard the ship. She haunts the Main Lounge (now the Queen's Salon) and is normally seen wearing a white, backless evening gown. The stories say that she usually strolls over to the grand piano as if listening to music only she can hear or dances alone for a few moments before vanishing without a trace. Who this woman might be is unknown but she has become a very real part of the haunted history of the ship.

These spirits may be the most frequented reported phantoms on board the ship, but they are far from the only ones who haunt the vessel. Security guards, crew, staff members and visitors have all been troubled by incidents that seem to have no explanation. Doors open and close on their own. They are locked one moment and then standing wide open the next, triggering alarms in the security office. This happens most often near the swimming pool and while the guards always look for the intruders, no one is ever found.

Other reports of unexplained happenings include strange noises (like footsteps when no one is there), banging and hammering (like work being done on equipment), voices, cold spots, inexplicable winds that blow through areas that are closed off, lights that turn on and off and much more!

And as we have wondered already, can we really be surprised by such reports? According to historical records, the death toll aboard the *Queen Mary* stands at 55 since her launch in 1936. The causes of these deaths range from heart attacks and accidents to suicides, poisonings and worse. Some even believe that the death toll here is much higher if the deaths of prisoners of war are taken into consideration. During the war years, besides being a troop transport for Allied soldiers, prisoners of war were sometimes taken aboard as well. Unconfirmed stories tell of suffocating heat below deck, which brought about deaths and burials at sea. Could these mistreated men still be lingering aboard the ship as well?

Carol Zalfini, a staff member aboard the *Queen Mary*, was passing an engine room door one evening after all of the workers had left for the day. She suddenly heard the sounds of banging and pounding inside. Thinking that someone was still there, she entered the engine room and walked to where she thought the sounds had come from. Not surprisingly (to the reader anyway), she found herself alone! When she climbed back toward the upper level, the sounds started up again. Puzzled, she turned to go down once more and the sounds immediately ceased. That was when she fled the engine room!

A Security Sergeant named Nancy Wazny may have once encountered the ghost of the woman who drowned in the ship's swimming pool. She was standing near the stairway that led to the pool one night when she spotted a middle-aged woman standing nearby and wearing a one-piece swimming suit. There wasn't supposed to be anyone in that area and the water had even been drained from the pool. The woman, who Wazny described as appearing to be "from the 1950s or earlier," was preparing to dive into the empty pool. Startled, the security officer screamed at the woman to stop and she abruptly vanished!

One night, a security guard was patrolling the ship with a trained dog and he heard a noise behind watertight door No. 13. The dog suddenly stopped and refused to go any further. A search of the area revealed that no one was nearby, but the guard couldn't help but remember that this same door had once crushed crewman John Pedder to death in 1966. Years after this incident, a tour guide was walking up some steps aboard the ship and felt the presence of someone behind her. She quickly turned around and for just a moment, saw the image of a young man that almost as suddenly, vanished. The guide, who didn't know about the horrible death that had occurred in Doorway 13, was later able to pick out a photograph of Pedder as the man she had seen on the stairs.

Another tour guide once told of hearing the sounds of children laughing and the sounds of footsteps on the deck above him as he was walking up an aft stairwell. The sounds continued until he neared the top of the stairs and then it stopped.

After the *Queen Mary* was docked in Long Beach, the stories of the staff member's strange encounters began to spread. Since that time, thousands of curious tourists, ghost hunters and skeptics have come to see for themselves. It comes as no surprise that many of these visitors and hotel guests have had their own bizarre experiences.

One guest, while on a guided tour of the ship, reported that someone continuously tugged on her purse and sweater throughout the tour. This would happen even when no one was standing next to her. Toward the end of the tour, she felt someone gently touch her hair, sending cold chills down her spine. She was standing at the end of the line at the time and there was no one near her at all!

Another guest was alone with a friend on the top deck. They went downstairs to the deck below and shortly after arriving there, they heard the footsteps of a large group of people coming from the deck where they had just been. Since they didn't recall seeing or hearing anyone when they had come down, they decided to climb back upstairs and see what was going on. They soon got a surprise though. The deck was completely empty!

An overnight visitor awoke from her sleep around midnight one night and saw a figure walking near the cabin door. Thinking that it was her sister, who was staying with her, she called out. There was no answer from the figure and just then, the woman turned over and saw that her sister was asleep beside her. She quickly sat up in bed...just in time to see the figure walk through the door and vanish into the corridor.

Two other guests spent the night with what may have been a

"practical joker ghost." They were relaxing in their room when they heard a soft tapping on the door. One of them asked who it was but received no reply. When they got up to open the door and looked out in the hall, there was no one there. "This happened later on in the night with the same results," the guest added. "Maybe it was someone playing a practical joke, although I think we knew it was something else."

And the stories of encounters and strange events go on and on. It seems almost certain that the events of the past have left an indelible impression on the decks, corridors and cabins of the *Queen Mary*. They repeat themselves, over and over again, and create a haunting that is rivaled by few others in the annals of the supernatural. The events of yesterday really do create the hauntings of today!

John L. Smith, a marine engineer who worked aboard the ship, was among the first to experience the most tragic reoccurrence from the *Queen Mary*'s past. It happened in 1967, when she was steaming toward the California coast. "I first heard men screaming while the old ship was still at sea," he said. "I was below deck at the bow, as far forward as anyone could get when it happened. It was the voices of horrified men, screaming in panic and followed by the terrible noise of crunching metal being ripped apart and the rush of water. It was coming from outside the bow where there was only sea."

Years later, after the ship was permanently berthed, the terrible sound of two ships colliding continued to be heard from inside of the Queen Mary. The screams and the shredding steel always came from outside of the ship's bow. Did the terrible events of 1942 somehow leave an impression on the atmosphere of this grand old ship? Or worse, is the crew of the Curacoa for some reason doomed to re-live that October afternoon for eternity?

The luxurious Queen Mary today

The famous Winchester Mystery House

THE WINCHESTER MYSTERY HOUSE

The Haunted History of America's Most Mysterious House

There is no single dwelling in America that more accurately fits the description of "most haunted house in the country" than the Winchester Mystery House in San Jose, California. If there is a house with a richer haunted history, a more mysterious origin and a greater reputation for ghosts, I can't think of it. With that in mind, there is no place that fits more easily into the category of "America's Most Haunted Places" than the Winchester House does.

While most ghost enthusiasts are familiar with the location, not everyone knows the story behind the story. The house is an enigma. It is a massive structure of which no accurate room count has ever been taken. Doors open to brick walls, staircases lead to nowhere, hallways end at blank facades, secret passages honeycomb parts of the building and all this combines to create a madhouse of gigantic proportions. But why? Who built this fantastic place, and for what reason? Why was an ordinary farm house turned into a labyrinth? And why did construction here never cease, continuing 24 hours a day, for decades?

The story of the mysterious mansion begins in September 1839 with the birth of a baby girl to Leonard and Sarah Pardee of New Haven, Connecticut. The baby's name was also Sarah and as she reached maturity, she became the belle of the city. She was well-received at all social events, thanks to her musical skills, her fluency in various foreign languages and her sparkling charm. Her beauty was also well known by the young men about town, despite her diminutive size. Although she was petite and stood only four feet, ten inches, she made up for this in personality and loveliness.

At the same time that Sarah was growing up, a young man was also maturing in another prominent New Haven family. The young man's name was William Wirt Winchester and he was the son of Oliver Winchester, a shirt manufacturer and businessman. In 1857, he took over the assets of a firm that made the Volcanic Repeater, a rifle that used a lever mechanism to load bullets into the breech.

Obviously, this type of gun was a vast improvement over the muzzle-loading rifles of prior times, but Winchester still saw room for advance. In 1860, the company developed the Henry Rifle, which had a tubular magazine located under the barrel. Because it was easy to reload and could fire rapidly, the Henry was said to average one shot every three seconds. It became the first true repeating rifle and a favorite among the Northern troops at the outbreak of the Civil War.

Money began to pour in and Oliver Winchester soon amassed a large fortune from government contracts and private sales. He re-organized the company and changed the name to the Winchester Repeating Arms Company. They soon began producing a new rifle, simply known as the Winchester, which improved once more on the earlier models. Cartridges were fed into the magazine through a small opening in the breech. It was easy to load and use and it became an immediate success, thanks to its fast action and the fact that its ammunition was interchangeable with a number of Colt revolvers. In that way, only one supply of ammo was needed for both rifle and pistol.

The family prospered and on September 30, 1862, at the height of the Civil War, William Wirt Winchester and Sarah Pardee were married in an elaborate ceremony in New Haven.

Four years later, on July 15, 1866, Sarah gave birth to a daughter named Annie Pardee Winchester. Just a short time later, the first disaster struck for Sarah, as her daughter contracted an illness known as marasmus, a child's disease in which the body wastes away. The infant died on July 24. Sarah was so shattered by this event that she withdrew into herself and teetered on the edge of madness for some time. In the end, it would be nearly a decade before she returned to her normal self but she and William would never have another child.

Not long after Sarah returned to her family and home, another tragedy struck. William, now heir to the Winchester empire, was struck down with pulmonary tuberculosis. He died on March 7, 1881. As a result of his death, Sarah inherited over $20 million dollars, an incredible sum, especially in those days. She also received 48.9 percent of the Winchester Repeating Arms Company and an income of about $1000 per day, which was not taxable until 1913.

But her new-found wealth could do nothing to ease her pain. Sarah grieved deeply, not only for her husband, but also for her lost child. The wound of the infant's death had been opened once more. She locked herself in her room, refused to leave the house, eat or take care of herself in any way. Her health naturally began to deteriorate. Friends urged her to leave New England and seek a warmer climate, which would relieve her health and ease the severe arthritis that she suffered from. Sarah refused to go. She did not want to leave the place where her loved ones were buried.

A short time later, a friend suggested that Sarah might speak to a Spiritualist medium about her loss. The well-meaning friend suggested that perhaps the medium might be able to ease her suffering and perhaps put her into contact with her late husband. This finally lured Sarah from her home. She attended a service conducted by a Boston medium named Adam Coons.

"Your husband is here," the medium told her and then went on to provide a description of William Winchester. "He says for me to tell you that there is a curse on your family, which took the life of he and your child. It will soon take you too. It is a curse that has resulted from the terrible weapon created by the Winchester family. Thousands of persons have died because of it and their spirits are now seeking vengeance."

Sarah was then told that she must sell her property in New Haven and head towards the setting sun. Her husband would guide her and when she found her new home in the west, she would recognize it. "You must start a new life," said the medium, "and build a home for yourself and for the spirits who have fallen from this terrible weapon too. You can never stop building the house. If you continue building, you will live. Stop and you will die."

Shortly after the seance, Sarah sold her home in New Haven and with a vast fortune at her disposal, moved west to California. She believed that she was guided by the hand of her dead husband and she did not stop traveling until she reached the Santa Clara Valley in 1884. Here, she found a six-room home under construction that belonged to a Dr. Caldwell. She entered into negotiations with him and soon convinced him to sell her the house, along with the 162 acres that it rested on. She tossed away any previous plans for the house and started building whatever she chose to. She had her pick of local workers and craftsmen and for the next 36 years, they built and rebuilt, altered and changed and constructed and demolished one section of the house after another. She kept 22 carpenters at work, year around, 24 hours each day. The sounds of hammers and saws sounded throughout the day and night.

As the house grew to include 26 rooms, railroad cars were switched onto a nearby line to bring building materials and imported furnishings to the house. The house was rapidly growing and expanding and while Sarah claimed to have no master plan for the structure, she met each morning with her foreman and they would go over the her hand-sketched plans for the day's work. The plans were often chaotic but showed a real flair for building. Sometimes though, they would not work out the right way, but Sarah always had a quick solution. If this happened, they would just build another room around an existing one. The foreman could never figure out where his employer got her ideas, but to Sarah, they came quite easily.

One of the first rooms that had been added to the house had been a seance room. It was located on the second floor in the center of the house. It had been designed with no windows and with a single entrance. There was only one key to the room, which had been painted a dark blue color. No one ever entered it but Sarah. She would go into this room and attempt to "commune with the spirits," sitting quietly in meditation until the spirits placed their

structural ideas for the house into her head. She would then pon-
der these ideas and place them on paper.

Sarah also had a bell tower installed on the house. The tower
was very high and virtually unreachable. The bell's rope hung down
through the inside of the bell tower shaft to a secret room in the
cellar. The room was only accessible through an underground tunnel that was known only to a Japanese servant and his apprentice.
The bell ringer carried an expensive pocket watch and in his quarters was a very expensive chronometer. Each day, he telephoned an
astronomical observatory in order to check the accuracy of his
timepieces. Sarah believed that time was very important to the
ringing of this bell, which she used to contact the spirits.

It was said that this bell tolled each night at midnight, one hour
later and then finally at two o'clock in the morning. It remained
silent the rest of the time. From her studies of the occult, or perhaps from the spirits themselves, Sarah learned that the element of
time was very important in regards to the arrival of visitors from
the other world.

As the days, weeks and months passed, the house continued to
grow. Rooms were added to rooms and then turned into entire
wings, doors were joined to windows, levels turned into towers
and peaks and the place eventually grew to a height of seven stories. Inside of the house, three elevators were installed, as were 47
fireplaces. There were countless staircases that led nowhere; a
blind chimney that stops short of the ceiling; closets that opened to
blank walls; trap doors; double-back hallways; skylights that were
located one above another; doors that opened to steep drops to the
lawn below; and dozens of other oddities. Even all of the stair posts
were installed upside-down and many of the bathrooms had glass
doors on them.

It was also obvious that Sarah was intrigued by the number
"13." Nearly all of the windows contained 13 panes of glass; the
walls had 13 panels; the greenhouse had 13 cupolas; many of the
wooden floors contained 13 sections; some of the rooms had 13

windows and every staircase but one had 13 steps. This exception is unique in its own right. It is a winding staircase with 42 steps, which would normally be enough to take a climber up three stories. In this case, however, the steps only rise nine feet because each step is only two inches high.

While all of this seems like madness to us, it all made sense to Sarah. In this way, she could control the spirits who came to the house for evil purposes, or who were outlaws or vengeful people in their past life. These bad men, killed by Winchester rifles, could wreak havoc on Sarah. The house had been designed into a maze to confuse and discourage the bad spirits.

Each night, at midnight, when the bell summoned Sarah and her spirit guides to the seance room, she would travel down the hallways in a strange course that would be sure to confuse any ghost who was following her. Besides the hellish corridors, Sarah also had access to secret panels that opened at the push of a button, windows that exited from one room to the next, and staircases that led both up and down to the same level in different parts of the house. It is sure that she could have easily lost any pursuer, earthly or otherwise.

In addition to trying to harass the vengeful spirits killed by Winchester rifles, Sarah also made an effort to appease the friendly ones too. The house was richly furnished and decorated with gold and silver chandeliers, art glass windows, Belgian crystal, art-molded bronze bathtubs, exquisite marble and even wonderful Tiffany glass windows that were said to have cost more than $1000 each. Two of these windows are located in Sarah's ballroom and are engraved with two quotes from Shakespeare: "Wide unclasp the tables of their thoughts" and "These same thoughts people this little world." The significance of these two quotations was known only to Sarah and remains a mystery today.

After her death, vast warehouses were discovered on the property and were found to contain supplies and fixtures that would have later been incorporated into the house. Among the pieces were elaborate light fixtures, ornate hardware, art glass windows and doors, wooden doors of cedar, oak, walnut, maple and mahogany, floor tiles, plumbing; and much more. Sarah had carefully cataloged all of it.

In addition to the eccentricity and the rich decor, the house also had a number of innovations that were far ahead of its time. In the laundry room, the wash trays had fitted washboards and center tubs to ease the laundering of clothing. The house was fitted with a hot water heater that warmed the water for all of the indoor plumbing. A thermostatically controlled shower was fitted into one bathroom that sprayed water from all directions. Sarah invented a crank that would open and close windows from the inside. The house had electricity and its own private gas plant, along with an extensive burglar alarm system and a heated spa which was designed to ease the pain of Sarah's arthritis. This room was designed with several fireplaces, large windows to let in the sun and numerous radiator vents. The heat generated here was her greatest remedy for aching joints.

Needless to say, the sort of building that was going on at the house did not exactly earn Sarah a worthy reputation in town. The stories carried home from the eccentric structure by the workmen alone would have been enough to raise many eyebrows. She went out of her way to have her groundskeepers plant large bushes along the property line, hoping to keep out the stares of the curious. In all of the years she lived in the house, she was observed in town only one time.

Because she never went calling on her neighbors, she did not expect people to call on her. In fact, she did not want anyone, save for the workmen, to even enter her home. Any curiosity-seeker, or even well meaning local, who approached the house was quickly turned away by a servant. Eventually, the front door of the house was ordered locked and boarded up and was never used again.

And Sarah did not discriminate when it came to turning away callers, whether they were famous or not. One such caller was President Theodore Roosevelt, a Winchester rifle and hunting enthusiast. He came to the house while on a western tour, but it is unknown whether he ever spoke with Sarah or not. His whole entourage was conducted to the rear carriage house, which had been designed so that Sarah's horse and buggy could actually enter into the mansion. There were several doors from the carriage area that led into various passageways, although one of them was only five feet high...a private entrance for Sarah herself. Roosevelt managed to get into the house, but no record remains as to whether he actually spoke with Sarah or not. Some visitors were not even that lucky. Prominent religious leader Mary Baker Eddy was actually turned away at the gate.

There was one visitor however, who not only was invited into the house, but with whom a private session with Sarah was actually allowed. He was famous illusionist Harry Houdini and his meeting with Sarah lasted for more then one hour. What they actually talked about, and what Houdini's reaction must have been to the house, is unknown. Houdini would never tell anyone what occurred behind the closed doors of the Winchester House.

The house continued to grow and by 1906, it had reached a towering seven stories tall. Sarah continued her occupancy, and expansion, of the house, living in melancholy solitude with no one other than her servants, the workmen and, of course, the spirits. It was said that on sleepless nights, when she was not communing with the spirit world about the designs for the house, Sarah would play her grand piano into the early hours of the morning. According to legend, the piano would be admired by passers-by on the street outside, despite the fact that two of the keys were badly out of tune.

Because of the number of bedrooms in the house, Sarah would often sleep in a different one each night. She did have a particular favorite though, and it became a place where she often spent the daylight hours also. She called it the Daisy Room, because of the daisies that had been cast into the stained glass windows. It was located on the second floor and here, Sarah would often sit and watch the wagons, horses and people pass by on the street outside. She often slept here at night, napping in the hours before midnight and returning here after her session with the spirit architects was completed. She loved this room very much....or at least she did until April 18, 1906.

On that night, Sarah was dozing when she was suddenly awakened by the bed shaking. In the dim light of the gas lamp, she saw that the walls of the room began to crack. The furniture began to shake and books and glass items fell to the floor from shelves and tables. Then, with horror, she saw the plaster ceilings start to crumble and collapse. She was certain that the spirits of those killed by the Winchester rifles had finally come for her soul!

The house began to collapse, sending wood and timber down into the room. Sarah struggled to get to the door and escape out in the corridor, but her path was blocked. Terrified, she ran to the internal communication system that she had installed in the maze-like house. She would call on her servants to save her! The intercom recorded her call, but not where she was. Finally, frightened and hysterical, Sarah fainted, still sure that the vengeful spirits had come for her.

The great San Francisco Earthquake of 1906 had struck. When it was all over, portions of the Winchester Mansion were nearly in ruins. The top three floors of the house had collapsed into the gardens and would never be rebuilt.

It was hours before the house servants and workmen were able to free Sarah from the Daisy Room. When they found her, she was a trembling wreck. She would never set foot in that bedroom again. She ordered it boarded up and sealed off. The room would never be used again during Sarah's lifetime and the private belongings, bedding and furniture were left just as they were.

For the next several months, the workmen toiled to repair the damage done by the earthquake, although actually the mammoth structure had fared far better than most of the buildings in the area. Only a few of the rooms had been badly harmed, although it had lost the highest floors and several cupolas and towers had toppled over.

The expansion on the house began once more. The number of bedrooms increased from 15 to 20 and then to 25. Chimneys were installed all over the place, although strangely, they served no purpose. Some believe that perhaps they were added because the old stories say that ghosts like to appear and disappear through them. On a related note, it has also been documented that only 2 mirrors were installed in the house. Sarah believed that ghosts were afraid of their own reflection.

Throughout the construction of the house, Sarah was always concerned about security. Besides having a burglar alarm, she also had locks installed so that every door required a key to open it. It was said that the number of keys needed for the house filled three large buckets. One has to wonder though if so many locks were really necessary? Rumors claimed that the Winchester Mansion was filled with treasure, gold and cash, yet no one ever attempted to rob the place. Imagine a bandit who slipped inside one night and entered the bizarre labyrinth of Sarah's mansion! In this case, the house's reputation served a very useful purpose.

In addition to the vast expanse of the house, Sarah also had a wonderful wine cellar constructed. She enjoyed sipping imported wines and liqueurs and it was said that the cellar was unequalled by any other similar structure on the West Coast.

One afternoon, she went down to the wine cellar and moments later, came running back upstairs, screaming all the way. On the cellar wall, she had discovered the black imprint of a large hand that she was sure had been left there as a warning from the spirit world. The servants tried to explain to her that the handprint had been there for years and had been left by one of the workmen but Sarah refused to listen. Leaving the cellar exactly as it was, she had the entrance bricked over and then hidden by so many other structures that the treasure trove of wine has never been found.

On September 4, 1922, after a conference session with the

spirits in the seance room, Sarah went to her bedroom for the night. At some point in the early morning hours, she died in her sleep at the age of 83. She left all of her possessions to her niece, France Marriott, who had been handling most of Sarah's business affairs for some time. In her will, Sarah had a couple of unusual requests. She asked that her casket be cared out of the house through the back door, consistent with Sarah's refusal to use the front entrance. She also requested that all subsequent owners of the house allow the ghosts of yesteryear to still be welcome there and that they keep the property in good repair and tell all visitors about Sarah's project.

Little did anyone know, but by this time, Sarah's large bank account had dwindled considerably. Rumor had it that somewhere in the house was hidden a safe containing a fortune in jewelry and a solid-gold dinner service with which Sarah had entertained her ghostly guests. Her relatives forced open a number of safes but found only old fishing lines, socks, newspaper clippings about her daughter's and her husband's deaths, a lock of baby hair, and a suit of woolen underwear. No solid gold dinner service was ever discovered.

The furnishings, personal belongings and surplus construction and decorative materials were removed from the house and the structure itself was sold to a group of investors who planned to use it as a tourist attraction. One of the first to see the place when it opened to the public was Robert L. Ripley, who featured the house in his popular column, "Believe it or Not."

The house was initially advertised as being 148 rooms, but so confusing was the floor plan that every time a room count was taken, a different total came up. The place was so puzzling that it was said that the workmen took more than six weeks just to get the furniture out of it. The moving men became so lost because it was a "labyrinth," they told the magazine, *American Weekly*, in 1928. It was a house "where downstairs leads neither to the cellar nor upstairs to the roof." The rooms of the house were counted over and over again and five years later, it was estimated that 160 rooms existed…although no one is really sure if even that is correct.

Today, the house has been declared a California Historical Landmark and is registered with the National Park Service as "a large, odd dwelling with an unknown number of rooms."

A House that had been built for the spirits? Most would say that such a place must still harbor at least a few of the ghosts who came to reside there at the invitation of Sarah Winchester. The question is: do they really haunt the place? Some would say that perhaps no ghosts ever walked there at all, that the Winchester mansion is nothing more than the product of an eccentric woman's mind and too much wealth being allowed into the wrong hands. Is the Winchester Mansion really haunted? You will have to decide that for yourself, although some people have already made up their minds.

In 1975, just one year after the house was placed on the National Register of Historic Places, Keith Kittle, who was the manager of the property, invited Jeanne Borgen to visit. She was, at that time, a well-respected psychic and Kittle thought that her visit would make a great publicity stunt for the Halloween season. He really didn't expect anything out of it, but it would garner a lot of attention for the house. Shortly after arriving, the psychic held a press conference and when asked if there were ghosts in the house, said that she had already seen one that morning. She also planned to hold a late night seance two evenings later.

When the time came for the seance, she chose one of Sarah's bedrooms for the event. A table was set up and another psychic, Joy Adams, sat down while Borgen paced back and forth, trying to locate cold spots. She said that all questions for the spirits should be directed to Adams, who by this time, had entered a trance-like state.

One of the reporters spoke up and asked if she liked living in the house. When the answer came from the mouth of Joy Adam's, it was in the voice of a much older woman. "Yes, I love it very much," she said and began to laugh, explaining that she had just remembered some of the wonderful things that had happened while staying in the house with her spirit friends. Then, she suddenly stopped laughing and said, rather sharply, "The townspeople. They always talk about me."

While Joy Adams was talking, Jeanne Borgen was still walking about the room with her hands outstretched, hoping to encounter patches of frigid air. She suddenly stopped and pointed at one of the reporters. According to witnesses, the previously clean-shaven man suddenly sported a spectral beard! He complained of being cold, while another reporter cried out that he felt hands pushing downward on his shoulders. The witnesses also said that Borgen's face suddenly appeared to age before their eyes. Her hair appeared to turn gray and her face became etched with lines. In moments, she was unable to stand and appeared to be suffering a heart attack. It only lasted for a moment and then was gone.

When it was over, Borgen stated that Sarah Winchester had graced them with her presence and that the discomfort that she had felt was due to the fact that there were so many people in the room. After all, Sarah had closely guarded her privacy.

In 1979, authors Richard Winer and Nancy Osborn visited the Winchester House while doing research for a book about haunted places. They got permission to spend the night there from Keith Kittle. They originally planned to sleep in the seance room, but were pointed to another room by one of the guides.

"It's the Daisy Room in the front that frightens me," the guide told them. "That's the room where Sarah Winchester was trapped during the 1906 earthquake." The guide really couldn't pinpoint any particular thing about the room which disconcerted her, but did say that sometimes the room would get very cold, but only in certain places.

With that in mind, Winer and Osborn decided to bed down on mats in what was once Sarah's favorite bedroom. They had not been there very long when Winer discovered an area of the room that was much colder than the surrounding atmosphere. Thinking that it might be a draft, he searched for a place where the wind might be coming from but could find nothing. He realized too that the cold air was not moving. It was perfectly still and it was occupying an area that would roughly be the size of a human body!

Convinced they were not alone in the room, they eventually lay down and went to sleep…but they wouldn't stay that way for long. Just after two in the morning, Nancy shook Winer awake. "Wake up! Do you hear it!" she asked him.

It was the sound of piano music, being played quite beautifully, except for the fact that two of the keys were flat. "Sarah Winchester's piano was supposed to have two flat keys," Winer said.

A short time later, they heard the sound of footsteps walking down the hallway outside of the bedroom. They looked to see who was there but found nothing. After that, neither one of them slept for the rest of the night.

The strange events at the Winchester House continued on for many years and continue today. Dozens of psychics have visited the house over the years and most have come away convinced, or claim to be convinced, that spirits still wander the place. In addition to the ghost of Sarah Winchester, there have also been many other sightings throughout the years.

But more compelling than the claims of psychics are the strange little stories passed on by staff members of the house. A number of years ago, a woman named Sue Sales took a tour through the house and encountered a small, gray-haired lady seated in the kitchen. At the end of the tour, she asked the guide about the lady dressed as Sarah Winchester and why this cleverly costumed woman had not been pointed out. The guide told her that there had been no one dressed in costume that day.

One night in 1979, several employees were buffing the floors on the second level of the house when they heard footsteps on the floor above them. They were the only ones in the building at the time.

In January 1981, Allen Weitzel was locking up the house for the night and as he walked the entire route of the tour, he shut down the lights as he went. He then locked the doors and walked out to the parking lot to get into his car. When he turned and looked back at the house, all of the lights on the third floor had been turned on again.

A security guard for the house once admitted that they often have a lot of false alarms at the house, with the security system being tripped, even though no one is ever found inside. Strangely, when they go to investigate, the alarms are usually found to have been triggered from the inside, even though the exterior alarms have not been bothered. In other words, someone, or something, is moving about inside of the mansion, even though there is no way that they could have gotten inside.

One summer afternoon, a tour guide named Gina Anging was on the third floor when the door to the servant's call station somehow slammed shut. There was no wind that could have closed the door and no one else on the floor at that time. Gina could offer no explanation for what happened.

One evening, a tour supervisor named Mike Bray was closing the house for the night. He was walking down an upstairs hallway when he heard the distinct sound of someone whispering his name. He searched all over for someone else in the house, but this occurred at the end of the day and the rest of the staff members had already left.

Another tour guide, named Amy Kinsch, was sweeping the floor in the front kitchen of the house when she caught the overpowering scent of chicken soup that was seemingly coming from the same room that she was in. She realized quickly that this wasn't possible, for she was certainly not cooking soup, and went in search of where the odor was coming from. The closest possible spot was from the caretaker's rooms, but once she walked toward them, she could no longer smell the soup. The event remained mysterious, even after another guide had an identical experience about six months later.

In the years that the house has been open to the public, employees and visitors alike have had unusual encounters here, as is evident from the anecdotes that have been related previously. There have been footsteps, banging doors, mysterious voices, windows that bang so hard they shatter, cold spots, strange moving lights, door-knobs that turn by themselves—and don't forget the scores of psy-chics who have their own claims of phenomena to report.

Obviously, these are all of the standard reports of a haunted house but are the stories merely wishful thinking? Are they reports of ghosts and spirits to continue the tradition of Sarah Winchester's bizarre legacy? Or could the stories be true? Was the house really built as a monument to the dead? Do phantoms still lurk in the maze-like corridors of the Winchester Mystery House?

I urge you to visit the house if you should ever get the chance. Perhaps that would be the best time to answer the questions that I have just posed to you. I can promise that you will find not anoth-er piece of American architecture like the Winchester mansion. And who knows what else you might find while you're there.

A GATEWAY TO HELL?

The Strange History of Stull Cemetery

There are graveyards across America, places with names like Bachelor's Grove and Stull Cemetery, that defy all definitions of a haunted cemetery. They are places that go beyond the legends of merely being haunted and enter into the realm of the diabolical. They are places said to be so terrifying that the Devil himself holds court with his worshippers there...and in the case of Stull Cemetery in Kansas, is one of the "gateways to hell" itself!

But just how terrifying are these places? While there are few of us who would challenge the supernatural presence of a place like Bachelor's Grove (see the next chapter), there are some who claim that Stull Cemetery does not deserve the blood-curdling reputa-tion that it has gained over the years.

Stull Cemetery, and the abandoned church that rests next to it, is located in the tiny, nearly forgotten Kansas town of Stull. There is not much left of the tiny village, save for a few houses, the newer church and about twenty residents. However, the population of the place allegedly contains a number of residents that are from beyond this earth! In addition to its human inhabitants, the town is also home to a number of legends and strange tales that are linked to the crumbling old church and the overgrown cemetery that can be found atop Stull's Emmanuel Hill. For years, stories of witch-craft, ghosts and supernatural happenings have surrounded the old graveyard. It is a place that some claim is one of the "seven gate-ways to hell."

The legends say that these stories have been linked to Stull for more than 100 years, but none of them made it into print until the 1970s. In November 1974, an article appeared in the University of Kansas student newspaper that spoke of a number of strange occur-rences in the Stull churchyard. According to the article, Stull was "haunted by legends of diabolical, supernatural happenings" and the legends asserted that the cemetery was one of the two places on earth where the devil appears in person two times each year. It said that the cemetery had been the source of many legends in the area, stories that had been told and re-told for over a century.

The piece also went on to say that most students learned of Stull's diabolical reputation from their grand-parents and older individuals, but that many of them claimed first-hand encounters with things that could not explain. One student claimed to have been grabbed by the arm by something unseen, while others spoke of unexplained memory loss when visiting the place. Like many other locations of this type, the tales of devil worship and witch-craft also figured strongly into the article. But were the stories actually true?

Not according to the residents of Stull, who claimed to have never even heard the stories before. They were bemused, annoyed and downright angered that such things were being said about their town. The pastor of the new church in Stull, located right across the road from the old one, indicated that he believed the stories to be the invention of students at the university.

But such stories have a strong hold on people, as evidenced by the reaction to the article that claimed that the devil would appear in Stull Cemetery on the night of the Spring Equinox and again on Halloween. On March 20, 1978, more than 150 people waited in the cemetery for the arrival of the devil. The word also spread that the spirits of those who died violent deaths, and were buried there, would return from the grave. Unfortunately, the only spirits that showed up that night came in bottles and cans…but this did not stop the stories from spreading.

All through the 1980s and up until today, stories have been told about Stull Cemetery and as time has passed, most have grown more horrifying and hard to believe. The problem seems to be that the cemetery has a lack of real, documented accounts of strange activity. The weird tales seem to be little more that urban legends and second-hand stories from teenagers and college students.

One story told of two young men who were visiting Stull Cemetery one night and became frightened when a strong wind began blowing out of nowhere. They ran back to their car, only to find that the vehicle had been moved to the other side of the highway and was now facing in the opposite direction. Another man claimed to experience this same anomalous wind, but inside of the church rather than in the graveyard. He claimed that the sinister air current knocked him to the floor and would not allow him to move for some time. Incidentally, it is inside of this same church where witnesses say that no rain will fall…even though the crumbling building has no roof!

The legends also say that the Devil has been appearing here since the 1850s and insist that the original name of the town was Skull and that the later corruption of that into Stull was simply to cover the fact that the area was steeped in black magic. It was said that the witchcraft-practicing early settlers were so repentant about their past deeds that they changed the name of the town. In truth, the town was called Deer Creek Community until 1899, when the last name of the first postmaster, Sylvester Stull, was adopted as the name of the village. The post office closed down in 1903, but the name stuck.

In 1980, an article appeared in the *Kansas City Times* that added further fuel to the rumors about Stull Cemetery and the abandoned church. The article was quoted as saying that the Devil chose two places to appear on Earth every Halloween. One of them was the "tumbleweed hamlet" of Stull, Kansas and the other, which occurs simultaneously at midnight, is someplace on the "desolate plain of India." From these sites, according to the article, the Devil gathers all the people who died violent deaths over the past year for a prance around the Earth at the witching hour.

But why in Stull? The article adds that he appears in Stull because of an event that took place in the 1850s, when "a stable hand allegedly stabbed the mayor to death in the cemetery's old stone barn. Years later, the barn was converted into a church, which in turn was gutted by fire. A decaying wooden crucifix that still hangs from one wall is thought to sometimes turn upside-down when passersby step into the building at midnight..." The story neglects to mention that, historically speaking, neither the Deer Creek Community nor Stull have ever had an official mayor.

Author Lisa Hefner Heitz has collected numerous legends that have added to the mythology of Stull Cemetery. Some of them include the "fact" that the Devil also appears at Stull on the last night of winter or the first night of spring. He comes to visit a witch that is buried there. Coincidentally, an old tombstone bearing the name "Wittich" is located fairly close to the old church. It should also be mentioned that there are rumors that an old tree in the graveyard, which was cut down a year or so ago, was once used as a gallows for condemned witches. There is also said to be a grave in the cemetery that holds the bones of a "child of Satan," who was born of the Devil and a witch. The child was so deformed that he only lived for a few days and the body was buried in Stull. Some say that his ghost may walk here, as there supposedly was a photo taken a few years ago that shows a "werewolf-like boy" peering out from behind a tree.

One of the strangest stories about Stull supposedly appeared in *Time* magazine (it didn't) in either 1993 or 1995 (depending on the version you hear). This story claims that Pope John Paul II allegedly ordered his private plane to fly around eastern Kansas while on his way to a public appearance in Colorado. The reason for this, the story claims, was that the Pope did not want to fly over unholy ground.

The legends grew and by 1989, the crowd at the graveyard on Halloween night had become so overwhelming that the Douglas County sheriff's department had to station deputies outside to send people on their way. They handed out tickets for criminal trespass to anyone caught on the property. It was believed that nearly 500 people came to the cemetery on Halloween night of 1988, doing damage to the church and gravestones, prompting a police response the following year.

As time passed, the local residents grew more irritated that vandals and trespassers were wreaking havoc in the cemetery where their loved ones and ancestors were buried. Finally, a chain link security fence was installed around the grounds and although the area is still regularly patrolled, the visits have died down somewhat, at least outside of October. In addition, there have been the signs posted against trespassing here and locals have made it clear that visitors are not welcome.

So, what about the stories? Were they true or the work of some student writer's imagination? Is the cemetery at Stull really haunted....or is the haunting merely the result of an urban legend gone berserk? That's a hard question to answer. Although undoubtedly the vast majority of the tales about the cemetery have been manufactured from horror fiction, they still beg that now-familiar question of how such stories got started in the first place? Is there a grain of truth to the dark tales? Did some isolated supernatural event take place here that led to embellishment over the years?

We have no idea and local residents are not talking. Strangely, although property owners have spoken out against both vandals and the macabre stories, they have done little to try and end the legends for good. For example, as so many of the paranormal events supposedly involve the ruin of the old church, why not tear it down? The building has been standing vacant 1922 and it has been badly damaged by vandalism over the years. In 1996, the remnants of the roof blew off and once exposed to the elements, the interior walls have been damaged by both weather and graffiti. Recently, a large crack also opened in one of the stone walls after the church was struck by lightning. So why not tear it down before it falls down on its own? Wouldn't this bring an end to the demonic tales circulating about the place?

To make matters worse, why chase away those who come to the cemetery at midnight on Halloween to see the Devil appear? Why not simply "control the chaos" and allow the curiosity-seekers to see that no spirits will run rampant on that fateful night? On Halloween night of 1999, reporters from a local newspaper and a television news crew joined a group of onlookers at the cemetery. Sheriff's deputies were on hand, but did not ask anyone to leave until 11:30pm. Why?

At precisely this moment, an unknown representative for the cemetery owners appeared and ordered everyone to leave the property. The officers had no choice but to go along with their wishes and the reporters and spectators had to leave. As Stull Cemetery and the land around it is private property, there was no option but to comply. The owners stated, through the representative, that they did not want media attention brought to the graveyard because it attracts vandals. But couldn't they have furthered their cause by allowing the camera crew to show that the Devil did not appear at midnight, thus debunking the legend forever? Makes you wonder, doesn't it?

HAUNTED ALCATRAZ

Doing Time for Eternity on the Rock

Alcatraz, which earned the nickname of the Rock, was the ultimate American prison. Bloodletters and badmen and assorted public enemies like Al Capone, Alvin Karpis and Machine-Gun Kelly and others, called this place the end of the line. For 29 years, the damp, fogged-in prison kept the country's most notorious criminals put away from the rest of the world. The heavy mists, cold wind and water and the foghorns of the bay made Alcatraz the loneliest of the prisons.

From the time it became a federal prison in 1934 until it was closed down in 1963, the steel doors clanged shut behind more than 1,000 hardened convicts, criminals and escape artists. Alcatraz was not conceived as a facility for rehabilitation. It was a place of total punishment and minimum privilege. And those who survived it often did so at the cost of their sanity…and some believe their souls.

Alcatraz Island, located in the mists off of San Francisco, received its name in 1775 when the Spanish explorers charted San Francisco bay. They named the rocky piece of land La Isla de los Alcatraces, or the Island of Pelicans. The island was totally uninhabited, plagued by barren ground, little vegetation and surrounding water that churned with swift currents.

In 1847, Alcatraz was taken over by the United States military. The Rock had extreme strategic value, especially during these times of tension between the United States and the Mexican government. Topographical engineers began conducting geological surveys and by 1853, a military fortress was started. One year later, a lighthouse was established (the first on the Pacific Coast) to guide ships through the Golden Gate.

A few years later, a military fort was erected on the island and in 1859, Alcatraz saw its first prisoners, a contingent of court-martialed, military convicts. Then in 1861, Alcatraz started to receive Confederate prisoners, thanks to its natural isolation created by the surrounding waters. Until the end of the Civil War, the number of prisoners here numbered from 15 to 50. They consisted of soldiers, Confederate privateers, and southern sympathizers. They were confined in the dark basement of the guardhouse and conditions were fairly grim. The men slept side-by-side, head to toe, lying on the stone floor of the basement. There was no running water, no heat and no latrines. Disease and infestations of lice spread from man to man and not surprisingly, overcrowding was a serious problem. They were often bound by six-foot chains attached to iron balls, fed bread and water and confined in sweat-boxes as punishment.

After the war ended, the fort was deemed obsolete and was no longer needed. The prison continued to be used though and soon, more buildings and cell houses were added. In the 1870s and 1880s, Indian chiefs and tribal leaders who refused to give into the white man were incarcerated on Alcatraz. They shared quarters with the worst of the military prisoners. The island became a shipping point for incorrigible deserters, thieves, rapists and repeated escapees.

In 1898, the Spanish-American War sent the prisoner population from less than 100 to over 450. The Rock became a holding pen for Spanish prisoners brought over from the Philippines. Around 1900 though, Alcatraz again became a disciplinary barracks for military prisoners. Ironically, it also served as a health resort for soldiers returning from the Phillipines and Cuba with tropical diseases. The overcrowding caused by a combination of criminals and recovering soldiers resulted in pardons to reduce the number of men housed on the island.

By 1902, the Alcatraz prison population averaged around 500 men per year, with many of the men serving sentences of two years or less. The wooden barracks on the island had fallen into a ramshackle state, thanks to the damp, salt air and so in 1904, work was begun to modernize the facility. Prisoner work crews began

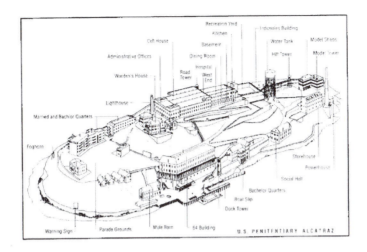

A diagram of the cell house and administrative offices on Alcatraz.
Featured in a manuscript called "Alcatraz Screw" by Velma Gregory.
Drawing by ArtWorks of San Anselmo, California and commissioned
by George H. Gregory (Courtesy of Rob and Anne Wlodarski)

extending the stockade wall and constructing a new mess hall, kitchen, shops, a library and a wash house. Work continued on the prison for the next several years and even managed to survive the Great Earthquake of 1906. The disaster left San Francisco in shambles and a large fissure opened up on Alcatraz, but left the buildings untouched. Prisoners from the heavily damaged San Francisco jail were temporarily housed on the island until the city's jail could be rebuilt.

Construction of the new buildings was completed in 1909 and in 1911, the facility was officially named the United States Disciplinary Barracks. In addition to Army prisoners, the Rock was also used to house seamen captured on German vessels during the First World War. Alcatraz was the Army's first long-term prison and it quickly gained a reputation for being a tough facility. There were strict rules and regulations with punishments ranging from loss of privileges to solitary confinement, restricted diet, hard labor and even a 12-pound ball and ankle chain.

Despite the stringent rules though, Alcatraz was still mainly a minimum-security facility. Inmates were given various work assignments, depending on how responsible they were. Many of them worked as general servants, cooking and cleaning for families of soldiers housed on the island. In many cases, the prisoners were even entrusted to care for the children of officers. However, this lack of strict security worked to the favor to those inmates who tried to escape. Most of those who tried for freedom never made it to the mainland and were forced to turn back and be rescued. Those who were not missed and did not turn back usually drowned in the harsh waters of the bay.

Other escape attempts were made by men who did not go into the water. During the great influenza epidemic of 1918, inmates stole flu masks and officer's uniforms and causally caught a military launch heading for the base at the Presidio. The convicts made it as far as Modesto, California before they were captured.

During the 1920s, Alcatraz gradually fell into disuse. The lighthouse keeper, a few Army personnel and the most hardened of the military prisoners were the only ones who remained on the island. The mostly empty buildings slowly crumbled, but a change was coming.

The social upheaval and the rampant crime of the 1920s and 1930s brought new life to Alcatraz. Attorney General Homer Cummings supported J. Edgar Hoover and the FBI in creating a new, escape-proof prison that would send fear into the hearts of criminals. They decided that Alcatraz would be the perfect location for such a penitentiary. In 1933, the facility was officially turned over to the Federal Bureau of Prisons and the Attorney General asked James A. Johnston of San Francisco to take over as warden of the new prison. He implemented a strict set and rules and regulations for the facility and selected the best available guards and officers from the federal penal system.

Construction was quickly started on the new project and practically the entire cellblock building was built atop the old Army fort. Part of the old Army prison was used but bars of hardened steel replaced the iron bars. Gun towers were erected at various points around the island and the cellblocks were equipped with catwalks, gun walks, electric locks, metal detectors, a well-stocked arsenal, barbed and cyclone wire fencing and even tear gas containers that were fitted into the ceiling of the dining hall and elsewhere. Apartments for the guards and their families were built on the old parade grounds and the lighthouse keeper's mansion was taken over for the warden's residence. Alcatraz had been turned into an impregnable fortress.

Wardens from prisons all over the country were polled and were permitted to send their most incorrigible inmates to the Rock. These included inmates with behavioral problems, those with a history of escape attempts and even high-profile inmates who were receiving privileges because of their status or notoriety. Each train that came from the various prisons seemed to have a celebrity on board. Among the first groups were inmates Al

Capone, Doc Barker (who was the last surviving member of the Ma Barker Gang), George "Machine Gun" Kelly, Robert "Birdman of Alcatraz" Stroud, and Floyd Hamilton (a gang member and driver for Bonnie & Clyde), and Alvin "Creepy" Karpis.

When they arrived on Alcatraz, the inmates were driven in a small transfer van to the top of the hill. They were processed in the basement area and provided with their basic amenities and a quick shower.

Al Capone arrived at the prison in August 1934. Upon his arrival, he quickly learned that while he may have once been famous, on Alcatraz, he was only a number. He made attempts to flaunt the power that he had enjoyed at the Federal prison in Atlanta and was used to the special benefits that he was awarded by guards and wardens alike. He was arrogant and unlike most of the other prisoners, was not a veteran of the penal system. He had only spent a short time in prison and his stay had been much different than for most other cons. Capone had possessed the ability to control his environment through wealth and power, but he was soon to learn that things were much different at Alcatraz.

Warden Johnston had a custom of meeting new prisoners when they arrived and he gave them a brief orientation. Johnston later wrote in his memoirs that he had little trouble recognizing Capone when he saw him. Capone was grinning and making comments to other prisoners as he stood in the lineup. When it became his turn to approach the warden, Johnston ignored him and simply gave him a standard prison number, just like all of the other men. During Capone's time on Alcatraz, he made a number of attempts to convince Johnston that he deserved special consideration. None of them were successful and at one point, Capone finally conceded that "it looks like Alcatraz has got me licked." And he wouldn't be the only one to feel that way.

Alcatraz was not a recreational prison. It was a place of penitence, just as the Quakers who had devised the American prison system had planned for all prisons to be. There were no trustees here. It was a place where the inmates had but five rights: food, clothing, a private cell, a shower once a week and the right to see a doctor.

Each of the cells in America's "first escape-proof prison" measured 4 x 8 feet, had a single fold-up bunk, a toilet, a desk, a chair and a sink. An inmate's day would begin at 6:30 in the morning, when he was awakened and then given 25 minutes to clean his cell and to stand and be counted. At 6:55, the individual tiers of cells would be opened and prisoners would march in a single file line to the mess hall. They were given 20 minutes to eat and then were marched out to line up for work assignments. The routine never varied and was completely methodical.

The main corridor of the prison was given the name Broadway by the inmates and the cells here were considered the least desirable. The ones on the bottom tier were always cold and damp and they were also the least private, since guards, inmates and staff members were always passing through this corridor. New prisoners were generally assigned to the second tier of B Block in a quarantine status for the first three months of their sentence.

The guards at Alcatraz were almost as hardened as the prisoners themselves. They numbered the inmates one to three, which was stunning considering that most prisons were at least one guard to every twelve inmates. Gun galleries had been placed at each end of the cell blocks and as many as 12 counts each day allowed the guards to keep very close tabs on the men on their watch. Because of the small number of total inmates at Alcatraz, the guards generally knew the inmates by name.

While the cells the prisoners lived in were barren at best, they must have seemed like luxury hotel rooms compared to the punishment cells. Here, the men were stripped of all but their basic right to food and even then, what they were served barely sustained the convict's life, let alone his health.

One place of punishment was the single Strip Cell, which was dubbed the Oriental. This dark, steel-encased cell had no toilet and no sink. There was only a hole in the floor that could be flushed from the outside. Inmates were placed in the cell with no clothing and were given little food. The cell had a standard set of bars with an expanded opening to pass food through, but a solid steel door enclosed the prisoner in total darkness. They were usually kept in this cell for 1-2 days. The cell was cold and completely bare, save for a straw sleeping mattress that the guards removed each morning. This cell was used a punishment for the most severe violations and was feared by the prison population.

The "Hole" was a similar type of cell. There were several of them and they were all located on the bottom tier of cells and were considered to be a severe punishment by the inmates. Mattresses were again taken away and prisoners were sustained by meals of bread and water, which was supplemented by a solid meal every third day. Steel doors also closed these cells off from the daylight, although a low wattage bulb was suspended from the ceiling. Inmates could spend up to 19 days here, completely silent and isolated from everyone. Time in the Hole usually meant psychological and sometimes even physical torture.

Usually, convicts who were thrown into the Hole for anything other than a minor infraction were beaten by the guards. The screams from the men being beaten in one of the four holes located on the bottom tier of D Block echoed throughout the block as though being amplified through a megaphone. When the inmates of D Block (which had been designated at a disciplinary unit by the warden) heard a fellow convict being worked over, they would start making noises that would be picked up in Blocks B and C and would then sound throughout the entire island.

Often when men emerged from the darkness and isolation of the Hole, they would be totally senseless and would end up in the prison's hospital ward, devoid of their sanity. Others came out with pneumonia and arthritis after spending days or weeks on the cold cement floor with no clothing. Some men never came out of the Hole at all.

And there were even worse places to be sent than the Hole. Located in front of unused A Block was a staircase that led down to a large steel door. Behind the door were catacomb-like corridors and stone archways that led to the sealed off gun ports from the days when Alcatraz was a fort. Fireplaces located in several of the rooms were never used for warmth, but to heat up cannonballs so that they would start fires after reaching their targets. Two of the other rooms located in this dank, underground area were dungeons.

Prisoners who had the misfortune of being placed in the dungeons were not only locked in, but also chained to the walls. Their screams could not be heard in the main prison. The only toilet they had was a bucket, which was emptied once each week. For food, they received two cups of water and one slice of bread each day. Every third day, they would receive a regular meal. The men were stripped of their clothing and their dignity as guards chained them to the wall in a standing position from six in the morning until six at night. In the darkest hours, they were given a blanket to sleep on. Thankfully, the dungeons were rarely used, but the dark cells of D Block, known as the Hole, were regularly filled.

Al Capone was in the Hole three times during his four and a half year stay at Alcatraz. The first years of Alcatraz were known as the "silent years" and during this period, the rules stated that no prisoners were allowed to speak to one another, sing, hum or whistle. Talking was forbidden in the cells, in the mess hall and even in the showers. The inmates were allowed to talk for three minutes during the morning and afternoon recreation yard periods and for two hours on weekends.

Capone, who remained arrogant for some time after his arrival, decided that the rule of silence should not apply to him. He ended up being sent to the Hole for two, 10-day stretches for talking to other inmates. He also spent a full 19 days on the Hole for trying to bribe a guard for information about the outside world. Prisoners were not allowed newspapers or magazines that would inform them of current events. Each time that Capone was sent to the Hole, he emerged a little worse for wear. Eventually, the Rock would break him completely.

Many of the prisoners who served time in Alcatraz ended up insane. Capone may have been one of them for time here was not easy on the ex-gangland boss. On one occasion, he got into a fight with another inmate in the recreation yard and was placed in isolation for eight days. Another time, while working in the prison basement, an inmate standing in line for a haircut exchanged words with Capone and then stabbed him with a pair of scissors. Capone was sent to the prison hospital but was released a few days later with a minor wound.

The attempts on his life, the no-talking rule, the beatings and the prison routine itself began to take their toll on Capone. After several fights in the yard, he was excused from his recreation periods, and, being adept with a banjo, joined a four-man prison band. The drummer in the group was "Machine-Gun" Kelly. Although gifts were not permitted for prisoners on the Rock, musical instruments were and Capone's wife sent him a banjo shortly after he was incarcerated. After band practice, Capone always returned immediately to his cell, hoping to stay away from the other convicts.

Occasionally, guards reported that he would refuse to leave his cell to go to the mess hall and eat. They would often find him crouched down in the corner of his cell like an animal. On other occasions, he would mumble to himself or babble in baby talk or simply sit on his bed and strum little tunes on his banjo. Years later, another inmate recalled that Capone would sometimes stay in his cell and make his bunk over and over again.

After more than three years on the Rock, Capone was on the edge of total insanity. He spent the last year of his sentence in the hospital ward, undergoing treatment for an advanced case of syphilis. Most of the time he spent in the ward, he spent playing his banjo. His last day on Alcatraz was January 6, 1939. He was then transferred to the new Federal prison at Terminal Island near Los Angeles. When he was paroled, he became a recluse at his Palm

Island, Florida estate. He died, broken and insane, in 1947.

And Al Capone was far from the only man to surrender his sanity to Alcatraz. In 1937 alone, 14 of the prisoners went rampantly insane and that does not include the men who slowly became stir crazy from the brutal conditions of the place. To Warden Johnston, mental illness was nothing more than an excuse to get out of work. As author Richard Winer once wrote, "it would be interesting to know what the warden thought of Rube Persful."

Persful was a former gangster and bank robber who was working in one of the shops, when he picked up a hatchet, placed his left hand on a block of wood and while laughing maniacally, began hacking off the fingers on his hand. Then, he placed his right hand on the block and pleaded with a guard to chop off those fingers as well. Persful was placed in the hospital, but was not declared insane.

An inmate named Joe Bowers slashed his own throat with a pair of broken eyeglasses. He was given first aid and then was thrown into the Hole. After his release, he ran away from his work area and scaled a chain-link fence, fully aware that the guards would shoot him. They opened fire and his body fell 75 feet down to the rocks below the fence.

Ed Wutke, a former sailor who had been sent to Alcatraz on murder charges, managed to fatally slice through his jugular vein with the blade from a pencil sharpener.

These were not the only attempts at suicide and mutilation either. It was believed that more men suffered mental breakdowns at Alcatraz, by percentage, than at any other Federal prisons.

In 1941, inmate Henry Young went on trail for the murder of a fellow prisoner and his accomplice in a failed escape attempt, Rufus McCain. Young's attorney claimed that Alcatraz guards had frequently beaten his client and that he had endured long periods of extreme isolation. While Young was depicted as sympathetic, he was actually a difficult inmate who often provoked fights with other prisoners. He was considered a violent risk and he later murdered two guards during an escape attempt. After that, Young and his eventual victim,

McCain, spent nearly 22 months in solitary confinement.

After the two men returned to the normal prison population, McCain was assigned to the tailoring shop and Young to the furniture shop, located directly upstairs. On December 3, 1940 Young waited until just after a prisoner count and then when a guard's attention was diverted, he ran downstairs and stabbed McCain. The other man went into shock and he died five hours later. Young refused to say why he had killed the man.

During his trial, Young's attorney claimed that because Young was held in isolation for so long, he could not be held responsible for his actions. He had been subjected to cruel and unusual punishment and because of this, his responses to hostile situations had become desperately violent.

The attorney subpoenaed Warden Johnston to testify about the prison's conditions and policies and in addition, several inmates were also called to recount the state of Alcatraz. The prisoners told of being locked in the dungeons and of being beaten by the guards. They also testified to knowing several inmates who had gone insane because of such treatment. The jury ended up sympathizing with Young's case and he was convicted of a manslaughter charge that only added a few years on this original sentence.

After the trial, he was transferred to the Medical Center for Federal Prisoners in Springfield, Missouri. After serving his Federal sentence, he was sent to the Washington State Penitentiary and was paroled in 1972. He had spent nearly 40 years in prison. He later disappeared, and it is unknown whether he is still alive today.

During the 29 years that Alcatraz was in operation, there were over 14 escape attempts in which 34 different men risked their lives to try and make it off the Rock. Almost all of the men were either killed or recaptured. Only one of the men was known to have made it ashore. John Paul Scott was recaptured when he was found shivering in the rocks near the Golden Gate Bridge. As for the men who vanished, it was believed that most of them succumbed to the cold water and the always churning currents that moved past the island. Although no bodies were ever recovered, the authorities always assumed that the men had drowned and marked the cases as closed.

Of all of the escape attempts though, two of them left a lasting mark on the history of the island. The most traumatic and violent of the two took place in 1946. It was later dubbed the Battle of Alcatraz and it began as a well-planned and well-organized break-out from the "escape-proof" prison.

In May 1946, six inmates captured a gun cage, obtained prison keys and took over a cell house in less than an hour. The breakout attempt might have succeeded if not for the fact that a guard, Bill Miller, didn't return one of the keys to the gun cage as soon as he finished using it, as was required by prison regulations. The strange twist of fate completely disrupted the escape attempt. When the cons captured the gun cage, they found all of the keys except for the one that would let them out of the cell building. This was the key that Miller failed to return to the guard cage. The breakout was grounded before it even began.

But the prisoners, Bernard Coy, Joe Cretzer, and Marvin Hubbard, Sam Shockley, Miran Thompson, and Clarence Carnes, would not give up. They took a number of guards hostage and before the escape attempts was over, three of the guards were dead and others were wounded. Two of them were murdered in cold blood in cells 402 and 403, which were later changed to C-102 and C-104.

Thousands of spectators watched from San Francisco as U.S. Marines invaded the island and barraged the cell block with mortars and grenades. The helpless inmates inside of the building took refuge behind water-soaked mattresses and tried to stay close to the floor and out of the path of the bullets that riddled the cells. But even after realizing that they could not escape, the six would-be escapees decided to fight it out.

Warden Johnston, unable to get a report on how many convicts were actually involved in the battle, came to believe that the safety of San Francisco itself might be at risk. With the entire prison under siege, he called for aid from the Navy, the Coast Guard, as well as the Marines. Before it was all over, two Navy destroyers, two Air Force planes, a Coast Guard cutter, a company of Marines, Army officers, police units, and guards from Leavenworth and San Quentin descended on the island.

The fighting lasted for two days. With no place to hide from the constant gunfire, Cretzer, Coy and Hubbard climbed into a utility corridor for safety. The other three men returned to their cells, hoping they would not be identified as participants in the attempt. In the bloody aftermath, Cretzer, Coy and Hubbard were killed in the corridor from bullets and shrapnel from explosives. Thompson and Shockley were later executed in the gas chamber at San Quentin and Carnes received a sentence of life, plus 99 years. His life was spared because he helped some of the wounded hostages. The cell building was heavily damaged and took months to repair.

While this may be the most violent escape attempt from Alcatraz, it is by all means not the most famous. This attempt was that of Frank Morris and brothers Clarence and John Anglin. In 1962, a fellow prisoner named Allen West helped the trio to devise a clever plan to construct a raft, inflatable life vests and human-like dummies that could be used to fool the guards during head counts. Over a several month period, the men used tools stolen from work sites to chip away at the vent shafts in their cells. They fabricated the life vests, the rafts and the dummies. They also ingeniously created replicated grills that hid the chipped away cement around the small vents. The quality of the human heads and faked grills was remarkable as they used only paint kits and a soap and concrete powder to make them. They also collected hair from the barbershop to make the dummies more lifelike. These painstaking preparations took over six months.

On the night of June 11, 1962, immediately following the head count at 9:30, Morris and the Anglin's scooted through the vents and scaled the utility shafts to the upper levels. Once they reached the roof, they climbed through a ventilator duct and made it to the edge of the building. After descending pipes along the cement wall, all three climbed over a 15-foot fence and made it to the island's shore, where they inflated the rafts and vests. They set out into the cold waters of the bay and were never seen again.

The next morning, when one of the prisoners failed to rise for the morning count, a guard jammed his club through the cell bars at the man. To his shock, a fake head rolled off the bunk and landed on the floor!

Almost 40 years later, it is still unknown whether or not the prisoners made a successful escape. The story has been dramatized in several books and was made into a gripping film starring Clint Eastwood. The FBI actively pursued the case but never found any worthwhile leads.

After this last escape attempt, the days of the prison were numbered. Ironically, the frigid waters around the island, which had long prevented escape, were believed to be the leading ruin of the prison. After the escape of Morris and the Anglin's, the prison was examined because of the deteriorating conditions of the structure, caused mostly by the corrosive effects of the salt water around it. In addition, budget cuts had recently forced security measures at the prison to become more lax. On top of that, the exorbitant cost of running the place continued to increase and over $5 million was going to be needed for renovations. According to U.S. Attorney General Robert Kennedy, the prison was no longer necessary to have open.

On March 23, 1963, Alcatraz closed it doors for good. After that, the island was essentially abandoned while various groups tried to decide what to do with it. Then, in 1969, a large group of American Indians landed on the island and declared that it was Native American property. They had great plans for the island, which included a school and a Native American cultural center. The Indians soon had the attention of the media and the government and a number of meetings were held about the fate of Alcatraz.

The volume of visitors to the island soon became overwhelming. Somehow, during the talks, the island had become a haven for the homeless and the less fortunate. The Indians were soon faced with the problem of no natural resources and the fact that food and water had to be brought over from the mainland. The situation soon became so desperate that island occupants were forced to take drastic measures to survive. In order to raise money for supplies, they began stripping copper wire and pipes from the island buildings to sell as scrap metal. A tragedy occurred around this same time when Yvonne Oakes, the daughter of one of the key Indian activists, fell to her death from the third story window. The Oakes family left Alcatraz and never returned.

Then, during the evening hours of June 1, 1970, a fire was started and raged out of control. It damaged several of the buildings and destroyed the Warden's residence, the lighthouse keeper's home and even badly damaged the historic lighthouse itself.

Tension now developed between Federal officials and the Indians as the government blamed the activists for the fire. The press, which had been previously sympathetic toward the Native Americans, now turned against them and began to publish stories about beatings and assaults that were allegedly occurring on the island. Support for the Indians now disintegrated, especially in light of the fact that the original activists had already left Alcatraz. Those who remained were seen as little more than squatters. On June 11, 1971, the Coast Guard, along with 20 U.S. Marshals descended on the island and removed the remaining residents. Alcatraz was empty once more.

In 1972, Congress created the Golden Gate National Recreation Area and Alcatraz Island fell under the purview of the National Park Service. It was opened to the public in the fall of 1973 and has become today one of the most popular of America's park sites.

During the day, the old prison is a bustling place, filled with tour guides and visitors; but at night, the building is filled with the inexplicable. Many believe that the energy of those who came to serve time on the Rock still remains, that Alcatraz is an immense haunted house, a place where strange things can and do happen today!

Every visitor who arrives by boat on Alcatraz follows the same path once walked by the criminals who came to do time on the Rock. The tourists who come here pass through the warden's office and the visiting room and eventually enter the cell house. After passing the double steel doors, a visitor can see just past C Block. If they look opposite the visiting room, they will find a metal door that looks as though it was once welded shut. Although the tour guides don't usually mention it, behind that door is the utility corridor where Coy, Cretzer and Hubbard were killed by grenades and bullets in 1946.

It was also behind this door where a night watchman heard strange, clanging sounds in 1976. He opened the door and peered down the dark corridor, shining his flashlight on the maze of pipes and conduits. He could see nothing and there were no sounds. When he closed the door, the noises started again. Again, the door was opened up, but there was still nothing that could be causing the sounds. The night watchman did not believe in ghosts, so he shut the door again and continued on his way. Some have wondered if the eerie noises may have been the reason why the door was once welded shut? Since that time, this utility corridor has come to be recognized as one of the most haunted spots in the prison.

Other night watchmen who have patrolled this cell house, after the last of the tourist boats have left for the day, say that they have heard the sounds of what appear to be men running from the upper tiers. Thinking that an intruder is inside the prison, the watchmen have investigated the sounds, but always find nothing.

One Park Service employee told author Richard Winer (anonymously, of course) that she had been working one rainy afternoon when the sparse number of tourists were not enough to keep all of the guides busy. She went for a walk in front of A Block and was just past the door that led down to the dungeons when she heard a loud scream from the bottom of the stairs. She ran away without looking to see if anyone was down there.

When Winer asked why she didn't report the incident, she replied "I didn't dare mention it because the day before, everyone was ridiculing another worker who reported hearing men's voices coming from the hospital ward and when he checked the ward, it was empty."

Several of the guides and rangers also expressed to Winer a strangeness about one of the hole cells: number 14D. "There's a feeling of sudden intensity that comes from spending more than a few minutes around that cell," one of them said.

Another guide also spoke up about that particular cell. "That cell, 14D, is always cold. It's even colder than the other three dark cells. Sometimes it gets warm out here—so hot that you have to take your jacket off. The temperature inside the cell house can be in the 70s, yet 14D is still cold…so cold that you need a jacket if you spend any time in it."

Oddly, the tour guides were not the only ones to have strange experiences in that particular cell. Authors Rob and Anne Wlodarksi were able to interview several former guards from the prison and one of them told of some pretty terrifying incidents that took place near the holes, and in particular, Cell 14D.

During the guard's stint in the middle 1940s, an inmate was locked in the cell for some forgotten infraction. According to the officer, the inmate began screaming within seconds of being locked in. He claimed that some creature with "glowing eyes" was locked in with him. As tales of a ghostly presence wandering the nearby corridor were a continual source of practical jokes among the guards, no one took the convict's cries of being attacked very seriously.

The man's screaming continued on into the night until finally, there was silence. The following day, guards inspected the cell and they found the convict dead. A horrible expression had been frozen onto the man's face and there were clear marks of hands around his throat! The autopsy revealed that the strangulation could not have been self-inflicted. Some believed that he might have been choked by one of the guards, who had been fed up with the man's screaming, but no one ever admitted it.

A few of the officers blamed something else for the man's death. They believed that the killer had been the spirit of a former inmate. To add to the mystery, on the day following the tragedy, several guards who were performing a head count noticed that there were too many men in the lineup. Then, at the end of the line, they saw the face of the convict who had recently been strangled in the Hole! As they all looked on in stunned silence, the figure abruptly vanished.

When authors Richard Winer and Nancy Osborn visited Alcatraz, they ventured down to this cell with a park ranger. As Osborn entered the cramped chamber, she immediately felt strong vibrations coming from inside. Winer and the ranger followed her inside and both experienced a tingling sensation in their hands and arms. They were convinced that something else was in the cell with them. According to the writers, the strongest energy seemed to come from the far corner of the cell. Here, naked and frightened prisoners would huddle in the darkness. Osborn stated that she had never felt such energy in one spot.

And that's not all. It may come as no surprise to many readers to learn that this same cell was the one where Henry Young was confined after his attempted jailbreak with Rufus McCain. He was confined here in the darkness for almost two years, and when he emerged, he was mad from the horrible isolation that he had endured. Just 11 days later, he killed McCain in the prison shop. Young found sympathy from the jury as it was said that his years of confinement in the Hole had deprived him of everything spiritual and human. Did Henry Young leave a piece of his insanity behind in Cell 14D, or did something already there give a piece of itself to Young?

If, as many believe, ghosts return to haunt the places where they suffered traumatic experiences when they were alive, then Alcatraz must be loaded with spirits.

According to Rob and Anne Wlodarksi, a number of guards who served between 1946 and 1963 experienced strange happenings on Alcatraz. From the grounds of the prison to the caverns beneath the buildings, there was often talk of people sobbing and moaning, inexplicable smells, cold spots and spectral apparitions. Even guests and families who lived on the island claimed to occasionally see the ghostly forms of prisoners and even phantom soldiers.

Phantom gunshots were known to send seasoned guards cringing in the belief that the prisoners had escaped and had obtained weapons. There was never an explanation. A deserted laundry room would sometimes fill with the smell of smoke, even though nothing was burning. The guards would be sent running from the room, only to return later and find that the air was clear.

Even Warden Johnston, who did not believe in ghosts, once encountered the unmistakable sound of a person sobbing while he accompanied some guests on a tour of the prison. He swore that the sounds came from inside of the dungeon walls. The strange sounds were followed by an ice-cold wind that swirled through the entire group. He could offer no explanation for the weird events.

And since the prison has been closed down, the ghostly happenings seem to have intensified. Famous psychic Peter James went to Alcatraz during the taping of a television show in 1992. During the filming, a number of the staff members confirmed the hauntings at the prison. Many of them had experienced the bizarre crashing sounds, cell doors that mysteriously closed and the intense feeling of being watched.

Peter James walked through the prison, hoping to get impressions about various parts of the place. At one point, he began to pick up the voices of souls that had been driven mad and unusual vibrations of abuse and pain. In one particular cell, he sensed that a man had been murdered. Having no idea of the history of that particular cell, he didn't realize that one of the guards who was killed during the 1946 escape attempt was shot down in that room.

Renowned ghost hunter and psychic Richard Senate also spent

the night on Alcatraz as part of a radio promotion. He chose to stay in Al Capone's old cell. According to Senate, emotions seemed to drip from every corner of the prison as the night progressed. He and another psychic visited a number of locations where rangers had reported marching feet and other strange sounds but nothing out of the ordinary happened.

Finally, Senate locked himself inside of the one of the Hole cells, 12D, where there have been reports of an angry ghost being present. As soon as the steel door clanged shut, Senate said that he felt icy fingers creep up the back of his neck. Every hair on his body seemed to stand on end! And while Senate found no trace of Al Capone in his former cell, there is a possibility that the famous gangster managed to leave a mark on the old prison anyway.

As Richard Winer and Nancy Osborn left Alcatraz on a foggy afternoon in the late 1970s, a Park Service employee approached them and asked if they were the ones writing the book about ghosts at Alcatraz?

"I overheard some of your conversations back on the island," he explained. "I myself heard something in the cell house early one morning. It was down in the shower room. A con killed his homosexual lover in there once—right in front of a guard. I guess it was a broken romance thing."

The man paused in his story as the ferryboat back to San Francisco lurched on the rough water of the bay. "It's kind of strange what I heard," he continued. "It was like banjo music. The room was empty, but I definitely heard banjo music coming from there. Maybe back in the days when it was a fort or Army stockade, there was some guy here who played that instrument."

As the boat continued on toward San Francisco, Winer said that he looked back at the Rock, which was now completely enshrouded in fog. "I thought of Al Capone during the most traumatic days of his life," he wrote," when, rather than risk going out to the exercise yard with the other inmates, he sat in the shower room strumming on his banjo."

And perhaps he sits there still, this lonesome and broken spirit, still plucking at the strings of a spectral musical instrument that vanished decades ago. For tour guides and rangers, who walk the corridors of the prison alone, still claim to hear and an occasional tune echoing through the abandoned building. Is it Al Capone? Or could it be merely another of the countless ghosts who continue to haunt this place, year after year.

YANKEE JIM AND OTHERS

The Hauntings of the Whaley House

There are few houses in America with so active a supernatural history as the Whaley House in San Diego, California. For decades, the residents and curators of the house have spoken of strange happenings, ghostly events and eerie experiences. Paranormal investigators, tourists and curiosity-seekers have all claimed an assortment of haunted events and even the United States government has gotten into the act. In the 1960s, the house was designated as haunted by the U.S. Commerce Department. It is one of only two houses to gain such a designation in California, the other being the Winchester House in San Jose.

But is there any truth to the reports of hauntings and ghostly incidents? Or are the stories merely the result of overactive imaginations and clever marketing? You be the judge, but I'll warn the skeptical reader in advance…The Whaley House may just have you believing in ghosts!

When Thomas Whaley first visited San Diego in 1849, the city was little more than a California desert outpost. El Pueblo de San Diego, as it was called by its Spanish residents, was a frontier settlement that has been founded around a mission in 1769. The legendary Padre Junipero Serra founded the San Diego de Alcala mission and by 1820, a cluster of homes and buildings began to grow around it. The community grew at the base of Presidio Hill, the site of the church, and what is now known as the historic district of Old Town.

The American flag was raised over the plaza here in 1846, ending Mexican rule over the region. Thomas Whaley arrived three years later and found the small town to be little more than rough adobe buildings and some wood-frame structures that had been erected by the first Americans to settle here. He didn't stay long. Whaley had been sent to California by the company that he worked for to start a mercantile business. Not finding what he wanted in San Diego, he went on to San Francisco instead. A few years later though, in 1851, he returned to San Diego and started a general store on the plaza. He took a partner, Thomas Crosthwaite, who later became the country clerk and the sheriff.

Whaley began designing his red brick home in 1855, drawing up plans for a Greek Revival mansion, a style that had never been seen in old California. That same year, he returned to New York and married Anna Eloise De Launay bringing her back with him to California.

But prior to the construction of the house, another event would take place on the site where the house would someday be. This event would play an integral role in the haunted history of the house that would later be built here. The lingering effects of the event are still being felt today!

Who exactly "Yankee Jim" Robinson may have been remains a mystery to this day. Descriptions of the man vary, but most seem to agree that he was a tall, mysterious drifter with blond hair and a reckless disposition. Some historians believe that he may have been a man named Santiago Robinson, who hailed from the island of Bermuda and who came to California in 1842. Regardless of who he was and where he came from, he was generally regarded as a shady character in the region.

On August 13, 1852, Robinson slipped aboard a schooner called the Plutus that was anchored in the San Diego harbor. The captain of the ship, James Keating, was on shore at the time and spotted Robinson rowing toward his vessel. He called out, believing that someone was trying to steal his ship, which was a hanging offense at the time. When Robinson did not answer his hail, he fired several shots at him but missed both the man and his rowboat. However, Robinson did start for shore and he headed inland toward a stand of scrub oak.

Keating waiting until the following morning to make a report to the authorities. Sheriff Reiner rounded up a posse and soon arrested two men who were thought to be Robinson's accomplices, William Harris (alias William Harney) and James Grayson Loring. Both were charged with grand larceny. The search continued for Robinson though. The sheriff warned the residents of False Bay, where Robinson put ashore, to be on the lookout for a tall man in a red shirt.

On Saturday, August 14, a man answering the fugitive's description knocked on the door of a Mexican couple in a settlement known as Rose's Ranch. He asked for something to eat, but quickly left when the residents began acting nervous. He ran from the house, but the Mexican man followed him. He managed to throw a lasso around the suspected fugitive and he hit him over the head with an old Spanish artillery sword. Bleeding and unconscious, Robinson was thrown over a horse and was taken to the sheriff's office.

Three days later, Yankee Jim was tried and was found guilty of grand larceny. On August 18, he was sentenced to hang exactly one month later. His alleged accomplices were let off with lighter sentences. Incidentally, Robinson almost didn't make it to the appointed date with the hangman. There was no jail in San Diego and on the day of the sentencing hearing, a group of citizens gathered outside and began discussing whether they should just string the convicted thief up on the spot. A few rational voices prevailed, and local men took turns guarding the prisoner until his appointed day of execution.

On September 18, 1852, Yankee Jim Robinson was placed in the back of a buckboard wagon and one end of the rope was knotted around his neck. The other was tied to the crude gallows that had been constructed. Robinson was asked if he had any final words, and the outlaw launched into a long speech that silenced the crowd of spectators. After more than 30 minutes, he was still talking! Finally, the frustrated sheriff had had enough. He gave the nod, and a crop was laid across the back of the horses pulling the wagon. They jerked forward and Robinson was thrown from the wagon, cutting him off in mid-sentence.

But a terrible error had been made! Robinson was a very tall man and the rough gallows had been built to hang much shorter criminals. Instead of breaking his neck when he fell, Robinson's toes actually scraped the ground. His boots kicked and scuffed at the earth, churning up a small cloud of dust as he danced his last dance. Minutes passed and his face turned red, then a ghastly shade of purple. The crowd watched in horrified silence as Robinson slowly strangled to death.

Among the spectators at the hanging was Thomas Whaley. Four years later, he would build his home on the same spot where Robinson had suffered a terrible death. And Whaley would find that Yankee Jim Robinson would not rest in peace.

In September 1855, Thomas Whaley purchased the old execution grounds and began making plans for a grand home to be built on the site. Construction began in May 1856 and was completed one year later.

The construction of the house called for materials that were not used in southern California, but Whaley wanted to avoid the high costs of having them shipped from the east. With that in mind, he decided to supply his own. He established a brickyard three hundred yards from the home site to create bricks for the exterior of the structure. He obtained roofing tar from the La Brea pits in Los Angeles and mixed plaster from horsehair, river sand and crushed seashells.

The main house contained seven rooms and included a kitchen, a parlor, a music room, a library and four bedrooms on the second floor that could be reached by a wide staircase. Whaley also built a granary that was later connected to the house. His wife, Anna, had a fine garden planted behind the house that was filled with a variety of roses.

It was not long before the Whaley House became the social center of the local American community. Politicians and citizens often came here for meetings and discussions and the house played host to overnight guests and visiting dignitaries. Presidents Ulysses S. Grant and Benjamin Harrison are known to have stayed the night, and Union General Thomas Sedgwick was headquartered here during the Civil War. Except for a period of about six years, when Thomas Whaley traveled to Alaska and established the city of Sitka, members of the Whaley family lived in the house as late as 1953.

Perhaps the most notable event to occur in the house took place in the late 1860s, when Whaley allowed the house to be used as the San Diego County Courthouse. He bore the expense of remodeling the granary and turning it into a courtroom, charging the county only $65 per year for rent.

This was a period of great unrest in San Diego and conflicts were brewing between the residents of the Old Town district and a development that was being referred to as New Town. There was some sentiment among officials that a bigger courthouse should be built in the city and located in a newer part of town. Thomas Whaley, along with many others, disagreed. The arguments became even more heated in the days to come and tensions flared to the point that martial law was declared in the city. Even though guards were posted at the courthouse, a group of armed men, led by county clerk and recorder Colonel Chalmers Scott, broke into the Whaley House on the night of March 31, 1871. They proceeded to steal all of the county records and wrecked the office. Whaley was away on a business trip to San Francisco at the time, and Anna was actually threatened at gunpoint when she walked in to investigate the noises in the county offices.

The intruders transported the records to the Wells Fargo building at Sixth and G Streets, which would end up being used as the courthouse until a new one was built in 1872. Whaley was left with a vandalized home, an empty courthouse and six months of unpaid rent that was never collected. He went to his grave in 1890, still angry over the poor treatment that he received from the county. He was never even reimbursed for the damages done to his home by Colonel Scott and his men.

But when did the Whaley House first come to be considered haunted? The first to suggest that ghosts lingered in the house was Corinne Lillian Whaley, Thomas and Anna's youngest daughter, who lived in the house until her death in 1953. According to the stories, she rarely ever went up to the second floor of the house and wrote that a force of some sort simply didn't want her up there. She told her friends that she had so many ghostly experiences in the house that she seldom slept peacefully at night.

Lillian was always a gracious host and frequently invited friends to visit here. The same strange experiences that she complained about also frightened her visitors. Many of them reported that when they would be visiting in the parlor, they would hear the sound of a man's boots walking back and forth upstairs. They often assumed that someone else was there, despite the fact that Lillian tried to ignore the sounds. As the day would wear on, they would realize that no living person was on the second floor.

Lillian often told people that it was Yankee Jim Robinson who haunted the house! She believed that only the hanged man's boots could walk the house and disturb the peace of those who tried to live on the spot where he was killed. Future staff members in the house have agreed and Robinson's ghost still does not rest, even after all of these years!

The Whaley House was scheduled for demolition in 1956. By this time, it had become run down, and little thought was given to its historic signifigance. A group of local citizens refused to let this happen, and they formed a Historic Shrine Foundation to buy the land and the building. San Diego County eventually agreed to preserve the house as a museum and to restore it to its former glory.

June Reading was one of the original members of the group who rallied to save the Whaley House and she spent more than 30 years as the museum's director. Even before the restoration of the house was completed in 1960, she had her first experience with one of the several ghosts believed to haunt the house.

One afternoon, she and a few men from the historical society were moving some large pieces of furniture into the house from storage. She went to the back door and opened it for the furniture to be brought inside. As the truck was backed up, Reading and some of the people inside heard the distinct sound of someone walking across the floor upstairs. It sounded like a big man who was wearing boots and his heels sounded loudly on the bare wood floors. They were sure that it was one of the helpers who was upstairs, but Reading didn't recall anyone going up there.

"I started up the stairs and got about halfway up," she recalled. "I did call out but I didn't get any response. Well, I turned around and came back down. I told them there was nobody up there. They looked kind of smug, then one of them said, 'Well, maybe old Thomas Whaley's come back to look the house over.' We all kind of laughed, but from that time on." Reading smiled and shrugged her shoulders.

Phantom footsteps have not been the only incidents to bother the staff either. A tour guide was eating lunch one day when she heard noises upstairs. She got up to investigate and saw a man wearing a frock coat at the top of the stairs. He was turned away from her and before she could call to him, he disappeared.

June Reading once saw what she believed to be the ghost of Thomas Whaley near the stairs on the second floor. She was in the house on a Sunday afternoon and a guide called her to see something. She looked up the stairs and saw a man in a long coat and a black hat with a wide brim. "He was all by himself, right in the middle of the landing," she said. "I couldn't believe my eyes."

Whaley has also been seen strolling through the garden at the back of the house and makes himself known in other ways as well. Some of the staff members are sometimes overwhelmed by the smell of cigar smoke. Whaley was known for smoking a distinctive type of Havana cigars. The odor is sometimes so strong that staff members have been forced to go outside for fresh air. In addition, the smell of baking food sometimes wafts through the house, as well as a strong woman's perfume. Jessie Keller, a longtime volunteer at the house, once said that the perfume was occasionally so heavy that it made her sick. She believed the perfume was connected to Anna Whaley because it is frequently encountered in her parlor. Anna Whaley has also made appearances in other ways too.

One of the most frequently recounted experiences in the house happened to television personality Regis Philbin. He visited the house in 1964, after its reputation was already becoming known. Before he had come, other famous would-be investigators visited the house, including *Twilight Zone* host and writer Rod Serling and actor Vincent Price. According to Gary Beck, the vice president of the California Historic Shrine Foundation, Philbin was a local television personality in San Diego at the time and decided to do a show on the Whaley House. "Regis thought it would make an interesting feature for his show but wound up getting the pants scared off him," Beck said.

Philbin reportedly came to the house and was accompanied by a very tough, gung-ho Marine officer who carried a gun and was not scared easily. At about 2:30 in the morning, the two of them were seated on a sofa and saw what they were convinced was the ghost of Anna Whaley coming toward them in a green haze. She materialized in the study, floated into the music room and into the parlor where Philbin and his friend were sitting. Philbin shined a flashlight at the apparition and she suddenly vanished.

"At that point, he said to the Marine: I've had enough, let's get out of here!" Gary Beck added.

While the ghostly reputation of the house exploded after this much-publicized encounter, accounts of Anna Whaley's ghost date back to even earlier times. June Reading remembered a story told to her by a local man who had delivered newspapers in the neighborhood when he was a boy. He said that he was would often stand across the street from the house in the early morning hours and wait for a delivery truck to drop off his bundle of papers. He said that he would often glance across the street and see a lady in a blue dress standing in an uncurtained window. The house was vacant at the time. In recent times, there have also been reports of a rocking chair in Anna's former bedroom that tends to rock back and forth on its own.

Anna Whaley may not be the only female ghost to haunt the house either. One of them is thought to be one of the Whaley daughters. In August 1976, June Reading reported that an unusually high amount of static electricity was plaguing the house. One afternoon, a tourist was in one of the upstairs bedrooms and reported a swarm of "tiny, glowing objects" flying about the room. She said that they looked like fireflies and that one of them fell to the floor and continued to glow.

Reading called the California Parapsychology Foundation about the mysterious orbs of light. Several group members came and conducted an investigation of the house and told her that they believed the lights were ectoplasm and that if they all came together, they would form a figure from the spirit world. Believe it or not, June Reading discovered they were right! A few days after their visit, she walked into the bedroom to discover the life-sized figure of a young woman at the end of the bed. She said that it looked as though the apparition was folding clothes or perhaps packing a suitcase. The scene lasted only a few seconds and then blinked out of sight.

Another encountered spirit in the house is the small ghost child who is known as the Washburn Girl. She was a playmate of the Whaley children and one day while she was running to join her friends in the backyard, she ran into a low hanging clothesline, fell and struck her head on a rock. She died in Thomas Whaley's arms as he carried her into the house. She has reportedly haunted the place ever since.

"She plays around on the stairs and moves things in the kitchen," June Reading stated. "One of the reasons we closed off the kitchen was that the meat cleaver on the rack in there would move. People were fascinated with that. We allowed visitors to walk through the kitchen, but we finally decided that it wasn't good practice. Everyone thought there was something mechanical that caused the meat cleaver to move."

The Whaley House continues to be haunted today, and strange occurrences are reported here on an almost weekly basis. Visitors who come here are apt to encounter just about anything, from unexplained scents to phantom footsteps, childish laughter, a piano that plays on its own, chairs that move by themselves, a ghostly dog or even the apparitions of Yankee Jim, Anna or even Thomas Whaley himself!

The house continues to hold a place in the west's haunted history but staff members will tell you that there is nothing to be scared of here. "It's not like there are poltergeists or furniture flies around or anything anyone needs to be afraid of," assures Wayne Cook, the curator of the house. "It's just a very old, very lovely house."

But that doesn't mean the place is not haunted! "I'm sure that other haunted structures abound," Cook adds, "before you make the government list you've got to have a history. This house certainly qualifies."

Chapter Five

HEARTLAND HAUNTINGS

Haunted History of Franklin Castle

For years, the gothic mansion known as Franklin Castle has been called the most haunted house in Ohio. During its long and strange history, the ghost stories have become an integral part of the lore. For years, tales have been told of doors that explode off their hinges, lights that spin on their own, electric circuits that behave erratically, the inexplicable sounds of a baby crying and even a woman in black who has been seen staring forlornly from a tiny window in the front tower room.

There are many ghosts here, the legends say. But what dark deeds caused this house to become so haunted? Are the stories of the murders committed here actually true, or the stuff of legend?

Franklin Castle is an eerie structure of dark and foreboding stone that has long been considered a spooky place by architects and the general public alike. There are over thirty rooms in the castle's four stories and the roof is designed in steep gables that give the place its gothic air. Secret passages honeycomb the house and sliding panels hide the doorways to these hidden corridors. It is said that a thirteen-year-old girl was once murdered in one of these hallways by her uncle because he believed her to be insane. In the front tower, it is told that a bloody ax murder once took place and it was here that one of the former owners found a secret cabinet that contained human bones. The Deputy coroner of Cleveland, Dr. Lester Adelson, who examined the bones shortly after they were found in January 1975, judged them to be of someone who had been dead for a very, very long time. Did they date back to the years of the original owners of the house?

It is hard to separate fact from fiction at Franklin Castle but we do know that a German immigrant named Hannes Tiedemann built the mansion in 1865. Tiedemann was a former barrel-maker and wholesale grocer who had gone into banking. This new source of wealth allowed him to spare no expense in building the house and he soon moved in with his wife, Luise. Over the next few years, Luise gave birth to a son, August, and a daughter, Emma, but life in the mansion was never really happy. By 1881, it had become tragic.

On January 16, fifteen-year-old Emma died from diabetes. In those days, death from the disease came as a horrible, lingering starvation for which there was no cure. A short time later, Tiedemann's elderly mother, Wiebeka, also died in the house. Over the next three years, the Tiedemanns buried three children, one of them just eleven-days-old. Rumors began to spread that there may have been more to these deaths than was first apparent.

To take his wife's mind off the family tragedies, Tiedemann enlisted the services of a prominent architectural firm to design some additions to the mansion. It was during this expansion that the secret passages, concealed rooms and hidden doors were added to the house. Gas lighting was also installed throughout the building and many of the fixtures are still visible today. A large ballroom was also added that ran the length of the entire house and turrets and gargoyles were also incorporated into the design, making it appear even more like a castle.

The hidden passages in the house also hide many legends. At the rear of the house is a trap door that leads to a tunnel that goes nowhere. Another hidden room once contained a liquor still, left over from the Prohibition era. During the 1920s, the house was allegedly used as a speakeasy and warehouse for illegal liquor. The most gruesome secret uncovered in the house came from another of the hidden rooms. Here, an occupant found literally dozens of human baby skeletons. It was suggested that they may have been the victims of a doctor's botched experiments or even medical specimens, but no one knew for sure. The medical examiner simply stated that they were "old bones."

On March 24, 1895, Luise died at the age of 57 from what was said to be liver trouble. Rumors continued to spread about the many untimely deaths in the Tiedemann family, especially when Hannes married again a few years later. By that time, he had sold the castle to a brewing family named Mullhauser and had moved to a grander home on Lake Road. The following summer, Tiedemann decided to vacation at a German resort, and there he met (or some have suggested became re-acquainted with) a young waitress named Henriette. He quickly married the woman and lived just long enough to regret it. He divorced her and left her with nothing.

By 1908, Tiedemann's entire family, including his son, August, and his children, had passed away. There was no one left to inherit his fortune or to comfort him in his old age. Tiedemann died later that same year, suddenly stricken while walking in the park one day. It is believed that he suffered a massive stroke.

Tiedemann's death did not end the speculation about strange events in the house however. Legend had it that Tiedemann had not been the faithful husband that he appeared to be. There were stories of affairs and sexual encounters within the vast confines of the house. Tangled in the distasteful stories were also rumors of murder.

One of the bloody tales was told about a hidden passage that extended beyond the castle's ballroom. It was here that Tiedemann allegedly killed his niece by hanging her from one of the exposed rafters. The stories say that she was insane and that he killed her to put her out of her misery. But it's possible this was not the truth, because others maintain that he killed her because of her promiscuity. He discovered her in bed with his grandson, it is said, and she paid the ultimate price for this transgression.

Tiedemann is also said to have murdered a young servant girl on her wedding day because she rejected his advances. Another version of the story says that the woman who was killed was Tiedemann's mistress, a woman named Rachel. She strangled to death in the house after Tiedemann tied her up and gagged her after learning that she wanted to marry another man. It's possible that Rachel's spirit is the resident "Woman in Black" who has been seen lurking around the old tower. Former residents say that they have heard the sound of a woman choking in this room.

More blood was spilled in the house a few years later, after the Mullhauser family sold the castle to the German Socialist Party in 1913. They used the house for meetings and parties, or so it was said. However, the legends of the house maintain that the Socialists were actually Nazi spies and that twenty of their members were machine-gunned to death in one of the castle's secret rooms. They sold the house fifty-five years later, and during the time of their residence, the house was mainly unoccupied.

It is believed that they may have rented out a portion of the house, as a Cleveland nurse recalled that she had cared for an ailing attorney in the castle in the early 1930s. She remembered being terrified at night by the sound of a small child crying. More than 40 years later, she told a reporter that she "would never set foot in that house again."

In January of 1968, James Romano, his wife, and six children moved into the house. Mrs. Romano had always been fascinated with the mansion and planned to open a restaurant there, but she quickly changed her mind. On the very day that the family moved in, she sent her children upstairs to play. A little while later, they came back downstairs and asked if they could have a cookie for their new friend, a little girl who was upstairs crying. Mrs. Romano followed the children back upstairs, but found no little girl. This happened a number of times, leading many to wonder if the ghost children might be the spirits of the Tiedemann children who died in the early 1880s.

Mrs. Romano also reported hearing organ music in the house, even though no organ was there, and sounds of footsteps tramping up and down the hallways. She also heard voices and the sound of glass clinking on the third floor, even though no one else was in the house. The Romanos finally consulted a Catholic priest about the house. He declined to do an exorcism of the place, but told them that he sensed an evil presence in the house and that they should leave.

The family then turned to the Northeast Ohio Psychical Research Society, a now defunct ghost-hunting group, and they sent out a team to investigate Franklin Castle. In the middle of the investigation, one of the team members fled the building in terror.

By September of 1974, the Romanos had finally had enough. They sold the castle to Sam Muscatello, who planned to turn the place into a church, but instead, after learning of the building's shady past, started offering guided tours of the house. He also had problems with ghostly visitors in the mansion encountering strange sounds, vanishing objects and the eerie woman in black.

He invited Cleveland radio executive John Webster to the house for an on-air special about hauntings and Franklin Castle. Webster claimed that while walking up a staircase, something tore a tape recorder from a strap over his shoulder and flung it down the stairs. "I was climbing the stairs with a large tape recorder strapped over my shoulder," Webster later recalled and then told how the device was pulled away from him. "I just stood there holding the microphone as I watched the tape recorder go flying down to the bottom of the stairs, where it broke into pieces."

A television reporter named Ted Ocepec, who also came to visit the castle, witnessed a hanging ceiling light that suddenly began turning in circular motions. He was also convinced that something supernatural lurked in the house. Someone suggested that perhaps traffic vibrations on the street outside had caused the movement of the light. Ocepec didn't think so. "I just don't know," he said, "but there's something in that house."

Muscatello's interest in the history of the house led him to start searching for the secret panels and passages installed by the Tiedemanns. It was he who made the gruesome discovery of the skeleton behind the panel in the tower room. This discovery apparently had a strange effect on Muscatello as he started becoming sick and lost over thirty pounds in a few weeks. He was never very successful at turning the place into a tourist attraction and eventually sold the place to a doctor, who in turn sold the house for the same amount to Cleveland Police Chief Richard Hongisto.

The police chief and his wife declared that the spacious mansion would make the perfect place in which to live but then, less than one year later, abruptly sold the house to George Mirceta, who was unaware of the house's haunted reputation. He had bought the castle merely for its solid construction and Gothic architecture. He lived alone in the house and also conducted tours of the place, asking visitors to record any of their strange experiences in a guest book before leaving. Some reported seeing a woman in white, babies crying and lights swinging back and forth. One women even complained of feeling like she was being choked in the tower room. Strangely, she had no idea of the legend concerning that room and the death of Tiedemann's mistress.

Even though he had a number of strange experiences while living there, Mirceta maintained that the castle was not haunted. If it was, he told reporters, he would be too scared to live there. "There has to be a logical explanation for everything," he told an interviewer.

In 1984, the house was sold once again, this time to Michael De Vinko, who attempted to restore the place. He claimed to have no problems with ghosts in the house but surmised that it may have been because he was taking care of the old place again. He spent huge sums of money in restoration efforts. He successfully tracked down the original blueprints to the house, some of the Tiedemann furniture, and even the original key to the front door, which still worked. Even after spending all of the money though, the house was put back on the real-estate market in 1994.

The castle was sold again in 1999 and the current owner is once again attempting to restore the place, even after an arson fire damaged it badly in November of that same year. As of this writing, work is still being completed on the structure. The owner plans to document the repairs and restoration on-line. Once it is completed, he hopes to open the house for tours once again.

But has the blood-soaked past of the house left a mark that is still being felt in the present? When asked if the castle is really haunted, the owner admits that he's not sure that it is, or if he even believes in ghosts at all. However, he does say that many of his friends and family have had had odd experiences here. "Most of them involve either unexplained sounds, or difficult-to-describe feelings."

He adds that the castle is not a scary place, but it is a little creepy, especially in the middle of the night. "I've heard strange sounds and hoped to see something or hear something that would prove to me that ghosts exist, but so far it hasn't happened," he said. "So far it's been no spookier than sleeping alone in any old house that creaks in the wind or has rattling pipes." Keep your fingers crossed for him that it stays this way!

SUICIDE & SPIRITS

The Haunted History of the Lemp Mansion

There is no place in the city of St. Louis, Missouri with a reputation that is quite as ghostly as the Lemp Mansion. It has served as many things over the years from stately home to boarding house to restaurant, but it has never lost the fame of being the most haunted place in the city. In fact, in 1980, *Life* Magazine called the Lemp Mansion "one of the ten most haunted places in America."

The Lemp family came to prominence in the middle 1800s as one of the premier brewing families of St. Louis. For years, they were seen as the fiercest rival of Anheuser-Busch and the first makers of lager beer in America but today, they are largely forgotten and remembered more for the house they once built than for the beer they once brewed. That house stands now as a fitting memorial to decadence, wealth, tragedy and suicide. Perhaps for this reason, there is a sadness that hangs over the place and an eerie feeling that has remained from its days of disrepair and abandonment. It has since been restored into a restaurant and inn, but yet the sorrow seems to remain. By day, the mansion is a bustling restaurant, filled with people and activity, but at night, after everyone is gone and the doors have been locked tight—something still walks the halls of the Lemp Mansion.

Are the ghosts here the restless spirits of the Lemp family, still unable to find rest? Quite possibly, for this unusual family was as haunted as their house is purported to be today. They were once one of the leading families in St. Louis but all that would change and the eccentricities of the family would eventually be their ruin.

The story of the Lemp brewing empire began in 1836, when Johann Adam Lemp came to America from Germany. He had learned the brewer's trade as a young man and when he came to St. Louis, after spending two years in Cincinnati, he opened a small mercantile store and began selling dry goods, vinegar and his own brand of beer. He soon closed the store and turned his attentions to a small factory that made strictly vinegar and beer. It is believed that during this period, Lemp introduced St. Louis to the first lager beer, which was a crisp, clean beer that required a few months of storage in a cool dark place to obtain its unique flavor. This new beer was a great change from the English-type ales that had previously been popular and the lighter beer soon became a regional favorite. Business prospered and by 1845, the popularity of the beer was enough to allow him to discontinue vinegar production and concentrate on beer alone.

His company expanded rapidly, thanks to the demand for the beer, and Lemp soon found that his factory was too small to handle both the production of the beer and the storage needed for the lagering process. He found a solution in a limestone case that was just south of the city limits at the time. The cave had been recently discovered and its proximity to the Mississippi River would make it possible to cut ice during the winter and keep the cave cold all year around.

Lemp purchased a lot over the entrance to the cave and then began excavating and enlarging it to make room for the wooden casks needed to store the beer. The remodeling was completed in 1845 and caused a stir in the city. Other brewers were looking for ways to model their brews after the Lemp lager beer and soon these companies also began using the natural caves under the city to store beer and to open drinking establishments. The Lemp's own saloon added greatly to the early growth of the company. It was one of the largest around and served only Lemp beer and no hard liquor. This policy served two purposes in that it added to beer sales and also created a wholesome atmosphere for families as beer was considered a very healthy drink, especially to the growing numbers of German immigrants in the city.

The Lemp's Western Brewing Co. continued to grow during the 1840s and by the 1850s was one of the largest in the city. Adam Lemp died on August 25, 1862, a very wealthy and distinguished man. The Western Brewery then came under the leadership of William Lemp, Adam's son, and it then entered its period of greatest prominence.

William Lemp had been born in Germany in 1836, just before his parents came to America. He spent his early childhood there and was brought to St. Louis by his father at age 12. He was educated at St. Louis University and after graduation, he joined his father at Western Brewery. At the outbreak of the Civil War, he enlisted in the Union Army and soon after leaving the military, he married Julia Feickert, and the couple would have nine children together.

After the death of Adam Lemp, William began a major expansion of the Western Brewery. He purchased a five-block area around the storage house on Cherokee, which was located above the lagering caves. Here, he began the construction of a new brewery and by the 1870s, the Lemp factory was the largest in the entire city. By 1876, it was producing 61,000 barrels of beer each year. A bottling plant was added the following year and artificial refrigeration was added to the plant in 1878. This would be the first year that the brewery's production would reach over 100,000 barrels.

By the middle 1890s, the Lemp brewery was known all over America. They had earlier introduced the popular Falstaff beer, which is still brewed by another company today although the familiar logo once had the name Lemp emblazoned across it. This beer became a favorite across the country and Lemp was the first brewery to establish coast-to-coast, and then international, distribution of its beer. The brewery had grown to the point that it employed over 700 men, and as many as 100 horses were needed to pull the delivery wagons in St. Louis alone. It was ranked as the eighth largest in the country and construction and renovation continued on a daily basis. The entire complex was designed in an Italian Renaissance style with arched windows, brick cornices and eventually grew to cover a five city blocks.

In addition to William Lemp's financial success, he was also well-liked and popular among the citizens of St. Louis. He was on the board of several organizations, including a planning committee for the 1904 World's Fair and many others. His family life was happy and his children were either involved in the business or successful in their own right.

During the time of the Lemp Brewery's greatest success, William Lemp also purchased a home for his family a short distance from the brewery complex. The house was built by Jacob Feickert, Julia Lemp's father, in 1868. In 1876, Lemp purchased it for use as a residence and as an auxiliary brewery office. Although already an impressive house, Lemp immediately began renovating and expanding it and turning it into a showplace of the period. The mansion boasted 33 rooms, elegant artwork, handcrafted wood decor, ornately painted ceilings, large beautiful bathrooms, and even an elevator that replaced the main staircase in 1904. The house was also installed with three room-sized, walk-in vaults where paintings, jewelry and other valuables were stored. It was a unique and wondrous place and one fitting of the first family of St. Louis brewing.

And the mansion was as impressive underground as it was above. A tunnel exited the basement of the house and entered into a portion of the cave that Adam Lemp had discovered for his beer lagering years before. Traveling along a quarried shaft, the Lemps could journey beneath the street, all the way to the brewery. The advent of mechanical refrigeration also made it possible to use parts of the cave for things other than business, as will be evident later in this account.

Ironically, in the midst of all of this happiness and success, the Lemp family's troubles truly began.

The first death in the family was that of Frederick Lemp, William Sr.'s favorite son and the heir apparent to the Lemp empire. He had been groomed for years to take over the family business and was known as the most ambitious and hard working of the Lemp children. In 1898, Frederick married Irene Verdin and the couple was reportedly very happy. Frederick was well-known in social circles and was regarded as a friendly and popular fellow. In spite of this, he also spent countless hours at the brewery, working hard to improve the company's future. It's possible that he may have literally worked himself to death.

In 1901, Frederick's health began to fail and so he decided to take some time off in October of that year and temporarily moved to Pasadena, California. He hoped that a change of climate might be beneficial to him. By December, he was greatly improved, and after his parents visited with him after Thanksgiving, William returned to St. Louis with hopes that his son would be returned to him soon. Unfortunately, that never happened. On December 12, Frederick suffered a sudden relapse and he died at the age of only 28. His death was brought about by heart failure, due to a complication of other diseases.

Frederick's death was devastating to his parents, especially to his father. Brewery secretary Henry Vahlkamp later wrote that when news came of the young man's death, William Lemp "broke down utterly and cried like a child...He took it so seriously that we feared it would completely shatter his health and looked for the worst to happen."

Lemp's friends and co-workers said that he was never the same again after Frederick's death. It was obvious to all of them that he was not coping well, and he began to slowly withdraw from the world. He was rarely seen in public and chose to walk to the brewery each day by using the cave system beneath the house. Before his son's death, Lemp had taken pleasure in paying the men each week. He also would join the workers in any department and work alongside them in their daily activities, or go personally among them and discuss any problems or any questions they had. After Frederick died though, these practices ceased almost completely.

On January 1, 1904, William Lemp suffered another crushing blow with the death of his closest friend, Frederick Pabst. This tragedy changed Lemp even more and soon he became indifferent to the details of running the brewery. Although he still came to the office each day, he paid little attention to the work and those who knew him said that he now seemed nervous and unsettled and his physical and mental health were both beginning to decline. On February 13, 1904, his suffering became unbearable.

When Lemp awoke that morning, he ate breakfast and mentioned to one of the servants that he was not feeling well. He finished eating, excused himself and went back upstairs to his bedroom. Around 9:30, he took a .38 caliber Smith & Wesson revolver and shot himself in the head with it. There was no one else in the house at the time of the shooting except for the servants. A servant girl, upon hearing the sound of the gunshot, ran to the door but she found it locked. She immediately ran to the brewery office, about a half block away, and summoned William Jr. and Edwin. They hurried back to the house and broke down the bedroom door. Inside, they found their father lying on the bed in a pool of blood. The revolver was still gripped in his right hand and there was a gaping and bloody wound at his right temple. At that point, Lemp was still breathing but unconscious.

One of the boys called the family physician, Dr. Henry J. Harnisch, by telephone and he came at once. He and three other doctors examined William but there was nothing they could do. William died just as his wife returned home from a shopping trip downtown. No suicide note was ever found.

Immediately after the shooting, the house was closed to everyone but relatives, and brewery employees were posted to intercept callers and newspapermen at the front gate. Funeral arrangements were immediately made, and services took place the next day in the mansion's south parlor. The brewery was closed for the day and employees came to pay their respects before the private service was held.

After the service, a cortege of 40 carriages traveled to Bellefontaine Cemetery, although Julia, Elsa and Hilda were too grief-stricken to go to the burial ground. Eight men who had worked for Lemp for more than 30 years served as pallbearers and honorary pallbearers included many notable St. Louis residents, including Adolphus Busch, the owner of the Anheuser-Busch brewery, who had liked and respected his principal competitor. William was placed inside the family mausoleum next to his beloved son, Frederick.

Lemp's terrible and tragic death came at a terrible time as far as the company was concerned. In the wake of his burial, all of St. Louis was preparing for the opening of the Louisiana Purchase Exposition, perhaps the greatest event to ever come to St. Louis. Not only had William been elected to the fair's Board of Directors, but the brewery was also involved in beer sales and displays for the event. William Jr. took his father's place and became active with the Agriculture Committee and with supervising the William J. Lemp Brewing Company's display in Agriculture Hall, where brewers and distillers from around the world assembled to show off their products.

In November 1904, William Lemp Jr. took over as the new president of the William J. Lemp Brewing Company. He inherited the family business and with it, a great fortune. He filled the house with servants, built country houses and spent huge sums on carriages, clothing and art.

In 1899, Will had married Lillian Handlan, the daughter of a wealthy manufacturer. Lillian was nicknamed the "Lavender Lady" because of her fondness for dressing in that color. She was soon spending the Lemp fortune as quickly as her husband was. While Will enjoyed showing off his trophy wife, he eventually grew tired of her and decided to divorce her in 1906. Their divorce, and the court proceedings around it, created a scandal that all of St. Louis talked about. When it was all over, the Lavender Lady went into seclusion and retired from the public eye.

But Will's troubles were just beginning that year. The Lemp brewery was also facing a much-altered St. Louis beer market in 1906 when nine of the large area breweries combined to form the

Independent Breweries Company. The formation of company left only Lemp, Anheuser-Busch, the Louis Obert Brewing Co. and a handful of small neighborhood breweries as the only independent beer makers in St. Louis. Of even more concern was the expanding temperance movement in America. The growing clamor of those speaking out against alcohol was beginning to be heard in all corners of the country. It looked as though the heyday of brewing was coming to an end.

The year 1906 also marked the death of Will's mother. It was discovered that she had cancer in 1905 and by March 1906, her condition had deteriorated to the point that she was in constant pain and suffering. She died in her home a short time later. Her funeral was held in the mansion and she was laid to rest in the mausoleum at Bellefontaine Cemetery.

In 1911, the last major improvements were made to the Lemp brewery when giant grain elevators were erected on the south side of the complex. That same year, the Lemp mansion ceased being a private residence and it was converted and remodeled into the new offices of the brewing company. Like most of its competitors, the Lemp brewery limped along through the next few years and through World War I. According to numerous accounts, Lemp was in far worse shape than many of the other companies. Will had allowed the company's equipment to deteriorate and by not keeping abreast of industry innovations, much of the brewing facilities had become outmoded. And to make matters worse, Prohibition was coming.

Brewers were stunned a short time later by the passing of an amendment that made the production, sales and consumption of alcohol illegal in America, and by the Volstead Act, which made prohibition enforceable by law. This seemed to signal the real death of the Lemp brewery. As the individual family members were quite wealthy aside from the profits from the company, there was little incentive to keep it afloat. Will gave up on the idea that Congress would suddenly repeal Prohibition and he closed the Lemp plant down without notice. The workers learned of the closing when they came to work one day and found the doors shut and the gates locked.

Will decided to simply liquidate the assets of the plant and auction off the buildings. He sold the famous Lemp Falstaff logo to brewer Joseph Griesedieck for the sum of $25,000. He purchased the recognizable Falstaff name and shield with the idea that eventually the government would see Prohibition for the folly that it was and that beer would be back. Lemp no longer shared the other man's enthusiasm, and in 1922 he saw the brewery sold off to the International Shoe Co. for just $588,000, a small fraction of its estimated worth of $7 million in the years before Prohibition. Sadly, virtually all of the Lemp company records were pitched when the shoe company moved into the complex.

With Prohibition finally destroying the brewery, the 1920s looked to be a dismal decade for the Lemp family. As bad as it first seemed, things almost immediately became worse with the suicide of Elsa Lemp Wright in 1920. She became the second member of the family to take her own life.

Elsa was born in 1883 and was the youngest child in the Lemp family. With the death of her mother in 1906, she became the wealthiest unmarried woman in the city after inheriting her portion of her father's estate. In 1910, she became even richer when she married Thomas Wright, the president of the More-Jones Brass and Metal Co. They moved into a home in Hortense Place in St. Louis' Central West End. During the years between 1910 and 1918, their marriage was reportedly an unhappy and stormy one. They separated in December 1918 and in February 1919, Elsa filed for divorce. Unlike the sensational divorce of her brother, Elsa's legal battle was kept quiet and the details of the divorce were not revealed. It was granted however in less than an hour and the reasons were cited as "general indignities."

By March 8, 1920 though, Elsa and Thomas had reconciled and the two were remarried in New York City. They returned home to St. Louis and found their house filled with flowers and cards from friends and well-wishers.

The night of March 19 was a restless one for Elsa. She suffered from frequent bouts of indigestion and nausea and her ailments caused periods of severe depression. She was awake for most of this night and slept very little. When her husband awoke the next morning, Elsa told him that she was feeling better but wanted to remain in bed. Wright agreed that this was the best thing for her and he went into the bathroom and turned on the water in the tub. He then returned to the bedroom for a change of underwear, retrieved them from the closet and went back into the bathroom. Moments after he closed the door, he heard a sharp cracking sound over the noise of the running water.

Thinking that it was Elsa trying to get his attention, Wright opened the door and called to his wife. When she didn't answer, he walked into the bedroom and found her on the bed. Her eyes were open and she seemed to be looking at him. When Wright got closer, he saw a revolver on the bed next to her. Elsa tried to speak but could not, and a few moments later, she was dead. No note or letter was ever found, and Wright could give no reason as to why she would have killed herself. He was not even aware that she owned a gun.

The only other persons present that morning were members of the household staff. None of them heard the shot and none of them saw any sign that Elsa intended to end her life. They quickly summoned Dr. M. B. Clopton and Samuel Fordyce, a family friend. Strangely, the police were not notified of Elsa's death for more than two hours and even then, the news came indirectly through Samuel Fordyce. Wright became "highly agitated" under the scrutiny of the police investigation that followed, and his only excuse for not contacting the authorities was that he was bewildered and did not know what to do.

And while the mysterious circumstances around Elsa's death have had some suggesting there was more to the story than was told, her brothers seemed to find little out of the ordinary about her demise. Will and Edwin rushed to the house as soon as they heard about the shooting. When Will arrived and was told what had happened, he only had one comment to make. "That's the Lemp family for you," he said.

Will was soon to face depression and death himself. He had already slipped into a dark state of mind following the end of the Lemp's brewing dynasty, but he took an even sharper turn for the worse after the sale of the plant to the International Shoe Co. Will soon began to follow in the footsteps of his father and he became increasingly nervous and erratic. He shunned public life and kept to himself, complaining often of ill health and headaches.

By December 29, 1922, he had reached the limit of his madness. On that morning, Lemp secretary Henry Vahlkamp arrived at the Lemp brewery offices around 9:00. When he came in the front door, he found Will already in his office. The two of them were joined shortly after by Olivia Bercheck, a stenographer for the brewery and Lemp's personal secretary.

Vahlkamp later recalled that Lemp's face was flushed that morning and that when he entered his employer's office, he had an elbow on the desk and he was resting his forehead on his hand. He asked Lemp how he was feeling and Will replied that he felt quite bad.

"I think you are looking better today that you did yesterday," Vahlkamp noted in an effort to cheer up the other man.

"You may think so," Will replied, "but I am feeling worse."

Vahlkamp then left and went to his own office on the second floor of the converted mansion.

Moments after this exchange, Miss Bercheck telephoned Will's second wife, Ellie, about instructions for the day's mail, and, as she was speaking to her, Lemp picked up the other line and spoke to his wife himself. The secretary recalled that he spoke very quietly, and she did not hear what turned out to be his last words to his wife. After Lemp finished the conversation, Bercheck asked him a question about some copying that she was doing from a blueprint. He first told her that what she had was fine, and then he changed his mind and suggested that she go down to the basement and speak to the brewery's architect, Mr. Norton.

While she was on her way downstairs, she heard a loud noise. Because there were men working in the basement, she thought nothing of it, assuming that someone had dropped something. When she came back upstairs though, she found Will lying on the floor in a pool of blood. Another employee had also been working upstairs but when he heard the same loud noises that Miss Bercheck later reported, he recognized it as a gunshot. He ran to find Will lying on the floor with his with his feet under the desk. He called for help and men from the office across the hall came over and put a pillow under Will's head.

Apparently, just after speaking to Miss Bercheck, Lemp had shot himself in the heart with a .38 caliber revolver. He had unbuttoned his vest and then fired the gun through his shirt. When discovered, Lemp was still breathing, but he had expired by the time a doctor could arrive.

Captain William Doyle, the lead police investigator on the scene, searched Lemp's pockets and desk for a suicide note, but as with his father and his sister before him, Will left no indication as to why he had committed suicide.

Oddly, Lemp seemed to have no intention of killing himself, despite being depressed. After the sale of the brewery, he had discussed selling off the rest of the assets, like land parcels and saloon locations, and planned to then just "take it easy." Not long after that announcement, he had even put his estate in Webster Groves up for sale, stating that he planned to travel to Europe for awhile. Even a week before his death, he had dined with his friend August A. Busch, who said that Lemp seemed cheerful at the time and that he gave no indication that he was worrying about business or anything else. "He was a fine fellow," Busch added, "and it is hard to believe that he has taken his own life."

The funeral of William Lemp Jr. was held on December 31 at the Lemp mansion. The offices were used as the setting for the services for sentimental reasons, staff members said. He was interred in the family mausoleum at Bellefontaine Cemetery, in the crypt just above his sister Elsa.

With William Jr. gone and his brothers involved with their own endeavors, it seemed that the days of the Lemp empire had come to an end at last. The two brothers still in St. Louis had left the family enterprise long before it had closed down. Charles worked in banking and finance, and Edwin had entered a life in seclusion at his estate in Kirkwood in 1911. The great fortune they had amassed was more than enough to keep the surviving members of the family comfortable through the Great Depression and beyond. But the days of Lemp tragedy were not yet over.

In 1933, Prohibition was officially repealed and almost immediately, beer was once again being brewed in St. Louis. The future was bright once more for many of the local companies but dark days were still ahead for the remaining members of the Lemp family.

By the late 1920s, only Charles and Edwin Lemp were left in the immediate family. Throughout his life, Charles was never much involved with the Lemp Brewery. His interests had been elsewhere and when the family home was renovated into offices, he made his residence at the Racquet Club in St. Louis. His work had mostly been in the banking and financial industries and he sometimes dabbled in politics as well. In 1929, Charles moved back to the Lemp mansion and the house became a private residence once more.

Despite his very visible business and political life, Charles remained a mysterious figure who became even odder and more reclusive with age. He remained a bachelor his entire life and lived alone in his old rambling house with only his two servants, Albert and Lena Bittner, for company. By the age of 77, he was arthritic and quite ill. Legend has it that he was deathly afraid of germs and wore gloves to avoid any contact with bacteria. He had grown quite bitter and eccentric and had developed a morbid attachment to the Lemp family home. Thanks to the history of the place, his brother Edwin often encouraged him to move out, but Charles refused. Finally, when he could stand no more of life, he became the fourth member of the Lemp family to commit suicide.

On May 10, 1949, Alfred Bittner, one of Charles' staff, went to the kitchen and prepared breakfast for Lemp as he normally did. He then placed the breakfast tray on the desk in the office next to Lemp's bedroom, as he had been doing for years. Bittner later recalled that the door to the bedroom was closed and he did not look inside. At about 8:00, Bittner returned to the office to remove the tray and found it to be untouched. Concerned, he opened the bedroom door to see if Charles was awake and discovered that he was dead from a bullet wound to the head. When the police arrived, they found Lemp still in bed and lightly holding a .38 caliber Army Colt revolver in his right hand. He was the only one of the family who had left a suicide note behind. He had dated the letter May 9 and had written "In case I am found dead blame it on no one but me" and had signed it at the bottom.

Oddly, Charles had made detailed funeral arrangements for himself long before his death. He would be the only member of the family not interred at the mausoleum at Bellefontaine Cemetery and while this might be unusual, it was nearly as strange as the rest of the instructions that he left behind. In a letter that was received at a south St. Louis funeral home in 1941, Lemp ordered that upon his death his body should be immediately taken to the Missouri Crematory. His ashes were then to be placed in a wicker box and buried on his farm. He also ordered that his body not be bathed, changed or clothed and that no services were to be held for him and no death notice published, no matter what any surviving members of his family might want.

On May 11, 1949, Edwin Lemp picked up his brother's remains at the funeral home and took them to the farm to be buried. And while these instructions were certainly odd, they were not the most enduring mystery to the situation. You see, even after all of these years, there is no indication as to where Charles Lemp's farm was located.

The Lemp family, which had once been so large and prosperous, had now been almost utterly destroyed in a span of less than a century. Only Edwin Lemp remained and he had long avoided the life that had turned so tragic for the rest of his family. He was known as a quiet, reclusive man who had walked away from the Lemp Brewery in 1913 to live a peaceful life on his secluded estate in Kirkwood. Here, he communed with nature and became an excellent cook, gourmet and animal lover. He collected fine art and entertained his intimate friends.

Edwin managed to escape from the family curse but as he grew older, he did become more eccentric and developed a terrible fear of being alone. He never spoke about his family or their tragic lives, but it must have preyed on him all the same. His fears caused him to simply entertain more and to keep a companion with him at his estate almost all the time.

His most loyal friend and companion was John Bopp, the caretaker of the estate for the last 30 years of Edwin's life. His loyalty to his employer was absolute and it is believed that Bopp was never away from the estate for more than few days at a time. He never discussed any of Lemp's personal thoughts or habits and remained faithful to Edwin, even after his friend's death.

Edwin passed away quietly of natural causes at age 90 in 1970. The last order that John Bopp carried out for him must have been the worst. According to Edwin's wishes, he burned all of the paintings that Lemp had collected throughout his life, as well as priceless Lemp family papers and artifacts. These irreplaceable pieces of history vanished in the smoke of a blazing bonfire and like the Lemp empire—were lost forever.

The Lemp family line died out with Edwin and while none of them remain today, it's almost certain that some of them are still around.

After the death of Charles Lemp, the grand family mansion was sold and turned into a boarding house. Shortly after that, it fell on hard times and began to deteriorate, along with the nearby neighborhood. In later years, stories began to emerge that residents of the boarding house often complained of ghostly knocks and phantom footsteps in the house. As these tales spread, it became increasingly hard to find tenants to occupy the rooms and because of this, the old Lemp Mansion was rarely filled.

One strange account from the days following Charles' death was told by a young woman who decided to sneak into the house with some friends one day in 1949. The house was still vacant at the time but the group managed to get into the front door and they started up the main staircase to the second floor. They climbed the steps to the first landing and then prepared to go up the last set of stairs to the upper level. Just as they reached the landing, they looked up and saw a filmy apparition coming down the steps toward them! The young girl much later described it as an almost human-shaped puff of smoke. The group took one look at it and ran! When she told this story for the first time in the late 1990s, the woman, who was quite elderly by this time, stated that she had never been back in the mansion again.

The decline of the house continued until 1975, when Dick Pointer and his family purchased it. The Pointers began remodeling and renovating the place, working for many years to turn it into a restaurant and an inn. But the Pointers were soon to find out that they were not alone in the house. The bulk of the remodeling was done in the 1970s and during this time, workers reported that ghostly events were occurring in the house. Almost all of the workers confessed that they believed the place was haunted and told of feeling as though they were being watched, spoke of strange sounds and complained of tools that vanished and then returned in different places from where they had been left.

At one point in the renovations, a painter was brought in to work on the ceilings and he stayed overnight in the house while he completed the job. One day, he was in his room and ran downstairs to tell one of the Pointers that he had heard the sound of horse's hooves on the cobblestones outside of his window. Pointer convinced the painter that he was mistaken. There were no horses and no cobblestones outside of the house. In time, the man finished the ceilings and left, but the story stayed on Pointer's mind. Later that year, he noticed that some of the grass in the yard had turned brown. He dug underneath it and found that beneath the top level of the soil was a layer of cobblestones! During the Lemp's residency in the house, that portion of the yard had been a drive to the carriage house! Pointer had the cobblestones removed and then used them as floor stones in one area of the mansion's basement.

Later in the restoration, another artist was brought in to restore the painted ceiling in one of the front dining rooms. It had been covered over with paper years before. While he was lying on his back on the scaffolding, he felt a sensation of what he believed was a "spirit moving past him." It frightened him so badly that he left the house without his brushes and tools and refused to return and get them. Some time after this event, an elderly man came into the restaurant and told one of the staff members that he had once been a driver for the Lemp family. He explained that the ceiling in the dining room had been papered over because William Lemp hated the design that had been printed on it. The staff members, upon hearing this story, noted that the artist had gotten the distinct impression that the spirit he encountered had been angry. Perhaps because he was restoring the unwanted ceiling?

During the restorations, Mr. Pointer's son, Richard "Dick" Pointer, lived alone in the house and became quite an expert on the ghostly manifestations. One night, he was lying in bed reading and he heard a door slam loudly in another part of the house. No one else was supposed to be in the house and he was sure that he had locked all of the doors. Fearing that someone might have broken in, he and his dog, a large Doberman named Shadow, decided to take a look around. The dog was spooked by this time, having also heard the sound, and she had her ears turned up, listening for anything else. They searched the entire house and found no one there. Every door had been locked, just as Pointer had left them. He reported that the same thing happened again about a month later, but again, nothing was found.

After the restaurant opened, staff members began to report their own odd experiences. Glasses were seen to lift off the bar and fly through the air, sounds were often heard that had no explanation, and some even glimpsed actual apparitions who appeared and vanished at will. In addition, many customers and visitors to the house reported some pretty weird incidents. It was said that doors locked and unlocked on their own, the piano in the bar played by itself, voices and sounds came from nowhere, and even the spirit of the Lavender Lady, Lillian Handlan, was spotted on occasion.

Late one evening, Dick was bartending after most of the customers had departed and the water in a pitcher began swirling around of its own volition. Pointer was sure that he was just seeing things but all of the customers who remained that night swore they all saw the same thing. Then one night in August 1981, Dick and an employee were startled to hear the piano start playing a few notes by itself. There was no one around it at the time and in fact, no one else in the entire building. The piano has continued to be the source of eerie occurrences as the years have passed. No matter where it has been located in the house, whether in the main hallway upstairs or in one of the guest rooms, the piano keys have reportedly tinkled without the touch of human hands.

And while the ghostly atmosphere of the place has admittedly attracted a number of patrons, it has also caused the owners to lose a number of valuable employees of the house. One of them was a former waitress named Bonnie Strayhorn, who encountered an unusual customer while working one day. The restaurant had not yet opened for business and yet she saw a dark-haired man seated at one of the tables in the rear dining room. She was surprised that someone had come so early, but she went over to ask if he would like a cup of coffee. He simply sat there are did not answer. Bonnie frowned and looked away for a moment. When she looked back, just moments later, the man was gone! She has continued to maintain that the man could not have left the room in the brief seconds when she was not looking at him. After that incident, she left the Lemp Mansion and went to work in a non-haunted location.

In addition to customers, the house has also attracted ghost hunters from around the country. Many of them have come due to the publicity that has been achieved by the house as a haunted location. The mansion has appeared in scores of magazines, newspaper articles, books and television shows over the years but it first gained notoriety back in the 1970s when it was investigated by the "Haunt Hunters." These two St. Louis men, Phil Goodwilling and Gordon Hoener, actively researched ghost stories and sightings in the area and during that period, even conducted a class on ghosts for St. Louis University. They promised their students that they would take them to a real haunted place and decided that the Lemp Mansion fit the bill. In October 1979, they brought the class to the house and brought along a local television crew to film the event.

Goodwilling and Hoener divided the students up into small groups and gave them all writing planchettes to try and contact the spirits. The devices, like Ouija boards, were used to spell out messages from the ghosts. Each of the groups of students was divided into groups of four. One of the groups asked: "Is there an unseen presence that wishes to communicate?"

"Yes," came the answer. It scrawled out on a large piece of paper as the planchette, with its pencil tip, moved across the surface.

The students asked another question: "Will you identify yourself?"

The planchette scratched out a reply: "Charles Lemp"

Goodwilling later noted that the students who received this message were the most skeptical in the class. He also noted that no one in the room that night, with the exception of Dick Pointer, had any idea that Charles had committed suicide. At that time, the history of the house had not been widely publicized.

After the name was revealed, the spirit added that he had taken

The legendary Lemp Mansion on the South Side of St. Louis

Bachelor's Grove Cemetery (Courtesy of Rob Johnson)

his own life. When asked why he did this, the spirit replied in three words: "Help, death, rest."

It might also be added that by the time this séance was over, the four students were no longer the most skeptical in the class.

In November, the Haunt Hunters returned to the house, and this time brought along a camera crew from the popular show of the era, *Real People*. Goodwilling and Hoener participated in a séance with two other participants, neither of which had any idea about the past history of the mansion. They once again made contact with a spirit who identified himself as Charles Lemp and he was asked again why he had committed suicide. The spirit reportedly used a derogatory term and then added, "damn Roosevelt." Apparently, the Lemps had not been fond of the politics practiced by Franklin D. Roosevelt during their time.

But the séance continued with the next question from the group: "Is there a message for someone in this house?"

The answer came: "Yes, yes, Edwin, money."

The group then asked if there was anything they could do to free the spirit from being trapped in the house? "Yes, yes," the ghost replied. Unfortunately though, they were unsuccessful in finding out what they could do to help.

Goodwilling felt that if the spirit was actually Charles Lemp, then he might have stayed behind in the house because of his suicide. He might have had a message for his brother, Edwin Lemp, who he tried to contact during the séance. He may have believed that Edwin was still alive and based on the conversation, was trying to pass along a message about money. Could this be what caused Charles Lemp's ghost to remain behind?

Most importantly perhaps to the reader is the question of whether the Lemp Mansion still remains haunted today? Most can tell you that it does although the current owners of the house accept this as just part of the house's unusual ambience. One of the owners, Paul Pointer, helps to maintain the place as a wonderful eating and lodging establishment. He takes the ghosts as just another part of the strange mansion. "People come here expecting to experience weird things," he said, " and fortunately for us, they are rarely disappointed."

BACHELOR'S GROVE CEMETERY

The Most Haunted Place in Chicagoland

Located near the southwest suburb of Midlothian is the Rubio Woods Forest Preserve, an island of trees and shadows nestled in the urban sprawl of the Chicago area. The rambling refuge creates an illusion that it is secluded from the crowded city that threatens its borders, and perhaps it is. On the edge of the forest is a small graveyard that many believe may be the most haunted place in the region. The name of this cemetery is Bachelor's Grove and this ramshackle burial ground may be infested with more ghosts than most can imagine. Over the years, the place has been cursed with more than 100 documented reports of paranormal phenomena, from actual apparitions to glowing balls of light.

There have been no new burials here for many years and as a place of rest for the departed, it is largely forgotten. But if you should ask any ghost hunter just where to go to find a haunting, Bachelor's Grove is usually the first place in Chicago to be mentioned!

The history of Bachelor's Grove has been somewhat shadowy over the years but most historians agree that it was started in the early part of the 1800s. In August 1933, the famous *Ripley's Believe it or Not* column featured a short piece on Bachelor's Grove Cemetery, stating that it was so unusual because even though it had been set aside as a burial ground for bachelors only, there were also women buried here. Unfortunately though, the column was inaccurate and this has been just one of the many myths and misconceptions created about the cemetery over the years. The name of the cemetery came not from the number of single men buried here but from the name of a family who settled in the area. The lore about the bachelor burial ground dates back to 1833 or 1834 when a man named Stephen H. Rexford settled in the region with a number of other unmarried men. Allegedly, they began calling the place Bachelor's Grove but this has been widely disputed by historians, who believe the name Batchelor's Grove was already in use at the time.

They believe that the name of the cemetery came from a settlement that was started in the late 1820s that consisted of mostly German immigrants from New York, Vermont and Connecticut. One family that moved into the area was called "Batchelder" and their name was given to the timberland where they settled, just as other timber areas like Walker's Grove, Cooper's Grove and Blackstone's Grove were named after families and individuals.

Regardless, the small settlement continued for some years as Batchelor's Grove, until 1850, when it was changed to Bremen by postmaster Samuel Everden in recognition of the new township name where the post office was located. In 1855, it was changed again to Batchelder's Grove by postmaster Robert Patrick but the post office closed down just three years later. Officially, the settlement ceased to exist and was swallowed by the forest around it.

The cemetery itself has a much stranger history— or at least a more mysterious one. The land was apparently first set aside to be used as a burial ground in 1844, when the first recorded burial took place here, that of Eliza (Mrs. Leonard H.) Scott. The land had been donated by the property owner, Samuel Everden, and it was named Everden in his honor. Strangely though, this first burial is disputed by an article that appeared in the *Blue Island Sun-Standard* in August 1935. According to this story, the first burial was that of a man named William B. Nobles, who died in 1838. The last burials to take place are believed to be that of Laura M. McGhee in 1965 and Robert E. Shields, who was cremated and buried in the family plot here in 1989.

Regardless of exactly when the cemetery started, the first legal record of it appeared when Edward Everden sold the property to Frederick Schmidt in 1864. A notation in the records stated that all of the land would be sold excepting "one acre used as a grave yard." This makes it clear that the cemetery was already in existence and had been created by Everden, not, as the Schmidt family later tried to claim, by Frederick Schmidt. However, the Schmidts did intend to expand the original property later on, but there is no evidence that this was ever done.

The last independent caretaker of the cemetery was a man named Clarence Fulton, whose family were early settlers in the township. According to Fulton, Bachelor's Grove was like a park for many years and people often came here to fish and swim in the adjacent pond. Families often visited on weekends to care for the graves of the deceased and to picnic under the trees. Things have certainly changed since then!

Problems began in and around the cemetery in the early 1960s, at the same time that the Midlothian Turnpike was closed to vehicle traffic in front of the cemetery. Even before that, the cemetery had become a popular spot along a lover's lane and when the road closed, it became even more isolated. Soon it began to show signs of vandalism and decay and was considered haunted. Although the amount of paranormal activity that actually occurs in the cemetery has been argued by some, few can deny that strange things do happen here. When the various types of phenomenon really began is unclear but it has been happening for more than three decades now. Was the burial ground already haunted? Or did the haunting actually begin with the destructive decades of the 1960s and 1970s?

The vandals first discovered Bachelor's Grove in the 1960s and probably because of its secluded location, they began to wreak havoc on the place. Gravestones were knocked over and destroyed, sprayed with paint, broken apart and even stolen. Police reports later stated that markers from Bachelor's Grove turned up in homes, yards and even as far away as Evergreen Cemetery! Worst of all, in 1964, 1975 and 1978, graves were opened and caskets removed. Bones were sometimes found to be strewn about the cemetery. Desecrated graves are still frequently found in the cemetery.

Was the haunting first caused by these disturbances? Most believe so, but others cite another source for the activity. Near the small pond that borders the cemetery, forest rangers and cemetery visitors have repeatedly found the remains of chickens and other small animals that have been slaughtered and mutilated in a ritualistic fashion. Officers that have patrolled the woods at night have reported seeing evidence of black magic and occult rituals in and around the graveyard. In some cases, inscriptions and elaborate writings have been carved in and painted on trees and grave markers and on the cemetery grounds themselves. This has led many to believe that the cemetery has been used for occult activities.

If you combine this sorted activity with the vandalism that has nearly destroyed the place, you have a situation that is ripe for supernatural occurrences. Could this be what has caused the blight on Bachelor's Grove? Even the early superstitions of the tombstone give credence to the idea that man has always felt that desecration of graves causes cemeteries to become haunted. Grave markers began as heavy stones that were placed on top of the graves of the deceased in the belief that the weight of it would keep the dead person, or their angry spirit, beneath the ground. Those who devised this system believed that if the stone was moved, the dead would be free to walk the earth.

There is no question that vandals have not been kind to Bachelor's Grove, but then neither has time. The Midlothian Turnpike bypassed the cemetery and even the road leading back to the graveyard was eventually closed. People forgot about the place and allowed it to fade into memory, just like the poor souls buried here.

Today, the cemetery is overgrown with weeds and is surrounded by a high, chain-link fence, although access is easily gained through the holes that trespassers have cut into it. The cemetery sign is long since gone. It once hung above the main gates, which are now broken open and lean dangerously into the confines of Bachelor's Grove.

The first thing noticed by those who visit here is the destruction. Tombstones seem to be randomly scattered about, no longer marking the resting places of those whose names are inscribed upon them. Many of the stones are missing, lost forever and perhaps carried away by thieves. These macabre crimes gave birth to legends about how the stones of the cemetery move about under their own power. The most disturbing things to visitors though are the trenches and pits that have been dug above some of the graves, as vandals have attempted to make off with souvenirs from those whose rest they disturb.

Near the front gate is a broken monument to a woman whose name was heard being called repeatedly on an audio tape. Some amateur ghost hunters left a recording device running while on an excursion to Bachelor's Grove and later, upon playback of the tape, they discovered that the recorder had been left on the ruined tombstone of a woman that had the same name as that being called to on the tape. Coincidence?

Just beyond the rear barrier of the cemetery is a small, stagnant pond that can be seen by motorists who pass on 143rd Street. This pond, while outside of the graveyard, is still not untouched by the horror connected to the place. One night in the late 1970s, two Cook County forest rangers were on night patrol near here and claimed to see the apparition of a horse emerge from the waters of the pond. The animal appeared to be pulling a plow that was steered by the ghost of an old man. The vision crossed the road in front of the ranger's vehicle, was framed for a moment in the glare of their headlights, and then vanished into the forest. The men simply stared in shock for a moment and then looked at one another to be sure that had both seen the same thing. They later reported the incident and, since that time, have not been the last to see the old man and the horse.

Little did the rangers know, but this apparition was actually a part of an old legend connected to the pond. It seems that in the 1870s, a farmer was plowing a nearby field when something startled his horse. The farmer was caught by surprise and became tangled in the reins. He was dragged behind the horse and it plunged into the small pond. Unable to free himself, he was pulled down into the murky water by the weight of the horse and the plow and he drowned. Since that time, the vivid recording of this terrible incident has been supernaturally revisiting the surrounding area.

In addition to this unfortunate phantom, the pond was also rumored to be a dumping spot for murder victims during the Prohibition era in Chicago. Those who went on a one-way ride were alleged to have ended the trip at the pond near Bachelor's Grove. Thanks to this, their spirits are also said to haunt the dark waters.

Strangely though, it's not the restless spirits of gangland execution victims that have created the most bizarre tales of the pond. One night, an elderly couple was driving past the cemetery and claimed to see something by the bridge at the edge of the pond. They stopped to get a closer look and were understandably terrified to see a huge, two-headed man come out from under the bridge and cross the road in the light from their headlights! Whatever this creature may have been, it quickly vanished into the woods.

Incredibly, even the road near Bachelor's Grove is reputed to be haunted. Could there be such a taint to this place that even the surrounding area is affected? The Midlothian Turnpike is said to be the scene of vanishing ghost cars and phantom automobile accidents. No historical events can provide a clue as to why this might be, but the unexplained vehicles have been reported numerous times in recent years. The stories are all remarkably the same too. People who are traveling west on the turnpike see the tail lights of a car in front of them. The brake lights go on, as if the car is planning to stop or turn. The car then turns off the road. However, once the following auto gets to the point in the road where the first vehicle turned, they find no car there at all! Other drivers have reported passing these phantoms autos, only to see the car vanish in their rearview mirrors.

One young couple even claimed to have a collision with one of these phantom cars in 1978. They had just stopped at the intersection of Central Avenue and the Midlothian Turnpike. The driver looked both ways, saw that the road was clear in both directions, and then pulled out. Suddenly, a brown sedan appeared from nowhere, racing in the direction of the cemetery. The driver of the couple's car hit the brakes and tried to stop, but it was too late to avoid the crash. The two vehicles collided with not only a shuddering impact, but with the sound of screeching metal and broken glass as well. To make the event even more traumatic, the couple was then shocked to see the brown sedan literally fade away! They climbed out of their car, which had been spun completely around by the impact, but realized that it had not been damaged at all. They had distinctly heard the sound of the torn metal and broken glass and had felt the crush of the two cars coming together, but somehow it had never physically happened!

It remains a mystery as to where these phantom cars come from, and where they vanish to. Why do they haunt this stretch of roadway? No one knows.

For those searching for Bachelor's Grove, it can be found by leaving the roadway and walking up an overgrown gravel track that is surrounded on both sides by the forest. The old road is blocked with chains and concrete dividers and a dented No Trespassing sign that hangs ominously near the mouth to the trail. The burial ground lies about a half-mile or so beyond it in the woods.

It is along this deserted road where other strange tales of the cemetery take place. One of these odd occurrences is the sighting of the "phantom farm house." It has been seen appearing and disappearing along the trail for several decades now. The reports date back as far as the early 1960s and continue today. The most credible thing about many of the accounts is that they come from people who originally had no idea that the house shouldn't be there at all.

The house has been reported in all weather conditions and in the daylight hours, as well as at night. There is no historical record of a house existing here but the descriptions of it rarely vary. Each person claims it to be an old frame farm house with two-stories, painted white, with wooden posts, a porch swing and a welcoming light that burns softly in the window. Popular legend states that should you enter this house though, you would never come back out again. As witnesses approach the building, it is reported to get smaller and smaller until it finally just fades away, like someone switching off an old television set. No one has ever claimed to set foot on the front porch of the house.

But the story gets stranger yet! In addition to the house appearing and disappearing, it also shows up at a wide variety of locations along the trail. On one occasion it may be sighted in one area and then at an entirely different spot the next time. Author Dale Kaczmarek, who also heads the Ghost Research Society paranormal investigation group, has interviewed dozens of witnesses about the paranormal events at Bachelor's Grove. He has talked to many who say they have experienced the vanishing farm house. He has found that while all of their descriptions of the house are identical, the locations of the sightings are not. In fact, he asked the witnesses to place an "X" on the map of the area where they saw the house. Kaczmarek now has a map of the Bachelor's Grove area with "X's" all over it!

Also from this stretch of trail come reports of "ghost lights." One such light that has been reported many times is a red, beacon-like orb that has been seen flying rapidly up and down the trail to the cemetery. The light is so bright, and moves so fast, that it is impossible to tell what it really looks like. Most witnesses state that they have seen a "red streak" that is left in its wake.

Others, like Jack Hermanski from Joliet, have reported seeing balls of blue light in the woods and in the cemetery itself. These weird lights have sometimes been reported moving in and around the tombstones in the graveyard. Hermanski encountered the lights in the early 1970s and chased a number of them. All of the lights managed to stay just out of his reach. However, a woman named Denise Travers did manage to catch up with one of the blue

lights in December 1971. She claimed to pass her hand completely through one of them but felt no heat or sensation.

Besides the aforementioned phenomena, there have been
many sightings of ghosts and apparitions within Bachelor's Grove
Cemetery itself. The two most frequently reported figures have
been the "phantom monks" and the so-called "Madonna of
Bachelor's Grove."

The claims of the monk-like ghosts are strange in themselves.
These spirits are said to be clothed in the flowing robes and cowls
of a monastic order and they have been reported in Bachelor's
Grove and in other places in the Chicago area too. There are no
records to indicate that a monastery ever existed near any of the
locations where the monks have been sighted, making them one of
the greatest of the area's enigmas.

The most frequently reported spirit is known by a variety of
names from the Madonna of Bachelor's Grove to the White Lady
to the affectionate name of Mrs. Rogers. Legend has it that she is
the ghost of a woman who was buried in the cemetery next to the
grave of her young child. She is reported to wander the cemetery
on nights of the full moon with an infant wrapped in her arms. She
appears to walk aimlessly, with no apparent direction and completely unaware of the people who claim to encounter her. There
is no real evidence to say who this woman might be but, over the
years, she has taken her place as one of the many spirits of this
haunted burial ground.

And there are other ghosts. Legends tell more apocryphal tales
of a ghostly child who has been seen running across the bridge from
one side of the pond to the other, a glowing yellow man, and even
a black carriage that travels along the old road through the woods.

Many of these tales come from a combination of stories, both
new and old, but the majority of first-hand reports and encounters
are the result of literally hundreds of paranormal investigations
that have been conducted here over the last forty years. Many of
the ghost hunters who come to this place are amateur investiga-

tors, looking for thrills as much as they are looking for evidence of the supernatural, while others are serious investigators looking for evidence of the supernatural.

In the end, we have to ask, what is it about Bachelor's Grove Cemetery? Is it as haunted as we have been led to believe? I have to leave that up to the reader to decide, but strange things happen here and there is little reason to doubt that this one of the most haunted places in the Midwest.

But haunted or not, Bachelor's Grove is still a burial ground and a place that should be treated with respect as the final resting place of those interred here. It should also be remembered that the cemetery is not a private playground for those who are intrigued by ghosts and hauntings. Thanks to the efforts of local preservation groups, it appears that Bachelor's Grove is not beyond restoration, but it should still be protected against the abuses that it has suffered in the past. It is a piece of our haunted history that we cannot afford to lose.

HAUNTINGS OF HICKORY HILL

The Legends of the Old Slave House

High on a windswept rise in southern Illinois is one of the region's most haunted spots. It is a place called Hickory Hill and over the years, it has been many things from plantation house to tourist attraction to chamber of horrors for the men and women once brought here in chains. Thanks to this dark blight on its history, Hickory Hill has long been known by its more familiar name, the Old Slave House.

For decades, travelers have come from all over Illinois and beyond to see this mysterious and forbidding place. The secrets of slavery that were hidden here were given up many years ago, but there are other dark whispers about the place. These stories claim that the dead of Hickory Hill do not rest in peace.

Hickory Hill was built by a man named John Hart Crenshaw, a descendant of old American family with ties to the founding of our country. His grandfather, John Hart, was one of the signers of the Declaration of Independence and a tree that once shaded the lawn of Hickory Hill was carried as a seed from the gravesite of George Washington. Crenshaw himself has a notable spot in the history of Illinois, thanks to both his public and private deeds.

He was born in November 1797 in a house on the borders of North and South Carolina. His family moved west and settled in New Madrid, Missouri, only to have their home destroyed by the great earthquake of 1811. A short time later, they moved to Saline County, Illinois and started a farm on the east side of Eagle Mountain. There was a salt well on the farm called Half Moon Lick.

Not long after settling in Illinois, William Crenshaw died and left his eldest son, John, to provide for his mother and six brothers and sisters. By the time he was 18, he was already toiling in the crude salt refinery at Half Moon Lick.

Today, it is hard for us to understand the demand that existed for salt in times past. In those days, salt was often used as money or as barter material when purchasing goods and supplies. In the early 1800s, there was great need for salt, thanks to the westward movement into the frontier. It could be used for both flavoring and as a preservative for meat.

Early on, a large salt reservation was discovered in southern Illinois and the land began to be leased out by the government in 1812. Individual operators rented tracts of land and hired laborers to work them. The work in these salt mines was brutal and in many cases, black men who would work cheaply were hired from the region. Many of them had escaped from slavery in the south, limiting them in the job market, but even free blacks from Illinois had a hard time finding other work. As these men made little money, and few had homes of their own, the mine operators constructed a small village called US Salines, where the blacks could live. In

1827, the town became Equality, Illinois.

In 1829, the government decided to sell off the salt lands to raise money for a new prison and other state improvements in Illinois. The individual operators were given the opportunity to purchase their holdings and one man who did so was John Hart Crenshaw. He made a number of such purchases over the years and eventually owned several thousand acres of land. At that time, he also owned a sawmill and three salt furnaces for processing.

Eventually, Crenshaw would become an important man in southern Illinois. In 1817, he had married Sinia Taylor and began developing wide-reaching business interests that would allow him to amass quite a fortune. In fact, at one point he made so much money that he paid one-seventh of all of the taxes collected in the state. He would become known as not only a salt operator but also as a toll bridge owner, farmer, land speculator, railroad builder, state bank director for a bank in Shawneetown, a supporter of the Methodist Church and an important figure in the Gallatin County Democratic party.

Despite all of these accomplishments, Crenshaw is best remembered today for Hickory Hill and his ties to Illinois slavery, kidnapping and illegal trafficking in slaves. But how is this possible in Illinois, a state where slavery was not allowed?

In the early years of the state's history, Illinois was far from a Northern state. Cairo, Illinois lies geographically further south than Richmond, Virginia and many of the settlers, especially in Little Egypt, came from southern states. They brought with them their customs and traditions, including slavery.

Illinois was technically a free state, although it did recognize three types of slavery. The slaves, and their descendants, of the French settlers along the Mississippi were protected under the Treaty of 1783. The state also allowed indentured servitude for a contracted length of time, and it also allowed slaves to be leased for one-year terms in the salt lands of Gallatin, Hardin and Saline counties.

Workers were always needed for the salt mines. They worked

the salt wells, cut trees and hauled wood for the fires that boiled the salt water in thirty or more cast-iron kettles. The work was backbreaking, hot and brutal, and attracted only the most desperate workers. Because of this, slavery became essential to the success of the salt operations. A provision for it to continue here was written into the 1818 Illinois Constitution, allowing the mine owners to lease slaves from Kentucky and Tennessee.

As imagined, the slaves had no protection under the law and free blacks had very little. There were a number of laws concerning slavery in Illinois. In the early days, it was discouraged but actually stopped short of being illegal. While the law did provide some small protection for free blacks living in Illinois, it did nothing to discourage the common practice of kidnapping them and selling them into slavery. Only civil prosecution was used to punish this practice and few officials ever interfered with the gangs of men who seized blacks in river towns and carried them down south for sale at auction.

Perhaps the most guilty of this practice were the night riders of the 1830s and 1840s. Originally, groups like this were formed when local residents felt that organized law had failed them but they were not always on the right side of the law either, and many blamed them for thievery, violence and corruption. In the 1840s, some of these bands were connected to the kidnapping of free blacks.

The night riders were alleged to always be on the lookout for escaped slaves and they posted men along the Ohio River at night. The slaves were then captured and could be ransomed back to their masters or returned for a reward. They also kidnapped free men, and their children, and sold them in the south. The night riders created a "reverse underground railroad," where slaves were spirited away to the southern plantations instead of to the northern cities and freedom.

Southern Illinois tradition has it that John Hart Crenshaw, who leased slaves to work the salt mines, kept a number of night riders in his employ to watch for escaped slaves. He used this as a profitable sideline to his legitimate businesses. By law, Crenshaw's men could capture the runaway slaves and turn them into a local law officer for a reward. If no reward had been offered for the runaway, the county paid a flat $10 fee. In addition to the fee, Crenshaw could then lease the slave from the county at a lower rate. However, many believe that Crenshaw had little interest in rewards and leases. He learned that he could make much more money by simply working the captured slaves himself or by selling them directly back into the southern market. While there exists no written evidence that Crenshaw was involved in illegally holding slaves, it has long been believed that he was.

Crenshaw was seen as a respected businessman and a pillar of the church and community. No one had any idea that he was holding illegal slaves or that he was suspected of kidnapping black families and selling them into slavery. They would have been even more surprised to learn that the slaves were being held captive in his home. In the third floor attic of Hickory Hill, barred chambers kept the men and women captive. The men were often subjected to cruelty and the women to the "breeding chamber." It was here, the stories say, the women and girls met a slave called Uncle Bob. He was a giant of a man who had been chosen as a stud slave because of his intelligence and physical size. He had been selected to breed better and stronger slaves and make more money for Crenshaw at auction. A pregnant slave on the southern market was worth nearly twice as much as a female with no child. Crenshaw was believed to have sold as slaves any workers that were in excess of what he needed on his farms and in the salt mines.

According to Uncle Bob, or Robert Wilson as he came to be called, he sired no less than three hundred children in a span of ten years at Hickory Hill. Historians have more than forty affidavits from people who met and talked with Wilson about his life in service to Crenshaw. After leaving southern Illinois, Wilson served in the Confederate Army during the Civil War. He lived to be 112 years old and died in the Elgin Veteran's Hospital in 1949.

Hickory Hill, the classic Greek plantation house, still stands today. It is located near the town of Equality, a short distance from Harrisburg. The border of Kentucky, where Crenshaw stationed his slave catchers on the river at night, is just a short horseback ride away.

Crenshaw contracted an architect to begin on the house in 1833, but he had little time to spend on the new project. Hickory Hill did not end up getting completed until 1842. It stands on a high hill, overlooking the Saline River. The structure was built in the Classic Greek style of the time period and rises three stories. Huge columns, cut from the hearts of individual pine trees, span the front of the house and support wide verandas. On the porch is a main entrance door and above it, on the upper veranda, is another door that opens onto the balcony. Here, Crenshaw could look out over his vast holdings. He furnished the interior of the house with original artwork and designs that had been imported from Europe. Each of the rooms, and there were thirteen on the first and second floors, were heated with separate fireplaces.

The house was certainly grand, but the most unusual additions to the place were not easily seen. Legend had it that there was once a tunnel that connected the basement to the Saline River, where slaves could be loaded and unloaded at night. In addition, another passageway, which was large enough to contain a wagon, was built into the rear of the house. It allowed the vehicles to actually enter into the house and, according to the stories, allowed slaves to be unloaded where they could not be seen from the outside. The back of the house is still marked by this carriage entrance today.

Located on the third floor of Hickory Hill are the infamous confines of the attic and proof that Crenshaw had something unusual in mind when he contracted the house to be built. The attic can still be reached today by a flight of narrow, well-worn stairs. They exit into a wide hallway and there are about a dozen cell-like rooms with barred windows and flat, wooden bunks facing the corridor. Originally, the cells were even smaller, and there were more of them, but some were removed in the past. One can only imagine how small and cramped they must have been because even an average-sized visitor to the attic can scarcely turn around in the ones that remain. The only cell that is really bigger than the rest is one that is designated as Uncle Bob's Room, but even this chamber only measures nine by twelve feet. The corridor between the cells extends from one end of the room to the other. Windows at the ends provided the only ventilation and during the summer months, the heat in the attic was unbearable. The windows also provided the only source of light.

The slaves spent their time secured in their cells, chained to heavy metal rings. There are still scars on the wooden walls and floors today and chains and heavy balls are still kept on display. There are also two frames that are said to have been whipping posts located in the attic. Slaves were often flogged for disobeying orders or failing to complete their work. It was written that the whipping posts were "built of heavy timber pegged together. A man of average height could be strung up by his wrists and his toes would barely touch the lower cross-piece."

Stories have long been told about the cruelties that Crenshaw inflicted on the slaves, from beatings to disfigurement. Owners of the house have told many of the stories but even worse are the stories passed on by descendants of the Crenshaw family. One relative recalled stories told by her grandmother about the family being forced to watch when the slaves were whipped. Other descendants swear that Crenshaw was unjustly accused of such crimes, while others in the family say that his actions went beyond inhumane and beyond the mere mistreatment of the slaves.

Earlier, it was mentioned that most local residents were unaware of Crenshaw's activities, but this was not the case with everyone. In the late 1820s, Crenshaw was actually indicted by a Gallatin County grand jury for kidnapping a free black family. A jury acquitted him of the charges and although it was later learned that the family had been sold to a plantation in Texas, Crenshaw could not be tried again for the same crime. He continued to maintain his standing in the community.

In 1842, Crenshaw was once again indicted on criminal charges. It was reported that he had engineered the kidnapping of a free black woman named Maria Adams and her children. According to the *Illinois Republican* newspaper in Shawneetown, Crenshaw had the family abducted from their home and kept them hidden for several days. They were then tied up in a wagon and were driven out of state. Unfortunately, the prosecutor in the case knew more than he could prove and Crenshaw was again set free.

Soon, rumors began to spread about Crenshaw's business activities. Around the same time, a newspaper account publicly declared that a nephew of Crenshaw was accusing him of cheating him out of his father's estate. These rumors and rumblings, combined with the Adams indictment, started to upset a lot of people in the area. On March 25, 1842, a steam mill that Crenshaw owned in Cypressville was burned to the ground. According to the *Sangamo Journal* newspaper, the burning of the mill touched off several events in the region:

"The steam mill of Mr. John Crenshaw, in Gallatin County, was burnt. It appears...that a short time previous, he sold a family of Negroes, on whose services he had claims, to a trader, and that these Negroes were shipped to the lower country, probably to be sold into perpetual slavery. By some it was believed that the mill was burnt by Negroes in revenge for this act...Great excitement followed and a band of "Regulators" had been raised with the design of driving all free Negroes out of Gallatin County."

The mill was burned just two days before Crenshaw's trial began in the Adams case and although no one was killed in the blaze, two of the workers were injured and badly burned. The fire was believed to have been started by a group of free black men, angry over Crenshaw's actions.

On April 2, after Crenshaw's acquittal, a group of night riders rode into Equality and began firing their guns into the air. They announced that they planned to return and lynch all of the blacks who had attacked John Crenshaw. After that, they declared that they would remove every black person from Gallatin County. All of the law enforcement officials, including attorneys, were warned not to interfere or they would be killed. The riders promised to return the following week as they rode out of town. True to their word, they returned the next Saturday, again brandishing weapons. They made more threats but the promises of death and violence were left unfulfilled. The incidents ended with no one harmed.

In 1846, Crenshaw's business holdings began to decline. In addition to several civil court actions against him, salt deposits were discovered in both Virginia and Ohio that proved to be more profitable than those in southern Illinois. To make matters worse, Crenshaw was also attacked by one of his slaves, resulting in the loss of one leg. The stories maintain that he was beating a woman in his fields one day when an angry slave picked up an ax and severed Crenshaw's leg with it. After that, most of the slaves were sold off, and his operations dwindled with the end of the salt mining.

During the Civil War, Crenshaw sold Hickory Hill and moved to a new farmhouse closer to Equality. He continued farming but also diversified into lumber, railroads and banks. He died on December 4, 1871 and was buried in Hickory Hill Cemetery, a lonely piece of ground just northeast of his former home.

Whether John Crenshaw rests in peace is unknown, but according to the tales of Little Egypt, many of his former captives most certainly do not. According to the accounts, "mysterious voices can be heard in that attic, sometimes moaning, sometimes singing the spirituals that comfort heavy hearts."

And those accounts, as the reader will soon learn, are just the beginning.

I have visited the Old Slave House more than a dozen times. The attic of the house, I believe, is still quite disturbing today. There has never been a time when I have climbed that old staircase to the third floor that I have not felt my heart clench a little. The remains of the slave quarters are often hot and cramped and at other times, are filled with mysterious chills that no one seems quite able to explain. I have yet to encounter one of the ghosts of Hickory Hill, but others have not been so lucky, leading me to believe that something lingers there. Could the tormented souls of the slaves still linger in the attic?

I have spoken with George Sisk, the last private owner of the house, on many occasions. I once asked him if he believed in ghosts and whether he thought there were any at Hickory Hill. "The house is haunted," he insisted, "I don't believe in ghosts but I respect them." This curious statement of non-belief was followed by the fact that he never goes into the attic of the place unless he has to. On those occasions, he never stays for long and, if no one else is in the house, the door to the attic is always kept locked.

Is the house haunted? Based on the stories, most likely it is, but despite what some people have claimed, the Sisk family did not create the ghost stories of Hickory Hill. That distinction belongs to the scores of visitors who have come to the house over the years and who have encountered something there that is beyond the ordinary. The house has been in the Sisk family since 1906, when George's grandfather purchased it from a descendant of John Hart Crenshaw. It was already a notorious place in the local area, but it would soon become even more widely known.

To locals, the house was known more as the Old Slave House than as Hickory Hill, thanks to the stories surrounding the place. In the 1920s, the Sisks began to have visitors from outside the area. They would come to the door at just about any hour and request a tour of the place, having heard about it from a local waitress or gas station attendant as they were passing through. This time period marked the early era of automobile vacations in America. As motor cars began to be more affordable to families, they began to travel, especially in the summer months. The Old Slave House, thanks to a savvy advertising campaign, became a destination point for many travelers, and the owners began charging an admission in 1930.

For just a dime, or a nickel if you were a child, you could tour the place where "Slavery Existed in Illinois," as the road signs put it.

Soon, Hickory Hill was one of the most frequently visited places in Little Egypt. And soon, it would gain a reputation for being the most haunted one!

Shortly after the house became a tourist attraction, visitors began reporting that strange things were happening in the place. They complained of odd noises in the attic especially, noises that sounds like cries, whimpers and even the rattling of chains. A number of people told of uncomfortable feelings in the slave quarters like sensations of intense fear, sadness and of being watched. Cold chills filled a number of the tales, along with being touched by invisible hands and feeling unseen figures brush by them. Soon, the stories spread that the Old Slave House was haunted!

Some have argued that the house could not be haunted because no records exist to say that anyone ever died there. Perhaps slaves did die in the house and it was not recorded but regardless, most experts believe that death may not be the only thing that causes ghosts to stay behind. Some feel the great trauma and horrific events that took place in the attic may have caused the spirits of the slaves to return to the house after death. Or perhaps the gruesome past replays itself, causing impressions of days gone by to remain in the atmosphere.

The rumored hauntings had little effect on tourist traffic and if anything, the stories brought more people to the house. Other legends soon began to attach themselves to Hickory Hill. The most famous is the story that "no one could spend the entire night in the attic." The story got started because of an incident involving a ghost chaser from Benton, Illinois named Hickman Whittington. The Benton newspaper, the *Post-Dispatch*, noted in a late 1920s edition that "whether ghost chaser Hickman Whittington expects to see a white or black ghost remains to be seen. He said he recently learned that cries have been heard coming from the post where slaves were whipped for disobedience, and he intended to do something about it."

George Sisk told authors Richard Winer and Nancy Osborn Ishmael that whatever happened to Whittington after coming to the house that night scared the life right out of him. He told them that "when he visited the place he was in fine health but just after he left here, he took sick and he died just hours after his visit…you might say that something scared him to death."

Winer asked him what he thought that "something" might have been, but Sisk had no answer. "I wouldn't want to be the one to say," he told them, "but it could have been the same thing that scared those two Marines that tried to stay in the attic overnight in 1966. They had the good sense to leave before anything disastrous happened…they came flying down the stairs at about one-thirty in the morning. Said they saw forms coming at them. They were in a state of shock. I really didn't get to talk to them very long. They tore out of here in a hurry…didn't even bother to go back upstairs to get their belongings."

What had they seen? The two Marines, who had both seen action in Vietnam, volunteered to spend the night in the attic. They were certainly not the first to attempt such a thing either. After the incident involving Hickman Whittington and the story that no one could make it through the night, literally dozens had tried. None of them had been successful, but the two veterans were sure they would be the first. Each of them scoffed when they were told that others had fled the house in terror and after several hours in the attic, they began to get bored. Finally, just as they were about to go to sleep, their kerosene lantern began to flicker. There were no drafts but the light began to get dimmer and dimmer. Then, an agonized moan filled the air, seeming to come from all around them. The moaning was followed by other voices and then, just before the lantern blew itself out, the Marines claimed to see "swirling forms" coming out of the shadows. Terrified, they fled the attic and never returned.

Other would-be thrill seekers followed the Marines, but for

one reason or another, no one managed to make it until daybreak in the attic of Hickory Hill. Eventually, the practice was ended because, as Mr. Sisk informed me later, a small fire got started one night by an overturned lantern. After that, he turned down requests for late night ghost hunting.

He only relented on one other occasion. In 1978, he allowed a reporter from Harrisburg named David Rodgers to spend the night in the attic as a Halloween stunt for a local television station. The reporter managed to beat out nearly 150 previous challengers and became the first person to spend the night in the slave quarters in more than a century. Sisk never believed that he would make it through the night and in fact announced that he would flee the house before one in the morning. "Other reporters before Rodgers had tried to stay the night, but none of them made it. They all said they heard shuffling feet and whimpering cries in the slave quarters at night," he told newspapers.

Rodgers later admitted that he was "queasy" going into the house and also said that his experience in the attic was anything but mundane. "I heard a lot of strange noises," he said the next morning. "I was actually shaking. The place is so spooky. The tape recorder was picking up sounds that I wasn't hearing." He felt pretty good about himself afterward, but confessed that he "didn't want to make the venture an annual event."

Stories from visitors and curiosity seekers have continued to be told over the years. One incident was even witnessed by George Sisk. A woman came down from the attic one day and asked about the peculiar things going on up there. He and his wife followed the woman back to the attic and she showed them how, in certain locations, all of the hair on her arms would stand on end. She demanded to know why it was happening, but of course, no one could tell her.

I have since spoken with others who have had similar experiences and with other witnesses who claim to have been touched and poked by fingers and who have heard the now famous voices and mumbling snatches of song that have long been reported on the third floor. The whispers and sounds are certainly unsettling, but more so are the encounters reported by those who have seen the ghosts here face to face!

For most visitors though, a visit to Hickory Hill is not so bizarre. Many experience nothing, while others say they feel unsettled or frightened in the attic. Often, emotions become very overwrought here and grown men have often been reduced to tears. Proof of the supernatural? Perhaps not, but the attic is certainly an odd place with a lot of odd energy.

The Sisks have also had their share of weird experiences at Hickory Hill over the years. Mr. Sisk has always maintained that he has never encountered any of the ghosts, but his wife can't say the same. She has talked about her experiences in the past. "The sounds here bother me a lot. I can make excuses for some of them...I tell myself that it's the wind but one night when we were lying in bed, I heard a loud crashing like glass breaking. Thinking that a window had broken, we got up to investigate. There was nothing broken...Another sound that shook me up tremendously happened one night when I was lying in bed. There was a sound like something, or someone, banging from under the floor with a hammer. I clearly heard it three times, but what it was, I don't know."

She also said that she never takes baths in the evenings anymore, but only in the morning or when her husband is home. The bathroom in the residence area of the house was located in the rear part of the building. She often heard the sound of someone calling her name when she took baths in the house alone. Mrs. Sisk eventually stopped trying to discover a source for the strange sounds and simply states that "I know now that there is something here."

Ever since the days of Hickman Whittington, the Old Slave House has been a frequent stopping place for ghost hunters, psychic investigators and supernatural enthusiasts. Sisk keeps a number of books and clippings related to some of these visits and has been interviewed (by myself and others) many times about the ghostly happenings here. Most of the ghost hunters, many of whom are historians at heart, come to the house looking for ghosts and hoping to soak up some of the rich history of the place. Others show up with offers of exorcisms. One couple even claimed that if they were not allowed to perform their ceremony, a negative energy would enter the bodies of the Sisk family and possess them. The Sisks declined the offer. "We decided that whatever's upstairs can stay there...I believe in leaving things like that alone."

In 1996, the Old Slave House was closed down, due to the declining health of Mr. and Mrs. Sisk. Although it looked as though the house might never re-open, it was finally purchased by the state of Illinois three years later. Plans are in the works (as of this writing) to open the house again in the future as a state historic site. What will become of the ghosts, or at least the ghost stories, is unknown. As many readers know, legends and lore don't often fare well at official state locations.

Regardless, if you should get the chance, mark Hickory Hill as a historical and haunted place to visit. If you climb those stairs to the attic, you will feel your stomach drop just a little and you might even be overwhelmed by sadness.

Is it your imagination or does the tragedy of the house still make itself felt here? I can't say for sure, but I can guarantee that you will find yourself speaking softly in the gloomy, third floor corridor as your voice lowers in deference to the nameless people who once suffered here. We must remember this part of the past, no matter how difficult this may be, because he who does not remember the past is doomed to repeat it.

SUMMERWIND

The History of Wisconsin's Most Haunted House

If a person were forced to choose what the greatest ghost story in Wisconsin might be, it would almost undoubtedly be the legend of Summerwind. This haunted mansion has spawned more strange tales and stories that any other location in the state. What dark secrets remain hidden in the ruins of this once grand estate? Were the stories of ghostly encounters and messages from beyond really true...or were they part of an elaborate publicity hoax?

Located on the shores of West Bay Lake, in the far northeast regions of Wisconsin, are the ruins of a once grand mansion that was called Summerwind. The house is long gone now, but the memories remain...as do the stories and legends of the inexplicable events that once took place there. Summerwind is perhaps Wisconsin's most haunted house, or at least it was, before fire and the elements of nature destroyed her. Regardless, even the ravages of time cannot destroy the haunted history of the house.

Robert P. Lamont built the mansion in 1916 as a summer home for his family. Nestled on the shores of the lake, the house caught the cool breezes of northern Wisconsin and provided a comfortable place for Lamont to escape the pressures of everyday life in Washington D. C., as he would later go on to serve as the Secretary of Commerce under President Herbert Hoover.

But life was not always sublime at Summerwind during the years of the Lamont family. For those who claim that the ghost stories of the house were created in later years, they forget the original tale of Robert Lamont's encounter with a spirit. Lamont actually fired a pistol at a ghost that he believed was an intruder. The bullet holes in the basement door from the kitchen remained for many years.

Upon the death of Robert Lamont, the house was sold...and sold again. It seemed that nothing out of the ordinary really happened here, save for Lamont's encounter with the phantom intrud-er, until the early 1970s. It was in this period that the family living in the house was nearly destroyed...supposedly by ghosts.

Arnold Hinshaw, his wife Ginger, and their six children, moved into Summerwind in the early part of the 1970s. They would only reside in the house for six months, but it would be an eventful period of time.

From the day that they moved in, they knew strange things were going on in the house. It had been vacant for some time but otherworldly visitors had apparently occupied it! The Hinshaws, and their children immediately started to report vague shapes and shadows flickering down the hallways. They also claimed to hear mumbled voices in darkened, empty rooms. When they would walk inside, the sounds would quickly stop. Most alarming was the ghost of the woman who was often seen floating back and forth just past some French doors that led off from the dining room.

The family wondered if they were simply imagining things, but continued events convinced them otherwise. Appliances, a hot water heater and a water pump would mysteriously break down and then repair themselves before a serviceman could be called.

Windows and doors that were closed would reopen on their own. One particular window, which proved especially stubborn, would raise and lower itself at all hours. Out of desperation, Arnold drove a heavy nail through the window casing and it final-ly stayed closed.

On one occasion, Arnold walked out to his car to go to work, and the vehicle suddenly burst into flames. No one was near it and it is unknown whether the source of the fire was supernatural in origin, but regardless, no cause was ever found for it.

Despite the strange activity, the Hinshaws wanted to make the best of the historic house so they decided to hire some men to make a few renovations. It was most common for the workers to not show up for work, usually claiming illness, although a few of them simply told her that they refused to work on Summerwind, which

Summerwind as it looked in its last years before destruction
(Courtesy of Todd Roll)

was, they said, haunted. That was when the Hinshaws gave up and decided to try and do the work themselves.

One day they began painting a closet in one of the bedrooms. A large shoe drawer was installed in the closet's back wall, and Arnold pulled it out so that he could paint around the edges of the frame. When he did, he noticed that there seemed to be a large, dark space behind the drawer.

Ginger brought him a flashlight and he wedged himself into the narrow opening as far as his shoulders. He looked around with the flashlight and then suddenly jumped back, scrambling away from the opening. He was both frightened and disgusted for there was some sort of corpse jammed into the secret compartment!

Believing that an animal had crawled in there and died many years ago, Arnold tried to squeeze back in for a closer look. He couldn't make out much of anything, so when the children came home from school, he recruited his daughter Mary to get a better look. Mary took the flashlight and crawled inside. Moments later, she let out a scream. It was a human corpse in the cabinet! She uncovered a skull, still bearing dirty black hair, a brown arm and a portion of a leg.

Why the Hinshaws never contacted the authorities about this body is unknown. Was the story concocted later to fit into the tales of haunted Summerwind? Or was their reasoning the truth...that the body had been the result of a crime that took place many years ago, far too long for the police to do anything about it now?

Had they been thinking things through, they might have realized that this body might have been the cause of much of the supernatural activity in the house. Removing it might have laid the ghost to rest, so to speak. Regardless, they left the corpse where they found it...but it will figure into our story once again.

Shortly after the discovery of the body in the hidden compartment, things started to take a turn for the worse at Summerwind.

Arnold began staying up very late at night and playing a Hammond organ that the couple had purchased before moving into the house. He had always enjoyed playing the organ, using it as a form of relaxation, but his playing now was different. His playing became a frenzied mixture of melodies that seemed to make no sense, and grew louder as the night wore on. Ginger pleaded with him to stop but Arnold claimed the demons in his head demanded that he play. He often crashed the keys on the organ until dawn, frightening his wife and children so badly that they often huddled together in one bedroom, crying and cowering in fear.

Arnold had a complete mental breakdown and, around the same time, Ginger attempted suicide.

Were the stories of strange events at Summerwind merely the result of two disturbed minds? It might seem so, but what about the children? They also reported the ghostly encounters. Were they simply influenced by their parents' questionable sanity...or were the stories real? The family's connection with the house would continue for years to come.

While Arnold was sent away for treatment, Ginger and the children moved to Granton, Wisconsin to live with Ginger's parents. Ginger and Arnold would eventually be divorced. Ginger later recovered her health, away from Summerwind at last, and she married a man named George Olsen.

Things seemed to be going quite well for her in her new peaceful life, until a few years later, when her father announced that he was going to buy Summerwind.

Raymond Bober was a popcorn vendor and businessman who with his wife Marie, planned to turn the old mansion into a restaurant and an inn. He believed that the house would attract many guests to the scenic location on the lake. They had no idea what had happened to their daughter in the house.

Ginger was horrified at her parents' decision. She had never given them the details about what had happened during the six months that she had lived in the house and she refused to do so now. What she did do was to beg them not to buy Summerwind.

Bober's mind was made up. He announced that he realized the

house was haunted, but this would not deter him. He claimed that he had spent time at the house and knew the identity of the ghost that was haunting the place.

According to Bober, the ghost was a man named Jonathan Carver, an eighteenth century British explorer who was haunting the house and searching for an old deed that had been given to him by the Sioux Indians. In the document, he supposedly had the rights to the northern third of Wisconsin. The deed had supposedly been placed in a box and sealed into the foundation of Summerwind. Bober claimed that Carver had asked his help in finding it.

Bober wrote a book about his experiences at Summerwind and his communications with Carver through dreams, trances and a Ouija board. The book was published in 1979 under the name of Wolffgang von Bober and was called *The Carver Effect*. It is currently out-of-print and very hard to find.

Shortly after Bober bought the house, he, his son Karl, Ginger and her new husband, George, spent a day exploring and looking over the house. The group had wandered through the place and as they were leaving the second floor, George spotted the closet where the secret compartment was hidden. He began pulling out the drawers and looking behind them, although Ginger begged him to stop.

George was confused. He had simply been curious as to what might be in the drawers. Up until then, Ginger had never told anyone about finding the body behind the closet. Sitting in the kitchen later, she would tell them everything.

After hearing the story, the men rushed back upstairs and returned to the closet. Ginger's brother, Karl, climbed into the space with a light and looked around. In a few moments, he climbed back out...it was empty!

Bober and George also inspected the small space and found nothing. Where had the corpse gone? Had it been removed, either by natural or supernatural forces? Or, most importantly, had it ever really been there at all?

Toward the end of that summer, Karl traveled alone to the old house. He had gone to get a repair estimate on some work to be done on the house and to check with someone about getting rid of the bats that inhabited the place. He also planned to do some yard work and to get the place cleaned up a little.

It started to rain the first day that he was there and he began closing some of the windows. He was upstairs, in the dark hallway, and heard a voice call his name. He looked around but there was no one there. Karl closed the window and went downstairs. He walked into the front room and heard what sounded like two pistol shots! He ran into the kitchen and found the room filled with smoke and the acrid smell of gunpowder. Apparently someone had fired a gun inside of the house!

Karl searched the place, finding the doors locked and undisturbed. There appeared to be no one inside and he returned to the kitchen. He began looking around the room and discovered two bullet holes in the door leading down to the basement. He examined them closely and realized that they were not new holes at all but old bullet holes that had worn smooth around the edges. They were apparently holes left behind from Robert Lamont's encounter with a ghost in the kitchen. Perhaps events from the past were replaying themselves at Summerwind!

No matter what the explanation, it was enough for Karl, and he left the house that afternoon.

The plans to turn the house into a restaurant did not go smoothly. Workmen refused to stay on the job, complaining of tools disappearing and feelings as if they were being watched. Marie Bober agreed with their complaints. She was always uneasy in the house and frequently told people that she felt as if she was followed from place to place whenever she was inside.

Most disturbing to Bober was the apparent shrinkage and expansion of the house. Bober would measure rooms one day and then find that they were a different size the next day. Usually, his measurements were larger than those given in the blueprints of the house...sometime greatly larger. At one point, Bober estimated that he could seat 150 people in his restaurant but after laying out his plans on the blueprints of Summerwind, he realized that the place could seat half that many.

Photographs that were taken of the house, using the same camera and taken only seconds apart, also displayed the variations of space. The living room was said to show the greatest enlargement. Bober compared his photos of the living room with those that Ginger had taken when she and Arnold moved in. Ginger's photos showed curtains on the windows that she took with her when she moved out. The curtains were physically absent in the room that Bober photographed but somehow they appeared in his photos!

Like the incident involving Karl and the pistol shots, could Summerwind be a place where time inexplicably repeats itself? Perhaps the place wasn't haunted at all, but instead, was a mysterious site where time was distorted in ways that we cannot understand. Perhaps the shadows and figures that were seen could have been people or images from the past (or the future) and perhaps the sound of someone calling Karl's name would happen in reality...several months later. We will never know for sure, but the idea is something worth considering.

Eventually, the project was abandoned and Bober would never see the dream of his restaurant and inn. Strangely, despite his claims that he was an earthly companion of the ghostly Jonathan Carver, the Bobers never spent the night inside of the house. They chose instead to sleep in an RV that they parked on the grounds. Also strange was the fact that Carver (if the ghost existed) chose to manifest himself in such malevolent ways, especially if he was looking for help in finding his deed.

Bober's explanation for this was that Carver resented anyone living in the house or trying to renovate the place, at least until the deed was found. Bober spent many days searching the basement for where it might be hidden, chipping the foundation and peering into dark holes and crevices. To this day, the mysterious deed has never been found.

In the years that followed Bober's abandonment of Summer-wind, a number of skeptics came forward to poke holes in some of Bober's claims. Many of their counter-claims have been nearly as easy to discredit as some of Bober's original ones.

Obviously, we are never going to know for sure if Summer-wind was really haunted. The house is gone now and we are left with only the claims, reports and witness accounts of Bober and his family.

But in 1983, a freelance writer named Will Pooley set out to gather the facts behind the story and discredit it. His research claimed that even if Bober had found Carver's deed, it would have been worthless. He based these findings on the fact that the British government ruled against an individual's purchase of Indian land and also that the Sioux had never claimed land west of the Mississippi River.

First of all, the land was not sold to Carver, it was given to him in return for assistance that he had given to the Indians, so British law would not have ruled against this. On the other subject, the Sioux Indians were not a single tribe, they were an entire nation, made up of many different tribes. It is possible, and very likely, that one tribe that belonged to the Sioux nation could have lived in Wisconsin. The white settlers pushed the Indians further and further west and as this particular tribe abandoned their lands, they could have deeded them to Carver.

Pooley also argued that the deed to the property had been located in the old land office in Wausau, Wisconsin in the 1930s and that it is unlikely that Carver even journeyed as far north as West Bay Lake.

But would he have had to travel to northern Wisconsin to hold a deed to the land? And why would there not have been another deed filed for that piece of land? Someone could have claimed it many years later, not even realizing that Carver already held the title to it.

He also argued that the deed could have never been placed in the foundation of the house anyway…Summerwind had been built more than 130 years after Carver died. To this, it can only be argued that many events of the supernatural world go unexplained.

One man that Pooley did talk to however, was Herb Dickman of Land 'O Lakes, Wisconsin. He had helped pour the foundation for the house in 1916 and recalled that nothing had been placed in the foundation. There was no box containing a deed or anything else. So, who really knows?

Apparently, Bober was not always the most credible person either. Residents who lived close to Summerwind said that Bober spent less than two summers at the estate. After abandoning plans for the restaurant, he tried to get a permit to operate a concession stand near the house but local ordinances prohibited this. Perhaps he was planning the idea of tours of the haunted house… an idea that would come along a little later.

There was even some uncertainty as to whether or not Bober even owned Summerwind. One area resident told Pooley that Bober had tried to buy the house on a contract-for-deed but the deal had fallen through. The house had been abandoned and no one laid claim to it, save for the bank, and they never realized what Bober was up to out there. This story has never been verified, and it cannot be proven that Bober did not own the place.

So how much of the story that Bober wrote about in his book is true? Was the house really haunted, or was the story of the haunting merely a part of a scheme by Raymond Bober to draw crowds to a haunted restaurant?

Those who live near the house claim that the idea that it is haunted has all come from the fact that the mansion was abandoned and from Bober's wild claims. But what else would they say?

These neighbors have often made it very clear that they resent the strangers who have come to the property, tramping over their lawns and knocking on their doors. They say that the chartered buses that once came and dumped would-be ghost hunters onto the grounds of Summerwind were also unwelcome. These are the last people to ask for an objective opinion on whether this house is actually haunted.

So there remains the mystery…was Summerwind really haunted? No one knows, and if they do, they aren't saying.

The house was completely abandoned in the early 1980s and fell deeper and deeper into ruin. Bats had already taken up residence years before and the house became a virtual shell, resting there in a grove of pines. The windows were shattered and the doors hung open, inviting nature's destructive force inside.

In 1986, the house was purchased by three investors who apparently thought that they could make a go of the place again. But it was not to be, for forces greater than man had other ideas. Summerwind was struck by lightning during a terrible storm in June of 1988 and burned to the ground.

Today, only the foundations, the stone chimneys, and perhaps the ghosts remain. And if they do reside here still, they share the space with our haunting memories of the house that once was.

Bibliography &
Recommended Reading

Adams, Charles J. III, *Philadelphia Ghost Stories* (1998)

Adelman, Garry E. & Timothy H. Smith, *Devil's Den* (1997)

Allen, John, *Legends and Lore of Southern Illinois* (1963)

American Weekly (April 1928)

Back, Mollie & Brian Wolle, *Ghost Encounters* (1998)

Belanger, Jeff, *Dudleytown* (1999/2001)

Bell, Charles Bailey, *A Mysterious Spirit* (1934)

Bell, Richard William, *Our Family Troubles* (1894)

Bettenhausen, Brad, "Batchelor's Grove Cemetery," *Where the Trails Cross* (1995)

Bielski, Ursula, *Chicago Haunts* (1998)

Bingham, Joan & Dolores Riccio, *More Haunted Houses* (1991)

Blue & Gray Magazine, *Guide to Haunted Places of the Civil War* (1996)

Brehm, H. C., *Echoes of the Bell Witch in the Twentieth Century* (1979)

Bullitt, Alexander Clark, *Rambles in Mammoth Cave* (1845)

Campbell, Bruce J., *Escape from Alcatraz* (1963/1976)

Chamberlain Jr., Paul Hilliard, *Dudleytown, Connecticut* (1964)

Citro, Joseph, *Passing Strange* (1996)

Daily Grind (Howard Co. Employee Newsletter) (1997)

Davis, Kenneth, *Don't Know Much About the Civil War* (1996)

Davis, William C & Bell I. Wiley, *The Civil War* (1998)

deLavigne, Jeanne, *Ghost Stories of Old New Orleans* (1946)

Drury, John, *Old Illinois House* (1948)

Edith Wharton Restoration, Inc. (www. edithwharton. org)

Floyd, Randall, *Great American Mysteries* (1990)

Frassanito, William, *Gettysburg: A Journey in Time* (1975)

Gallagher, Trish, *Ghosts & Haunted Houses of Maryland* (1988)

George, Angelo, *Mummies, Catacombs & Mammoth Cave* (1994)

Ghosts of the Prairie, www. prairieghosts. com

Guiley, Rosemary Ellen, *Encyclopedia of Ghosts & Spirits* (2000)

Hauck, Dennis William, *Haunted Places: The National Directory* (1996)

Heitz, Lisa Hefner, *Haunted Kansas* (1997)

Holzer, Hans, *Yankee Ghosts* (1963)

Howard County News (various editions)

Ingram, M. V., *An Authenticated History of the Bell Witch* (1894)

Jarman, Rufus, "Mystery House on Elm Street," *Yankee Magazine* (1971)

Jarvis, Sharon, *Dark Zones* (1992)

Jarvis, Sharon, *Dead Zones* (1992)

Klein, Victor C., *New Orleans Ghosts* (1993)

Kaczmarek, Dale, *Windy City Ghosts* (2000)

Lyons, Joy Medley, *Mammoth Cave: Story Behind the Scenery* (1991)

May, Antoinette, *Haunted Houses of California* (1990)

McCloy, James F. & Ray Miller, Jr., *The Jersey Devil* (1976)

McCloy, James F. & Ray Miller, Jr., *Phantom of the Pines* (1998)

Meloy, Harold, *Mummies of Mammoth Cave* (1996)

Miller, Harriet Parks, *The Bell Witch of Middle Tennessee* (1930)

Murray, Earl, *Ghosts of the Old West* (1988)

Murray, Robert K. & Robert W. Brucker, *Trapped! The Story of Floyd Collins* (1979)

Myers, Arthur, *Ghost Hunter's Guide to Haunted Landmarks* (1993)

Myers, Arthur, *The Ghostly Register* (1986)

Nesbitt, Mark, *Ghosts of Gettysburg* (1991)

Nesbitt, Mark, *More Ghosts of Gettysburg* (1992)

Nesbitt, Mark, *Ghosts of Gettysburg III* (1995)

Nesbitt, Mark, *Ghosts of Gettysburg IV* (1998)

Norman, Michael & Beth Scott, *Haunted America* (1994)

Norman, Michael & Beth Scott, *Historic Haunted America* (1995)

Norris, Curt, *Ghosts I have Known* (1994)

Owens, Joseph A., "Dudleytown Never Had a Chance," *Yankee Magazine* (1971)

Phillips, Ben, *Eastern State Penitentiary: 140 Years of Reform* (1996)

Price, Charles Edwin, *The Infamous Bell Witch of Tennessee* (1994)

Rainey, Rich, *Haunted History* (1992)

Riccio, Delores & Joan Bingham, *Haunted Houses USA* (1989)

Saxon, Lyle, Edward Dreyer & Robert Tallant, *Gumbo Ya-Ya* (1945)

Sandlass, Virginia, *16 Howard County Ghosts* (1980)

Scott, Beth & Michael Norman, *Haunted Heartland* (1985)

Senate, Richard, *Ghost Stalker's Guide to Haunted California* (1998)

Sifakis, Carl, *Encyclopedia of American Crime* (1982)

Smith, Susy, *Prominent American Ghosts* (1967)

Snow, Edward Rowe, *Boston's Lady in Black* (Yankee Magazine 1971)

Stackpole, Gen. Edward J., *They Met At Gettysburg* (1956)

Sullivan, Jack, *Penguin Encyclopedia of Horror &The Supernatural* (1986)

McArdle, Stacy & Taylor, Troy, *Summerwind: Ghosts of the Prairie* (1998)

Taylor, Troy, *Beyond the Grave* (2000)

Taylor, Troy, *Haunted Illinois* (2001)

Taylor, Troy, *Haunted New Orleans* (2000)

Taylor, Troy, *No Rest for theWicked* (2001)

Taylor, Troy, *Season of theWitch* (1999)

Taylor, Troy, *Spirits of the CivilWar* (1999)

von Bober, Wollfgang, *The Carver Effect* (1979)

Wagoner, John J. & Lewis D. Cutliff, *Mammoth Cave* (1985)

Walker, Stephen, *Lemp:The Haunting History* (1988)

Warnell, Norman, *Mammoth Cave* (1997)

Winer, Richard, *Ghost Ships* (2000)

Winer, Richard & Nancy Osborn, *Haunted Houses* (1979)

Winer, Richard, *Houses of Horror* (1983)

Winer, Richard & Nancy Osborn Ishmael, *More Haunted Houses* (1981)

Wlodarski, Robert & Anne, *Guide to the Haunted Queen Mary* (1995 / 2000)

Wlodarski, Robert & Anne, *Haunted Alcatraz* (1998)

Wlodarski, Robert & Anne, *HauntedWhaley House* (1997)

Personal Interviews & Correspondence.

About the Author

TROY TAYLOR is the author of 40 books about history, hauntings and the unexplained in America, including *Haunted Illinois*, *Haunted Chicago*, *Weird Illinois* and many others.

Taylor is the president of the American Ghost Society, a network of ghost hunters, which boasts more than 600 active members in the United States and Canada. Along with writing about the unusual, Taylor is also a public speaker on the subject and has spoken to literally hundreds of private and public groups on a variety of paranormal subjects. He has appeared in newspaper and magazine articles about ghosts and hauntings. He has also been fortunate enough to be interviewed hundreds of times for radio and television broadcasts about the supernatural. He has also appeared in a number of documentary films, several television series, and in one feature film.

Born and raised in Illinois, Taylor has long had an affinity for things that go bump in the night;" he published his first book in 1995. For seven years, he was also the host of the popular, and award-winning, Haunted Decatur ghost tours of the city for which he sometimes still appears as a guest host. Taylor is the co-owner and manager of the Illinois Hauntings Tour Co., with tours in Alton, Chicago and Springfield and of the Bump in the Night Tour Co., which hosts overnight excursions to haunted places throughout the Midwest.

He currently resides in Central Illinois with his wife, Haven, in a decidedly non-haunted house.